Event History Modeling

Event History Modeling provides an accessible up-to-date guide to event history analysis for researchers and advanced students in the social sciences. The substantive focus of many social science research problems leads directly to the consideration of duration models, and many problems would be better analyzed by using these longitudinal methods to take into account not only whether the event happened, but when. The foundational principles of event history analysis are discussed and ample examples are estimated and interpreted using standard statistical packages, such as STATA and S-Plus. Recent and critical innovations in diagnostics are discussed, including testing the proportional hazards assumption, identifying outliers, and assessing model fit. The treatment of complicated events includes coverage of unobserved heterogeneity, repeated events, and competing risks models. The authors point out common problems in the analysis of time-to-event data in the social sciences and make recommendations regarding the implementation of duration modeling methods.

Janet M. Box-Steffensmeier is Vernal Riffe Professor of Political Science at Ohio State University. She was chair of the R.H. Durr Award Committee for the best paper applying quantitative methods to a substantive issue that was presented at the 2002 Annual Meeting of the Midwest Political Science Association in 2002–3. She is Vice President (2003–5) and a member of the Executive Committee of the Political Methodology Section of the American Political Science Association.

Bradford S. Jones is Associate Professor of Political Science at the University of Arizona. He has served as a Section Officer for the Society for Political Methodology and as a guest editor for a special issue of *Political Analysis* on causal inference. His research on methodology includes work on reliability analysis, duration modeling, and models for categorical data. Professor Jones received his Ph.D. from the State University of New York at Stony Brook. Apart from methodology, Professor Jones's research interests include racial and ethnic politics, public opinion, and representation.

Event History Modeling

A Guide for Social Scientists

Janet M. Box-Steffensmeier
Ohio State University

Bradford S. Jones
University of Arizona

CAMBRIDGE
UNIVERSITY PRESS

PUBLISHED BY THE PRESS SYNDICATE OF THE UNIVERSITY OF CAMBRIDGE
The Pitt Building, Trumpington Street, Cambridge, United Kingdom

CAMBRIDGE UNIVERSITY PRESS
The Edinburgh Building, Cambridge CB2 2RU, UK
40 West 20th Street, New York, NY 10011-4211, USA
477 Williamstown Road, Port Melbourne, VIC 3207, Australia
Ruiz de Alarcón 13, 28014 Madrid, Spain
Dock House, The Waterfront, Cape Town 8001, South Africa

http: // www.cambridge.org

First published 2004

Printed in the United States of America

Typefaces Times New Roman 10/12 pt. and Helvetica   *System* LaTeX 2$_\varepsilon$ [TB]

A catalog record for this book is available from the British Library.

Library of Congress Cataloging in Publication Data

Box-Steffensmeier, Janet M., 1965–
Event history modeling : a guide for social scientists / Janet M. Box-Steffensmeier, Bradford S. Jones.
    p.   cm.
Includes bibliographical references and index.
ISBN 0-521-83767-7 – ISBN 0-521-54673-7 (pbk.)
1. Event history analysis – Computer simulation.   2. Social sciences – Methodology.
3. History – Methodology.   I. Jones, Bradford S., 1965–   II. Title.
H61.B6366   2004
001.4'32–dc22   2003056923

ISBN 0 521 83767 7 hardback
ISBN 0 521 54673 7 paperback

To Michael, whose "duration" of love and support was unmeasurable, and to Andrew, Zachary, Nathaniel, and Elizabeth, the most exciting "events" and true blessings in my life.
—Jan Box-Steffensmeier

To Arlen, for her tremendous love and support, and to Mitchell, Daniel, and little Jackson, for their love and their ability to help me keep things in perspective. Also, to Grandpa.
—Brad Jones

Contents

Figures

Tables

Preface

Our work on event history began in graduate school. We met as graduate students attending the Political Methodology Society's annual meeting in 1993 at Florida State University in Tallahassee, Florida. A small group of us at the meeting were interested in event history modeling and we saw its great potential for unlocking new answers to old questions and for revealing new questions in political science. We are indebted to the Political Methodology Group for bringing us together, providing a forum for us to present subsequent work, and providing ready and constructive critics and supporters. We are also indebted to our home departments for surrounding us with highly talented graduate students and interesting, stimulating colleagues. Meetings subsequent to our initial one in 1993, collaborations, and prodding from students and colleagues across the country who were interested in event history methodology, led to this manuscript.

This work has several goals. Our first goal in writing this book was to connect the methodology of event history to a core interest that social scientists, and indeed many scientists in fields as diverse as biostatistics and engineering, are interested in, namely understanding the causes and consequences of change over time. Scholars are commonly interested in "events." For example, political scientists who study international relations might investigate the occurrence of a militarized dispute or criminologists might study instances of victimization. Events such as these connote change and frequently, this concern with events is concomitantly tied to an interest in the "history" preceding the event. Understanding an "event history" entails a consideration of not only whether something happens, but also when something happens. Event history analysis, which is also referred to as survival, duration, and reliability analysis, is a growing but often underutilized, statistical approach for testing theories about dynamics in many areas of social science.

A second goal of the book is to present the fundamental steps when estimating event history models and to highlight the nuances of social science data that require special consideration. We challenge scholars to evaluate, justify, and test whether their modeling assumptions are valid. For example, we highlight the importance of checking the fundamental proportional hazards assumption and argue for more widespread use of the Cox model, which does not impose parametric assumptions on the data. Social science data also has inherently different characteristics that affect modeling choices. The repeatability of events in the social sciences is common (in contrast to the biological sciences where the typical study is of death, which only occurs once). Repeatability requires critical modeling adjustments to account for potential correlation over time. Such issues have been overlooked by much of the substantive literature applying event history models.

A third goal of the book is to provide a presentation that goes beyond introductory material so that scholars could use current statistical research conclusions to best answer their substantive questions. Interest in event history modeling is growing, and thus providing a reference book for social scientists was a timely and needed objective.

There are many people and institutions to thank for assisting us in this work. Janet Box-Steffensmeier would like to thank the National Science Foundation for financial support, specifically the Methodology, Measurement, and Statistics Program in the Division of Social, Behavioral, and Economic Research and Statistics and Probability Program in the Division of Mathematical Sciences (SES-0083418) as well as Ohio State University for their support of her sabbatical. Brad Jones would like to thank the National Science Foundation (SES-9708936) for its financial support during the early stages of this project. We owe a debt to our home departments of the Ohio State University and the University of Arizona for the rich and intellectually stimulating environment in which we are pleased to be working. Parts of this book were completed while Brad Jones was in the Political Science Department at the State University of New York at Stony Brook. Brad Jones would like to thank his colleagues in that department for their tremendous support. We also benefitted from presenting our work at several workshops and to several political science departments including the 2001 Speaker Series for The Center for Biostatistics and The School of Public Health, Division of Epidemiology and Biometrics, Ohio State University; State University of New York at Binghamton; Director's Series Luncheon at the Mershon Center, Ohio State University; Texas A&M University; University of California, San Diego; and the University of Kentucky.

We thank numerous colleagues for their comments, discussion, support, and questions, including Bill Anderson, Chris Anderson, Brandon Bartels, Larry Baum, Paul Beck, Fred Boehmke, Jon Bond, Jake Bowers, Sarah Brooks, Tom Brunell, Greg Caldeira, Valeria Sinclair Chapman, Dave Clark, Aage Clausen, Renato Corbetta, Brian Crisp, Dave Darmofal, Bill Dixon, Stanley Feldman, Rich Fleisher, Rich Fording, John Freeman, Jeff Gill, Sandy Gordon, Paul Gronke, Rick Hermann, Tim Hellwig, Craig Jenkins, Jenn Jerit, Gregg Johnson, David Judkins, Kris Kanthak, April Kelley, John Kessel, Dean Lacy, Laura Langer, Stan Lemeshow, Miller McPherson, Ken Meier, Bill Mishler,

Mel Moeschberger, Will Moore, Barbara Norrander, Mark Peffley, Sal Peralta, Dave Peterson, Jon Pevehouse, Dan Powers, Kathy Powers, Peter Radcliffe, Dan Reiter, Rip Ripley, Kira Sanbonmatsu, Mark Schneider, Jeff Segal, Paul Senese, Renee Smith, Michael Sobel, Jim Stimson, Alex Thompson, Rich Timpone, Steve Voss, Chen Lung Wang, B. Dan Wood, and Jack Wright. We apologize if anyone was inadvertently left out as we have had e-mail conversations too numerous to count that inevitably raised the quality of our work as well. We owe a special and heartfelt thanks to: Scott Bennett, Gina Branton, Suzanna DeBoef, Charles Franklin, Jeff Gill, Gary Goertz, Jonathan Golub, Sam Kernell, Katherine Tate, Terry Therneau, Herb Weisberg, Rick Witmer, and Chris Zorn. We wish to thank our students who took our event history classes at the University of Arizona, Ohio State University, and the ITV Program, which includes students from the University of Illinois, University of Minnesota, and the University of Wisconsin at Madison. Students who worked with us as teaching or research assistants over the course of the project also have our gratitude: Andy Farrell, Tobin Grant, Scott Meinke, Kevin Scott, Kevin Sweeney, and Andy Tomlinson. We sincerely thank the series editors, Mike Alvarez and Neal Beck, for their comments, support, and tremendous assistance throughout the process. We thank Sarah Mann, Andrea Olson, and Jeremy Shine for their assistance. Finally, at Cambridge University Press, we thank Malinda Barrett and especially Ed Parsons for their expert guidance.

CHAPTER 1

Event History and Social Science

Social scientists often examine events, for example, the occurrence of a militarized dispute, unemployment, or adoption. Events like these connote change or represent a transition from one state to another. Frequently, this concern with events is tied to an interest in the history preceding the event, for example, the number of years leading up to a war or the number of months a child is in foster care before adoption. History, thought of in this way, involves timing, and for many research questions, the timing of social change is at least as interesting as understanding the event culminating the history. Such questions naturally lend themselves to an examination of both the occurrence of an event and the history leading up to the event's occurrence.

The issues of timing and change are relevant for social science and bear on many hypotheses and theories with which social scientists regularly work. Such hypotheses and theories may have observable implications related to timing and change. Moreover, methods accounting for timing and change often naturally follow from hypotheses or theoretical expectations embedded in the research question. Understanding an "event history" entails a consideration of not only *if* something happens, but also *when* something happens. An event history is longitudinal and event history *analysis* typically involves the statistical examination of longitudinal data collected on a set of observations. While a wide variety of statistical models may be constructed for event history data, at the most basic level, all event history models have some common features.

The dependent variable measures the duration of time that units spend in a state before experiencing some event. Generally, a researcher knows when the observations enter the process and when the process ends (with the occurrence or nonoccurrence of some event). Analysts are frequently interested in the relationship between the length of the observed duration and independent variables, or *covariates*, of theoretical interest. A statistical model may then be constructed linking the dependent variable to the covariates. Inferences can be made regarding the influence of the covariates on the length of the duration and the occurrence (or nonoccurrence) of some event. In the remainder of this

1

chapter, we point out why event history models are suitable to a wide range of issues dealt with by social scientists.

The Substantive Motivation for Event History Analysis

Many of the problems, hypotheses, and theories underlying social science research have, at their core, an implicit or explicit interest in the notions of timing and change. Even if a researcher does not explicitly think in terms of "duration," that is, how long something persists before it changes, many interesting problems in the social sciences have observable implications that *are* longitudinal. By thinking of problems in terms of the longitudinal implications embedded in them, a potentially richer understanding of the social process underlying the problems can be achieved. We point out how some of the common themes and concerns in social science analysis are directly relevant to an event history model.

An Implicit Interest in "Survival"

Event history models are often referred to as survival models. Indeed, the class of models discussed in this book have a wide variety of names: duration models, survival models, failure-time models, reliability models, and so forth. The nomenclature arises from the different kinds of applications for which these models have been employed. For example, in engineering research, industrial reliability testing has led to the consideration of duration models, as these models naturally address questions of interest: How long does a mechanical component work (or "survive") until it fails? Similarly, many of the kinds of questions asked in social science are implicitly related to a conception of survival: Why do political parties maintain control or fail to maintain control of a legislature? How do politicians keep their seats over time, even when political conditions are unfavorable to them? How does the number of children affect the duration of marriage? Why do military conflicts persist or fail to persist? Why does the "peace" between one set of countries last longer than the peace between another set? Why are some families seemingly stuck in poverty?

Each of these questions beckons the notion of survival. Political parties or politicians, in order to maintain control of a legislature or of a seat, must survive over a series of elections. The length of a military conflict, or conversely, the duration of peace between countries invokes the idea of survival. Disputes can "survive"; peace can persist. Most of the important theoretical issues social scientists grapple with have implications regarding survival. For example, one facet of democratic theory suggests that a functioning and healthy democracy should permit some semblance of citizen control over its elected officials. If politicians are habitually dependent upon voter support, political "survival" may be a natural implication of such fundamental concepts as representation and citizen control. Theorists studying patterns of democratization in developing countries may treat as an implication of democratic stability, the duration with which regimes persist. Theorists of political institutions may be interested in the relationship between institutional design and rules and the duration of time that politicians survive or stay within the institution. Criminologists study the effectiveness of alternative rehabilitation programs on whether and when someone returns to prison. Health economists study the duration of hospitalization. Examples abound; the point is, the concept of survival is pervasive in social science. Event history analysis, or *survival* analysis, is explicitly premised on the notion of survival.

An Implicit Interest in Risk

Just as many social science theories have implications relevant for survival, the concept of "risk" is equally prevalent and important in social science research. It is difficult to consider survival without also explicitly considering risk: given that a political party has maintained control of the legislature for three elections, what is the risk the party will fall subsequently? The notion of risk in political science, or in any scientific field for that matter, implies a conditional relationship with survival. As something persists—as it survives— what is the risk it will subsequently end? Usually, political science questions pertaining to survival and risk are asked in more complicated ways: given a change in electoral rules, what is the risk that a party which has held control of the legislature for three elections will fall in the subsequent election? This question, which invokes the notions of survival and risk, ties these concepts to some tangibly interesting factor: an observable change to the rules governing elections. The kinds of questions that relate survival and risk to important theoretical factors are replete in social science. We demonstrate throughout this book how this notion of risk is directly incorporated into an event history model.

Event History Analysis *Is* Comparative Analysis

Social science research often strives or purports to be comparative. Indeed, at some basic level, just about every empirical question asked in social science is comparative in nature: given variation across some theoretical attribute, how do cases vary on values of the dependent variable? This question is rudimentary, but comparative. Likewise, event history models are explicitly comparative statistical models. Unlike traditional time-series models, where a single entity is typically examined over time, event history data contains information on many observations (i.e. individuals, politicians, wars, conflicts, convicts, parties, patients, countries, and so on) over time. Inferences from event history models can be very powerful. Not only can some claims be made regarding survival and risk, but also, explicit comparative inferences can be made regarding differences across the cases.

For example, in studying the duration of time coalitional governments survive (King, Alt, Burns and Laver 1990; Warwick 1992; Diermeier and Stevenson 1999), event history methods permit researchers to make claims not just about the factors that precipitate the risk a government will fall (or "stop surviving"), but also, how differences across political systems are related to this risk. The inference is comparative in nature. Given that event history data are longitudinal and generated across many observations, comparative inferences are naturally obtained from *any* event history model. It is not unreasonable to claim that *all* event history models are comparative. Certainly, the analyst may choose not to think of his or her results in comparative terms, but this kind of interpretation is forthcoming from an event history model.

Growing Body of Longitudinal Data

Social scientists are amassing an ever-growing body of longitudinal data. In part, the accrual of this kind of data has simply been a function of consistent and long-term research programs and data collection efforts. The accumulation of this kind of data has also stemmed from the recognition among social scientists that much more powerful inferences and theory-testing is possible with longitudinal data. Concomitantly, in the social science methodology literature, research on methods for time series, panel data, time-series cross-section designs, event counts, and event history data has flourished in recent decades. An equally burgeoning literature has emerged regarding the application of these kinds of models to substantive social science problems.

The fact that a considerable body of longitudinal data exists, or can be readily constructed from extant data sources, helps to motivate the consideration of event history models. But data availability alone is not sufficient to motivate the use of a statistical model. Rather, given the readily increasing availability of longitudinal data, *coupled with* social scientists' interest in the notions of survival and risk, one is directly led to the consideration of event history models. It is one of the aims of this book to demonstrate that the event history model is a valuable method for addressing substantive social science problems. Application of the models herein should be a matter of course when one has a substantive problem that requires the comparative analysis of longitudinal data. Since these problems abound in the social sciences, the event history model is a natural model for analyses.

Conclusion

It is incontrovertible that the substantive focus of many social science research problems leads directly to the consideration of duration models. This will be one of the principal claims we make throughout this book. As a road map for what is to come, in Chapter 2, we discuss the foundational principles of event history analysis. We consider the structure of event history data and introduce some important issues that will be of concern to us throughout the book. Additionally, we present the mathematical "building blocks" upon which event history analysis rests and then proceed to explain why traditional statistical models are problematic in the face of duration data.[1]

In Chapters 3-6, we consider in detail, estimation and interpretation of duration models for so-called "single-spell" durations. Specifically, Chapter 3 deals with parametric duration models—that is, models where the underlying hazard rate is parameterized in terms of a distribution function. In Chapter 4 we present the nonparametric alternative to the models considered in Chapter 3. In particular, we discuss the critical innovations of Cox (1972). We will make the argument that in general, the Cox model in most applied settings *will be preferable* over its parametric alternatives. In Chapter 5, we consider so-called "discrete-time" event history models. As we will point out later, the "discrete-time" label can be misleading inasmuch as discrete-time models often are good approximations of otherwise continuous-time processes. Chapter 6 provides a discussion of model selection, including further elaboration on the issue of parametric versus nonparametric estimation.

In Chapters 7-10, we discuss complications that emerge in event history data. Specifically, Chapter 7 deals with the inclusion of time-varying covariates in duration models; Chapter 8 discusses the implementation of model diagnostics; Chapter 9 considers the issue of unobserved heterogeneity; and Chapter 10 considers models for multiple events. By "multiple events," we mean the case when events can occur repeatedly, or the case where different/multiple kinds of events can occur. In the last chapter, Chapter 11, we summarize our principal arguments, revisit some of the issues raised regarding the relevance of the event history framework for social science, and make some recommendations regarding the implementation of duration modeling methods.

---

[1] We do not present the Bayesian approach to event history analysis in this book. Interested readers should see Ibrahim, Chen, and Sinha 2001.

CHAPTER 2

The Logic of Event History Analysis

The lexicon of event history analysis stems from its historical roots in biostatistics. Terms like "death," "failure," and "termination" are natural for analyses of medical survival data, but may seem awkward for social science analysis. In the context of medical research, survival data usually consist of longitudinal records indicating the duration of time individuals survive until death (if death is observed). In analyzing survival data, medical researchers are commonly interested in how long subjects survive before they die. The "event" is death, while the duration of time leading up to the death, the "history," is the observed *survival time*. Analysts working with survival data may be interested in assessing the relationship between survival times and covariates of interest such as drug treatments.

Likewise, social scientists frequently work with "survival data," although such data are generally not thought of in terms of survival and death. Nevertheless, much of the data social scientists use are generated from the same kinds of processes producing survival data. Concepts like "survival," "risk," and "failure" are directly analogous to concepts with which social scientists work. Thus, the concept of survival and the notion of survival and failure times are useful starting points to motivate event history analysis.

Event history data are, as Petersen (1995) notes, generated from *failure-time processes*. A failure-time process consists of units (individuals, governments, countries, dyads) observed at some natural starting point or time-of-origin. At the time-of-origin, the units are in some state (for example, holding some elected office) and are observed over time. A unit, at any given point in the process, is "at risk" of experiencing some event. An event represents a change or transition from one state to another state (for example, losing office in an election). After the event is experienced, the unit is either no longer observed or is at risk of experiencing another kind of event (or returning to the previously occupied state). In some instances, units are not observed experiencing an event, i.e., no transition is made from one state to another. Such

7

cases are treated as *censored*, because although the event may be experienced, subsequent history after the last observation point is unobserved.

Such a process may be called a "failure-time" process because units are observed at an initial point, survive for some length of time or spell, and then "fail" (i.e. experience the event of interest) or are censored. The notion of failure is, of course, directly relevant to medical research or mechanical engineering, for example, where units *really do* fail: patients die, generators seize. But in social science applications, the "failure" is more appropriately thought of as an event, where the event denotes a transition from one state to another. The "failure time" represents the duration of time units survive until they fail. In political science applications, the failure time is analogous to the duration of time a unit is in some political state until it experiences an event.

Event History Data Structures

To make the notion of a failure-time process tangible, we consider some typical event history data structures. The "event" in event history analysis represents a change or transition from one state or condition of interest to another. For example, if a researcher is interested in studying the duration of a militarized intervention, the intervention is observed from its origin time until it ends. The termination of the intervention is the event and it represents the transition from one state (being "in a dispute") to another state (being "out of a dispute").

The premise of event history analysis is to model *both* the duration of time spent in the initial state *and* the transition to a subsequent state, that is, the event. At a minimum, event history data contain information on when the units begin the process under study and information on the timing of the event's occurrence (if an event is observed within the span of the observation plan). The starting time is usually treated as some natural beginning point of a process or state. For example, if one is interested in studying legislative career paths in the U.S. Congress, a natural starting point for observing House members is after their first successful election.

Defining an appropriate starting point for a process is a theoretical issue, not a statistical issue. For example, in analyzing the timing until a strong challenger emerges against an incumbent in a legislative election, the researcher must specify what the natural starting time of an election is. Because there is no officially sanctioned "start time" for campaigns, the time-of-origin is determined by the researcher, using theoretical guidance.

Knowing the time-of-entry into the process is important because it provides a natural baseline from which to compare units and observe subsequent history. Each unit in an event history data set is presumed to enter the process at the same time. In terms of "calendar time," the time-of-origin may vary across observations, but in terms of "clock time," the starting point is generally treated as equivalent for all observations. Continuing the example of

TABLE 2.1: Example of Event History Data: Military Interventions

Intervention	Intervenor	Target	Duration	Contiguity[a]	C[b]
1	U.K.	Albania	1	0	0
46	El Salvador	Honduras	657	1	0
81	U.S.	Panama	274	0	1
184	Bulgaria	Greece	12	1	0
236	Taiwan	China	7456	1	0
278	Botswana	S. Africa	1097	1	0
332	Uganda	Kenya	409	1	1
467	Israel	Egypt	357	1	0
621	Malawi	Mozambique	631	1	1
672	India	Pakistan	173	1	0

[a] Intervenors and Targets separated by 150 miles of water or less are coded as contiguous; [b]C denotes"censored": disputes on-going as of 31 Dec. 1988 are treated as right-censored. Data are Pearson-Baumann Militarized Intervention Data (ICPSR 6035).

congressional careers, the entry time begins after the first election. However, this start time varies across members of Congress, e.g., some members may be first elected in 1992 and others in 1994. Although the calendar time differs (1992 versus 1994), the "clock" begins 'ticking" at the same relative position: after the first election to Congress.[1]

Aside from giving information on starting times, event history data also provide information on the occurrence of the event. After some initial start time, units are observed in a state until at a later date, an event is experienced and a transition from one state to another is observed. The length of time that passes between entry into the process and occurrence of the event is the survival time or the duration time. Since the event must occur after the starting time, survival times must be positive. Note that events may or may not be observed for all individuals in a study. By the time the last observation period ends, some units may still be surviving. Units not experiencing an event by the last observation period are known as "right censored" observations because history subsequent to the last observation is unobserved. To illustrate what event history data look like in the context of a social science data set, consider Table 2.1. Here, we reproduce a portion of the International Military Intervention data set constructed by Pearson and Baumann (1993; see also Pearson and Baumann 1989 and Pearson, Baumann, and Bardos 1989). In the table, 10 of the 520 interventions from the data set are displayed.

The first column of data is the intervention number, the second and third columns list the intervening state and the target state of the dyad. The fourth column denotes the duration (in days) that the intervention lasted. The fifth

---

[1] In practical applications of event history analysis, sometimes the time-of-origin is unobserved, as an observation enters the study already in the process. Such an observation is referred to as "left truncated" because all history prior to, or "left" of, the initial observation point is unobserved, or truncated. Later in this chapter we discuss the problem of left truncation in more detail.

column lists the values of a binary variable indicating whether the intervenor and target are geographically contiguous states. And the sixth column indicates whether the intervention is right-censored. Contained in the duration time are two important pieces of information. We know how long the intervention "survives" or lasts from its onset until its termination date. The duration time indicates both the length of the intervention and the time at which the event occurred. The event is the termination (or "failure") of the intervention. For right-censored interventions, note that the duration time only provides information on the intervention up to the last observation point; no information is revealed on when the intervention terminates. So for example, although cases 46 and 621 have similarly recorded duration times (657 and 631 days), we know that the dispute between El Salvador and Honduras (case 46) ended on the 657th day after its onset; the only thing we know about the dispute between Malawi and Mozambique (case 621) is that as of the last observation point, the dispute had survived for 631 days. The similarity in duration times is illusory: one intervention has ended, the other has not. It is not uncommon for event history data sets to contain numerous right-censored observations. Analyses that fail to distinguish uncensored and censored cases can produce misleading conclusions. This point is elaborated later in this chapter.

Finally, Table 2.1 includes information regarding a variable of interest, contiguity status. Typically, analysts are interested in studying the relationship between duration times and covariates. In the case of these data, it may be interesting to ask whether duration times of interventions vary according to contiguity status of the intervenor and target (cf. Goertz and Diehl 1992, Mansfield and Snyder 1995, Mitchell and Prins 1999). A model may be constructed treating the duration time as some function of contiguity status. From the model, a researcher could assess if this covariate is associated with longer or shorter duration times. Using the risk terminology discussed previously, one can assess if the "risk" of an intervention ending increases or decreases with contiguity status. The contiguity covariate in Table 2.1 is known as a "time-independent" covariate, as its values do not change within observations over time. However, researchers frequently will be interested in covariates that have values that change within observations over time. Such covariates may be referred to as "time-varying" covariates (TVCs). The use of TVCs helps to motivate event history analysis, but raises special problems as well. These problems are discussed in Chapter 7.

So far, our interest has implicitly centered on "single-spell" processes, or single event processes. In our discussion of militarized interventions, for example, we referred to the duration of *an* intervention and (conveniently) ignored the possibility that a state may become involved in multiple interventions. Likewise, in our example of House careers, we side-stepped the obvious issue that a career could end in a variety of ways, for example through electoral defeat or through retirement from office. In short, we have assumed there is a

TABLE 2.2: Disputes between Nicaragua and Costa Rica

Date of Dispute Onset	Date of Dispute Termination	Duration	Outcome
Dec. 11, 1948	Mar. 9, 1949	89	Stalemate
April 1, 1954	Feb. 24, 1955	330	Compromise
May 3, 1957	June 23, 1957	51	Stalemate
Oct. 10, 1977	Oct. 15, 1977	6	Stalemate
Sept. 12, 1978	Dec. 27, 1978	107	Stalemate
Sept. 28, 1983	Sept. 3, 1984	342	Stalemate
May 31, 1985	June 5, 1985	6	Stalemate
April 16, 1986	April 16, 1986	1	Stalemate
Sept. 2, 1987	Sept. 2, 1987	1	Stalemate

singular event of interest: the termination of a single spell. For many research questions, however, the focus on a single event (or transition) is limiting. Event histories are often complicated. The most general form of an event history can encompass multiple events of the same type, or multiple events of different types. Moreover, the complications that emerge in event history structures can directly influence the modeling strategy one chooses.

To illustrate some of the issues that emerge in complicated event history data structures, consider the data in Table 2.2. These data are taken from a large data set recording the occurrence and duration of militarized interstate disputes, or MIDs (see Jones, Bremer, and Singer 1996 and Maoz 1999 for details on the MID data). The MID data have been widely used in studies of international conflict because the structure of the data set permits one to examine, longitudinally, disputes that occur between pairs of countries, commonly referred to as "dyads." In Table 2.2, we give the event history data for disputes that have occurred between Nicaragua and Costa Rica in the post World War II era;[2] hence, the data in Table 2.2 provide a comprehensive account of the dispute history between this dyad. We see that in this era, the two countries were involved in 9 disputes varying in length from 1 day (the MID began and ended on the same day) to 342 days. The data help to illustrate several points regarding event history data structures.

First, note that there are *multiple* spells, or duration lengths, each corresponding to a separate MID. This implies that this dyad has *repeatedly* engaged in disputes with one another. Second, note also that there are *multiple* events, or outcomes, in the dispute history between Nicaragua and Costa Rica: one dispute ended in compromise, the other disputes ended in a stalemate. Third, note that there is an implied duration time *between* disputes. That is, between dispute spells, there are nine "peace" spells, corresponding to the length of time between the termination of a prior dispute and the onset of a subsequent dispute. In piecing together the full dispute history for this dyad, an event

---

[2]This dyad was arbitrarily chosen from the MID Data to illustrate event history structures.

history structure emerges that is considerably more complicated than a single-spell data structure.

Since we know MIDs can terminate for one of several reasons, it may be useful to distinguish among the different possible kinds of outcomes. To explain, one can imagine a MID could end because one state wins a military victory over the other state, one state yields to the other state, a compromise is reached, or a stalemate is reached. A more nuanced understanding of dispute behavior may result if these multiple kinds of events are taken into account, rather than simply defining the event as "MID terminates." Additionally, *how* a MID ends *may* have some implications for the subsequent duration of "peace" that is observed for the dyad. Hence, it may be useful to not only account for MID durations, but also account for "peace" spells, or durations of non-dispute activity. Indeed, for this dyad, the total number of spells is 18. Nine of the spells are dispute spells, and the intervening "peace" spells comprise the additional nine spells.

The complications illustrated in the dispute history for Nicaragua and Costa Rica illuminate a larger concern of this book. In some settings, one-way transition models (or single spell models) may be applicable; however, in other settings, more complicated event history models may be required. We consider a variety of modeling choices that are suitable to a wide range of event history data structures. Now that the basic features of event history data have been discussed, we consider more formally, some basic mathematical principles underlying event history analysis.

Mathematical Components of Event History Analysis

We begin by defining T as a positive random variable denoting survival times. We assume that T is absolutely continuous (the discrete case is considered in detail in Chapter 5). The actual survival time of a unit is a realization or value of T, which can be denoted as t. The possible values of T have a *probability distribution* that is characterized by a probability density function, $f(t)$, and a cumulative distribution function, $F(t)$.

The distribution function of random variable T is given by

$$F(t) = \int_0^t f(u)d(u) = \Pr(T \leq t), \tag{2.1}$$

which specifies the probability that a survival time T is less than or equal to some value t. For all points that $F(t)$ is differentiable, we define a density function $f(t)$

$$f(t) = \frac{dF(t)}{d(t)} = F'(t), \tag{2.2}$$

implying that

$$f(t) = \lim_{\Delta t \to 0} \frac{F(t + \Delta t) - F(t)}{\Delta t}. \tag{2.3}$$

The density function, $f(t)$, gives the unconditional failure rate of event occurrences in an infinitesimally small differentiable area. This can also be seen by expressing $f(t)$ in terms of probability. By the definition of the distribution function, (2.1), the probability density may be written as

$$f(t) = \lim_{\Delta t \to 0} \frac{\Pr(t \leq T \leq t + \Delta t)}{\Delta t}, \tag{2.4}$$

where (2.4) gives the *instantaneous* probability an event will occur (or a unit will fail) in the infinitesimally small area bounded by t and $t + \Delta t$. Both (2.3) and (2.4) demonstrate that the density function is an unconditional failure rate. Either $F(t)$ or $f(t)$ can be used to specify an equivalent distribution. If $F(t)$ is differentiable, then $f(t)$ must exist. Thus, either the distribution function or the density function may be used to characterize the distribution of failure times.

Another important concept in event history analysis is the *survivor function*, $S(t)$. This can be expressed mathematically as

$$S(t) = 1 - F(t) = \Pr(T \geq t). \tag{2.5}$$

The survivor function denotes the probability a survival time T is equal to or greater than some time t. Similarly, $S(t)$ can also be thought of as the proportion of units surviving beyond t. At the origin time, $t = 0$ and $S(0) = 1$, indicating all units in the study are surviving. As time passes, the proportion of surviving units must decrease as units in the study fail (or remain flat if no units fail); hence, $S(t)$ is a strictly decreasing function. Theoretically, if the study continued indefinitely, all observations would fail so the survivor curve at the last observation point would equal 0. If there are no censored observations, then $S(t) = 0$ at this point. Empirically, an estimate of the survival function will resemble a step function because with observed data, cases fail at specifically recorded times. The time between observed failures is therefore "flat," thus producing the step function.

Having defined the survivor function and the density of failure times, we have an idea of how "survival" and "death" are accounted for in the event history framework. How the notions of failure and survival relate to one another is captured by an important facet of duration analysis: the *hazard rate*. The relationship between failure times and the survival function is captured through the hazard rate in the following way:

$$h(t) = \frac{f(t)}{S(t)}. \tag{2.6}$$

The hazard rate gives the rate at which units fail (or durations end) by t given that the unit had survived until t. Thus, the hazard rate is a *conditional* failure rate. To see this more clearly, note that (2.6) can be expressed as

$$h(t) = \lim_{\Delta t \to 0} \frac{\Pr(t \leq T \leq t + \Delta t \mid T \geq t)}{\Delta t}, \tag{2.7}$$

where (2.7) denotes the rate of failure per time unit in the interval $[t, t + \Delta t]$, conditional on survival at or beyond time t. This rate may be increasing such that the likelihood of failure increases as time passes, or the rate may be decreasing, such that the likelihood of failure decreases as time passes. The rate can also take a variety of shapes, such as increase and then decrease, or decrease and then increase, over time.

The hazard rate, survivor function, and distribution and density functions are mathematically linked. If any one of these is specified, the others are fully determined. To illustrate these relationships, note first that the density function in (2.2) can be equivalently written as

$$f(t) = \frac{-dS(t)}{dt},$$

leading to the hazard rate being expressed as

$$h(t) = \frac{-dS(t)/dt}{S(t)}, \tag{2.8}$$

which is thus equivalent to

$$h(t) = \frac{-d \log S(t)}{dt}. \tag{2.9}$$

By integrating (2.9) using $S(0) = 1$, the survivor function can be written as

$$S(t) = \exp\left(-\int_0^t h(u)du\right) = \exp^{-H(t)}, \tag{2.10}$$

where the term

$$H(t) = \int_0^t h(u)du$$

is the so-called *integrated hazard rate* or, equivalently, the cumulative hazard rate. By (2.10), it is noted that $H(t)$ can be expressed in terms of the log survivor function:

$$H(t) = -\log S(t). \tag{2.11}$$

This relationship will be useful for us when we discuss model diagnostics in Chapter 8. Also by (2.10), note that the density function can be expressed in terms of the integrated hazard

$$f(t) = h(t) \exp^{-H(t)}, \tag{2.12}$$

and so it follows that

$$h(t) = \frac{h(t) \exp^{-H(t)}}{\exp^{-H(t)}},$$

which is equivalent to $h(t) = f(t)/S(t)$, that is, equation (2.6). It is evident that any one function determines the other functions. Commonly, analysts focus attention on the hazard rate and so we consider $h(t)$ in more detail.

The hazard rate, unlike the density function or the survivor function, describes the risk a unit incurs of having a spell or duration end in some period, given that the spell has lasted up to or beyond some length of time. "Failure" is conditional on "survival": the event is conditional on its history.

In the social sciences, examination of the hazard rate naturally stems from many types of research questions: Given that a drug addiction has lasted t periods, what is the likelihood it will end in the subsequent period? Given that a prisoner has been released for t months, what are the chances he or she will return to prison in the subsequent month? Given a legislative district has supported one political party for t elections, what is the probability the district will stop supporting this party in the next election? Such "conditional" questions are routinely asked in social science research and as such, the answers to these questions beckon the notion of risk. Further, analysts are frequently interested in understanding how the hazard rate varies with respect to covariates of interest. The interpretation afforded the covariates has a natural appeal: given differences in the values of the covariates, how does the risk of an event occurring (or analogously, a spell ending) increase or decrease? If the hazard rate is treated as having a dependency on time as well as covariates, then we can reexpress the hazard rate as

$$h(t \mid \mathbf{x}) = \lim_{\Delta t \to 0} \frac{\Pr(t \leq T \leq t + \Delta t \mid T \geq t, \mathbf{x})}{\Delta t} \qquad (2.13)$$

to accommodate this dependency. In (2.13), $\mathbf{x}$ are the covariates and the other terms are defined as before. Various statistical models may be constructed to describe (2.13); however, it is useful to note that the substantive interpretation of covariates in event history analysis is directly interpretable in terms of risk. For social science analysis, where many questions implicitly lead to a consideration of risk, modeling the hazard rate naturally follows the research question. We now turn toward deriving statistical models for event history data. To do this, we first demonstrate why traditional statistical methods are problematic with duration data.

Problems with Modeling Duration Data

Duration data present special challenges for statistical models thus rendering traditional linear regression models like OLS regression problematic. In standard OLS applications, the mean response (or some function of it) is usually modeled as a function of covariates (Collett 1994); however, as duration data must be positive, it is often the case that the response variable will exhibit considerable asymmetry, particularly if some observations have exceptionally long duration times. One common "fix" to this problem is to transform the response variable, for example, by taking the natural log, and then applying OLS. The resultant model mitigates the skewness problem, but does not avoid other, more serious problems. We discuss some of these problems below.

Censoring and Truncation

Censoring occurs whenever an observation's full event history is unobserved. Thus, we may fail to observe the termination or the onset of a spell. In this sense, censored observations are akin to missing data, insofar as the portion of the history that is censored is, in fact, missing. *Right*-censoring is commonly observed in event history data sets. Typically, we encounter right-censoring because the time-frame of a study or observation plan concludes prior to the completion or termination of survival times. The ubiquity of right-censoring in social science data sets provides a strong motivation for event history models.

To explain more clearly what is meant by right-censoring, consider two hypothetical incumbents in the study of U.S. House member careers. Suppose that the last observation point for a study is the election of 2002. Imagine one incumbent was reelected in the 2002 election and imagine the other incumbent was defeated. Further, suppose that *up until* the 2002 election, both incumbents had served five terms (or survived over five election periods) in Congress. Hence, at the sixth election period, one incumbent "fails" (i.e. loses) and the other incumbent "survives" (i.e. wins). For both incumbents, the last recorded duration time would be "6" for both cases, yet the two observations are clearly dissimilar: one has failed, the other has not. The "surviving" incumbent would be considered right-censored because the subsequent history for this incumbent is unknown. The basic problem is that if censored and uncensored cases are treated equivalently, then parameter estimates from a model treating the duration time as a function of covariates may be misleading (that is, the relationship between the covariates and the duration times may be under- or over-stated). In general, the standard regression framework does not distinguish between uncensored and right-censored observations.

In contrast to right-censoring, some observations in an event history data set may be truncated. Left-truncation emerges in event history data sets when history *prior to* the first observation point is unobserved.[3] For example, suppose we have data on international militarized conflicts and suppose that the first observation period for these data is the year 1900. Suppose further that we know some observations are already engaged in military conflict prior to

---

[3] We refer to left-censoring as observations that experience an event prior to the beginning of the study and thus are not part of the study.

1900. The portion of "history" not included in the analysis is referred to as left-truncated. In the context of the standard regression model, left-truncated observations are usually treated as having equivalent entry times to all non-left-truncated observations, even though they do not. Event history methods can accommodate the presence of left-truncated observations. In some instances, however, accounting for left-truncation in the duration model framework is nontrivial (we discuss left-truncation in more detail later). Nevertheless, as a general matter, right-censoring and left-truncation problems provide one impetus for the use of event history methods in social science.

Accounting for Censoring

The question then naturally arises as to how event history methods handle the problems of censoring. To understand this, it is instructive to return to the hazard rate. Formally, the hazard rate, $h(t)$, of a random variable is the ratio of the probability density to the survival function at value t. This is easily seen in (2.6). To illustrate further, it is also noted that $h(t)$ may be equivalently expressed in terms of the integrals of $f(t)$ and $S(t)$:

$$h(t) = \frac{\int_t^{t+\Delta t} f(u)du}{\int_t^\infty f(u)du}. \tag{2.14}$$

The area bounded by the definite integral in the numerator gives the probability of unconditional failure, while the denominator gives the area (or probability) of survival. The hazard gives the ratio of unconditional failure to survival. In practical applications, the upper limit of the integral of $S(t)$ is generally not ∞, because this limit is usually known to be some value $t = C_i$, where C_i denotes a *known right-censoring point* for the ith unit. That is, by the time the observation period ends, some units may be right-censored and so the integral of $S(t)$ is thus given by

$$S(t) = \int_t^{t=C_i} f(u)du. \tag{2.15}$$

For left-truncated observations, the true entry time into the process may occur before the initial observation point, t. This suggests that the lower limit of the integral of $S(t)$ in (2.14) will, in reality, occur prior to t, but unobserved in the observation period. We can think of the survivor function for left-censored cases as being

$$S(t) = \int_{t_L}^\infty f(u)du, \tag{2.16}$$

where t_L denotes the time period, i.e. the clock time, that the left-truncated observation actually enters the observation period.

   The presentation of the survivor functions in (2.15) and (2.16) is nonstandard, but it serves a useful pedagogical purpose. It is clear from (2.15) that right-censored cases *only* contribute information on survival up to the known censoring point, C_i; no information is contributed to $f(t)$, the numerator in (2.14). Likewise, by (2.16), it is clear that left-truncated observations *only* contribute information to the survivor function from point t_L forward.

If the censoring points are known in the data, it is possible to construct a likelihood function to accommodate censoring. To illustrate, suppose we have n observations on which the full duration time, t, is observed. In this case, there are no censored observations. To derive a likelihood for the sample, we need only specify a probability density function, $f(t)$. The likelihood of the sample under these conditions is given by

$$\mathcal{L} = \prod_{i}^{n} f(t_i).$$

However, suppose that in the sample, some observations are right-censored. For censored cases, the duration, t_i, is observed only up to the last observation period t^*, after which the duration continues, but is unobserved. The observed duration for right-censored cases is t_i^*, denoting that the duration time for the ith censored case is equal to the time of the last observation period (even though it is continuing beyond t^*). For uncensored observations, the full duration time is observed within the observation period, $t_i \leq t^*$. Under these conditions, it is clear that uncensored cases contribute information regarding failure times (as the event of interest is experienced), while censored observations only contribute information on survival. This suggests that the likelihood of the sampled observations will consist of two parts: the density of failure times, $f(t)$, and the survivor function, $S(t)$:

$$\mathcal{L} = \prod_{t_i \leq t^*} f(t_i) \prod_{t_i > t^*} S(t_i^*).$$

This likelihood function can be rewritten to explicitly show how censored and uncensored cases are treated. To see this, let us first define a censoring indicator, δ_i, in the following way:

$$\delta_i = \begin{cases} 1 & \text{if } t_i \leq t^* \\ 0 & \text{if } t_i > t^*. \end{cases}$$

When $\delta_i = 1$, the observation is uncensored; when $\delta_i = 0$, the observation is right-censored. Incorporating our knowledge of δ_i into the likelihood function, the likelihood of the sampled duration times may be expressed as

$$\mathcal{L} = \prod_{i=1}^{n} \left\{ f(t_i) \right\}^{\delta_i} \left\{ S(t_i) \right\}^{1-\delta_i}, \tag{2.17}$$

thus illustrating the point that censored duration times contribute to the overall likelihood only through $S(t)$, while uncensored duration times contribute to the overall likelihood through $f(t)$. Consequently, it becomes clear how event history methods can account for both censored and uncensored observations.

Moreover, the event history approach is clearly preferable to the alternative "solution" of omitting censored cases from the data set. By deleting censored cases from the analysis, we may induce a form of case selection bias into the results. If censored cases are systematically different from uncensored cases, then simply deleting the latter cases will produce a nonrepresentative "sample" and render coefficient estimates biased due to the case selection process. The implications of selection bias are well known, and should be avoided. A "fix" to this problem is to convert the response variable to a binary indicator, and then model the likelihood (using logit or probit) that a spell will terminate. This approach, as Petersen (1995) notes, is troublesome, because it belies the logic of duration modeling; usually, we are concerned *both* with the occurrence or nonoccurrence of some event *as well as* the length of time the unit survived until the event occurred. This strategy precludes this kind of information. Fortunately, as discussed in this section, event history methods are quite capable of handling censoring.

Time-Varying Covariates

Another complication with the traditional regression-based approach is the inability of the model to account for covariates having values that change over time, that is, time-varying covariates. Analysts are frequently interested in TVCs; however, the traditional regression model approach implicitly treats all covariates as if they are time-invariant. This is a substantial limitation of the OLS model, and thus provides another motivation for event history methods. In the context of event history modeling, TVCs may be readily incorporated into the analysis in a variety of ways; however, as we explain in Chapter 7, TVCs can induce certain complications in both the estimation and interpretation of event history models. Nevertheless, we simply note for now that while traditional modeling approaches cannot easily account for TVCs, event history methods can. The inclusion of TVCs in event history analysis can lead to novel information regarding how the risk of an event occurrence (or duration termination or failure) changes in relation to changes in the value of the TVC. This kind of risk-based interpretation of TVCs is naturally forthcoming from event history methods, where the hazard rate is often modeled directly.

Conclusion

The shortcomings of the regression model provide a statistical motivation for event history analysis. In recognizing that the duration modeling approach can overcome the obvious problems with the traditional linear model, our path is set toward consideration of a wide variety of statistical modeling choices. In this chapter, we have sought to introduce the core conceptual and mathematical concepts underlying event history analysis. We have argued throughout that event history methods naturally follow many research questions of interest to social scientists. Moreover, traditional OLS-type modeling strategies are not always compatible with event history data structures. In the remainder of this book, we consider in detail several possible modeling strategies for event history data. We begin by considering parametric duration models.

CHAPTER 3

Parametric Models for Single-Spell Duration Data

The basic logic underlying parametric event history models is to directly model the time dependency exhibited in event history data. This is easily done by specifying a distribution function for the failure times. If the researcher suspects that the risk of an event occurrence is increasing, or "rising" over time, for example, then one may specify a distribution function that accounts for such a relationship. Social scientists, and in particular, political scientists, have made use of parametric methods to understand such phenomena as coalition durations (King et al. 1990; Warwick 1992), the survival of political leaders (Bueno de Mesquita and Siverson 1995), and the duration of military conflicts (Bennett and Stam 1996). Parametric models for political analysis would seem most reasonable when there exists a strong theoretical expectation regarding the "shape" of the hazard rate (or by extension, survival times), conditional on the covariates included in the model. Under such conditions, correctly specifying the distribution function will yield slightly more precise estimates of the time dependency in the data as well as more precise estimates of covariate parameters than nonparametric approaches in small samples (Collett 1994); however, if the distribution of failure times is parameterized *incorrectly* (for any size sample) then the nice interpretations afforded parametric models may not hold (Bergström and Edin 1992).

We make this cautionary note primarily because parametric methods directly specify the shape of the hazard rate. This will happen even if the parameterization is wrong. But if wrong, the researcher still has the job of interpreting this distribution, which may or may not make substantive sense. Even inferences regarding the relationship between the covariates and the duration time could be misleading since covariate estimates can be sensitive to the distribution function specified. Since the shape of the baseline hazard, given its parameterization, can be highly sensitive to included (or omitted) covariates, the ancillary parameters that give the form of the baseline hazard in a parametric model may widely vary across different submodels. Because of this, we adopt the perspective that time dependency or "duration dependency," in event history models can largely be thought of as a statistical "nuisance."

When one is modeling the hazard rate as a function of covariates, the distribution function specified is conditional on the covariates included in the model. Therefore, the nature of the time dependency exhibited in the data may dramatically change depending on the kinds (and even the number) of covariates included in the model. Therefore, although there may be some *a priori* theoretical basis to select some distribution function, the substantive import of the estimated time dependency should be interpreted as a function of the model.

With these issues in mind, we now consider some of the more common types of parametric event history models. We begin with the exponential model. Because there are few applied settings in social science where the exponential would reasonably hold, we then consider the more flexible Weibull distribution (under which the exponential is nested). After this, we examine the log-normal, log-logistic and Gompertz distribution functions and present applications. We conclude the chapter by discussing estimation methods and approaches to adjudicate among competing parametric forms.

The Exponential Model

The exponential model is a good pedagogical place to start our consideration of parametric duration models due to its simplicity. The defining feature of the exponential model is that its characterization of the baseline hazard rate is flat. This implies that the risk of an event occurring or a transition happening, conditional on covariates, is the *same* at all time points. Because the risk of an event occurrence under the exponential is flat with respect to time, this would imply that the hazard rate is constant. The exponential hazard is given by

$$h(t) = \lambda \qquad t > 0, \lambda > 0, \tag{3.1}$$

where λ is a positive constant. The hazard is "flat" in that the risk or the rate of event occurrences is equal to λ, and is the same at all observation points. Furthermore, if $h(t)$ is expressed as above, the survivor function, $S(t)$, and density function, $f(t)$, are defined from (2.10) and (2.12) as

$$S(t) = \exp^{-\lambda(t)} \tag{3.2}$$

and

$$f(t) = \lambda(t) \exp^{-\lambda(t)}. \tag{3.3}$$

If the density function is specified as in (3.3), then the duration time T has an exponential distribution with mean λ^{-1}. Graphically, the hazard rate plotted against time would be a flat line where the location of $h(t)$ would be fully determined by the value of λ. The mean survival time under the exponential distribution is computed by λ^{-1}, while the percentiles of the duration times for the exponential model are derived from the formula

$$t(\text{p'tile}) = \lambda^{-1} \log \left(\frac{100}{100 - \text{p'tile}} \right), \tag{3.4}$$

where $t(\text{p'tile})$ is the percentile of interest. Thus, for the median survival time, $t(\text{p'tile})$ in (3.4) is equal to 50 percent and is found by $\lambda^{-1} \log 2$.

The exponential distribution is fully determined by the parameter λ, and so modeling the dependency of the hazard rate or of the expected duration time, λ^{-1}, on covariates entails constructing a model that ensures a nonnegative hazard rate or similarly, a nonnegative expected duration time. This is the case because duration times must be positive. A common way the exponential model is parameterized is in terms of a *log-linear* model. The log-linear form of the exponential is given by

$$\log(T) = \beta_0 + \beta_1 x_{i1} + \beta_2 x_{i2} + \ldots + \beta_j x_{ij}, \tag{3.5}$$

and it is easy to see that in this form, (3.5) is a linear model for the log of the survival times (the log-linear approach is discussed in more detail in the next section). We can derive a model for the expected duration time. Letting $\lambda_i^{-1} = E(t_i)$, the following model could be estimated:

$$E(t_i) = \exp(\beta_0 + \beta_1 x_{i1} + \beta_2 x_{i2} + \ldots + \beta_j x_{ij}), \tag{3.6}$$

where $E(t_i)$ is the expected duration time for the ith observation, x_{ij} are the covariates, and β_j are the parameters (with β_0 denoting the constant term in the regression model). The model in (3.6) can be rewritten in more compact form using vector notation:

$$E(t_i) = \exp^{\beta' \mathbf{x}}, \tag{3.7}$$

where the first element of β is the constant term. A model treating the hazard rate as a function of covariates can be easily written using (3.7). Since T is exponentially distributed, conditional on the covariates, the parameter λ can be expressed as

$$\lambda = \exp^{-(\beta' \mathbf{x})}. \tag{3.8}$$

Consequently, the hazard rate (with covariates) for the exponential model is obtained by substituting (3.8) into (3.1):

$$h(t \mid \mathbf{x}) = \exp^{-(\beta' \mathbf{x})}. \tag{3.9}$$

We can rewrite (3.9) to demonstrate an important property of the exponential model:

$$h(t \mid \mathbf{x}) = \exp^{(-\beta_0)} \exp^{-(\beta' \mathbf{x})}, \qquad (3.10)$$

where β_0 is the constant term. Expressed in this way, it is easy to see that the *baseline hazard rate* is equal to β_0, a constant. Any increase or decrease to the baseline hazard rate is solely a function of the covariates. Changes to the baseline hazard in (3.10) are a multiple of the baseline hazard rate. Suppose there is a single binary covariate, x_1, with parameter β_1. The baseline hazard rate in this case would be $\exp(-\beta_0)$, and the hazard rate for the case of $x_1 = 1$ would be $\exp(-\beta_0) \times \exp(-\beta_1 x_1)$ or equivalently, $\exp(-\beta_0 - \beta_1 x_1)$. Since the increase (or decrease) in the hazard rate when $x_1 = 1$ is a multiple of the baseline hazard rate, the change in the hazard rate is proportional to the baseline hazard and is assumed to hold for all time points. This is seen more clearly by noting that the ratio of the two hazards

$$\frac{h_i(t \mid x_1 = 1)}{h_i(t \mid x_1 = 0)} = \exp^{-\beta_1} \qquad (3.11)$$

is equal to the multiple of the baseline, i.e., $\exp^{-\beta_1}$. This result is known as the *proportional hazards* property. As we will show, other types of event history models also have this important property. It is important to note that this property may not hold for all (or some) covariates in a model. Consequently, it will be important for researchers to test the proportional hazards assumption when applying models where this assumption is maintained. In Chapter 8, we discuss this issue in detail.

The simplicity of the exponential model is appealing; however, this simplicity is its major shortcoming. The exponential distribution is a "memoryless" distribution. The probability of an individual surviving beyond some time t_1 conditional on having survived to t_0 is equal to

$$\Pr(T \geq t_1 \mid T \geq t_0) = \frac{\Pr(T \geq t_1)}{\Pr(T \geq t_0)},$$

which by (2.5) is equal to $S(t_1)/S(t_0)$, that is, the ratio of the survivor functions.[1] Since $S(t) = \exp^{-\lambda t}$ (given by [3.2]), then

$$\Pr(T \geq t_1 \mid T \geq t_0) = \exp^{-\lambda(t_1 - t_0)}.$$

---

[1] Formally, this is obtained by a result from conditional probability. Specifically,

$$\Pr(T \geq t_1 \mid T \geq t_0) = \frac{\Pr(T \geq t_1) \cap \Pr(T \geq 0)}{\Pr(T \geq t_0)},$$

but since $t_1 > t_0$, this conditional probability reduces to

$$\Pr(T \geq t_1 \mid T \geq t_0) = \frac{\Pr(T \geq t_1)}{\Pr(T \geq t_0)},$$

which is equivalent to $S(t_1)/S(t_0)$. Collett (1994) discusses this result in more detail.

This implies that the survival time observed beyond t_0 *also* has an exponential distribution (with mean λ^{-1}). The exponential distribution is "memoryless" because the distribution of the increased survival time is not affected by knowing the observation had survived for a certain length of time (Collett 1994). This is a strong assumption and one that is likely to be inappropriate for most applications.

An additional feature of the exponential distribution is that the distribution is fully determined by a single parameter, λ. The mean of the exponential distribution is λ^{-1} and the variance is the square of the mean, that is $(\lambda^{-1})^2$. Once the mean is estimated, the variance is fixed and may not be estimated separately from the data. This is extremely restrictive; a more flexible alternative to the exponential may be preferable. In the next section, we consider an alternative parameterization.

The Weibull Model

A more flexible alternative to the exponential distribution is the Weibull distribution. The defining feature of the Weibull parameterization of the baseline hazard is that it is characterized as monotonic. The baseline hazard given by the Weibull can be monotonically increasing, monotonically decreasing or flat with respect to time. Because a flat hazard can be produced by the Weibull, it turns out that the exponential distribution is simply a special case of the Weibull. It is important to point out that just as the assumption of a flat hazard seems unrealistic for many applied social science questions, *so too* does the assumption of ever-increasing or ever-decreasing hazard rates. While the Weibull permits the hazard to change (in one direction) with respect to time, this characterization of the hazard rate is probably only slightly less implausible for many research questions. Nevertheless, models parameterized in terms of the Weibull are ubiquitous in applied social science research and so we consider the Weibull in some detail.

If a researcher suspects the hazard rate is increasing or decreasing then a Weibull distribution function may be appropriate. To illustrate how the Weibull hazard can monotonically vary with respect to time, we can express hazard rate for the Weibull distribution as

$$h(t) = \lambda p (\lambda t)^{p-1} \qquad t > 0, \lambda > 0, p > 0, \qquad (3.12)$$

where λ is a positive scale parameter and p is known as the shape parameter. The p term gets its name because the shape of the hazard rate depends on the value of this term. When $p > 1$, the hazard rate is *monotonically* increasing with time; when $p < 1$, the hazard rate is *monotonically* decreasing with time; when $p = 1$, the hazard is flat, taking a constant value λ. For the case of $p = 1$, the hazard rate has an exponential distribution. It is easy to see that the Weibull distribution is more flexible than the exponential since it is a function of two parameters, λ and p, and not a single parameter.

The survivor and density functions for the Weibull are, respectively,

$$S(t) = \exp^{-(\lambda t)^p}, \tag{3.13}$$

and

$$f(t) = \lambda p (\lambda t)^{p-1} \exp^{-(\lambda t)^p}. \tag{3.14}$$

The mean duration time, or equivalently, the expected value of the random variable T is given by

$$E(T) = \frac{\Gamma(1 + \frac{1}{p})}{\lambda}, \tag{3.15}$$

where Γ denotes the gamma function. Since the Weibull density in (3.14) is defined for $0 \le t \le \infty$, the Weibull distribution will be right-skewed and the median may be a better summary of the duration times. The percentiles of the Weibull distribution are computed by

$$t(\text{p'tile}) = \lambda^{-1} \log \left(\frac{100}{100 - \text{p'tile}} \right)^{1/p}, \tag{3.16}$$

so for the median duration time, $t(\text{p'tile})$ in (3.16) is 50 percent, and is computed by $\lambda^{-1} \log(2)^{1/p}$.

A common way to parameterize the Weibull model in terms of covariates is by constructing a linear model for $\log(T)$ (recall [3.5]). This involves the specification of a log-linear model and treating the log of the survival times as the response variable. This parameterization is convenient since it permits easier comparison with the traditional linear model. The Weibull expressed as a log-linear model has the following form:

$$\log(T) = \beta_0 + \beta_1 x_{i1} + \beta_2 x_{i2} + \ldots + \beta_j x_{ij} + \sigma \epsilon, \tag{3.17}$$

and in vector notation,

$$\log(T) = \beta_j' \mathbf{x} + \sigma \epsilon, \tag{3.18}$$

where β_j are the regression coefficients, x_{ij} are time independent covariates, ϵ is a stochastic disturbance term with a type-1 extreme-value distribution scaled by σ, which is equivalent to $1/p$.[2] Because the regression parameters in (3.18) are expressed in terms of the log of the duration times, the coefficients convey information regarding expected failure times. For this reason, this model is

---

[2]There is a close connection between the Weibull distribution and the extreme value distribution. Specifically, the distribution of the log of a Weibull distributed random variable gives rise to the type-1 extreme value distribution. Hence, the log of a Weibull random variable is a type-1 extreme value random variable (indeed, sometimes this parameterization is referred to as a log-Weibull distribution).

sometimes referred to as a "log expected failure time model" or more conventionally as an *accelerated failure time* (AFT) model.

Like the exponential model, the Weibull model is a proportional hazards model. One way to see this property is to express the hazard rate for the Weibull as a function of a baseline hazard and of covariates:

$$h(t \mid \mathbf{x}) = h_{0t} \exp(\alpha_1 x_{i1} + \alpha_2 x_{i2} + \ldots + \alpha_j x_{ij}), \qquad (3.19)$$

where h_{0t} is the baseline hazard rate and is equivalent to $\exp(\alpha_0) p t^{p-1}$ (where α_0 is the parameter for the regression constant term). We use α to denote the parameters in order to distinguish this model from the model given by (3.18). Rewriting (3.19) to explicitly account for the constant term, we obtain

$$h(t \mid \mathbf{x}) = \exp(\alpha_0) p t^{p-1} \exp(\alpha_1 x_{i1} + \alpha_2 x_{i2} + \ldots + \alpha_j x_{ij}), \qquad (3.20)$$

and in more compact form,

$$h(t \mid \mathbf{x}) = p t^{p-1} \exp(\alpha_j' \mathbf{x}), \qquad (3.21)$$

where the first element of α_j now includes the parameter α_0. The Weibull distribution is a function of two parameters, the scale parameter and the shape parameter. In the parameterization shown in (3.21), the scale parameter can be thought of as $\exp(\alpha_j' \mathbf{x})$, and the shape parameter is p. The impact of the covariates is to alter the scale parameter, while the shape of the distribution remains constant. Therefore, because the impact of the covariates are a multiple of the baseline hazard (which is most clearly shown in (3.20)), it is clear that the Weibull model is a member of the proportional hazards family of models. Indeed, the parameterization given by (3.21) is commonly referred to as the *proportional hazards* parameterization.

Example 3.1: Weibull Model of U.N. Peacekeeping Missions

To illustrate the Weibull model, we analyze data on the duration of United Nation peacekeeping missions from 1948 (the start of the first U.N. Peacekeeping Mission) to 2001. These data were originally analyzed in Green, Kahl, and Diehl (1998). There are two binary covariates to denote the three types of conflicts precipitating a U.N. peacekeeping force. The first covariate denotes whether or not the mission occurs in response to a civil war and the second whether or not the mission occurs in response to an interstate conflict. The omitted category (when both covariates are 0) is the baseline category and denotes an internationalized civil war.

The results of the estimation are shown in Table 3.1. There are three sets of parameter estimates. To facilitate comparison of the Weibull with the exponential, the first column of estimates corresponds to an exponential model. The

TABLE 3.1: Weibull Model of U.N. Peacekeeping Missions

| | Model Parameterized As: | | |
	Exponential Model	Weibull A.F.T.	Weibull Prop. Hazards
Variable	Estimate (s.e.)	Estimate (s.e.)	Estimate (s.e.)
Constant	4.35 (.21)	4.29 (.27)	−3.46 (.50)
Civil War	−1.16 (.36)	−1.10 (.45)	.89 (.38)
Interstate Conflict	1.64 (.50)	1.74 (.62)	−1.40 (.51)
Shape Parameter		$\sigma = 1.24$ (.15)	$p = .81$ (.10)
N	54	54	54
Log-Likelihood	−86.35	−84.66	−84.66

The baseline category denoted by the constant term represents the category of "internationalized civil wars." The column labeled "Accelerated Failure Time" presents the Weibull model estimates parameterized in terms of the model in Equation (3.21). The column labeled "Proportional Hazards" presents the Weibull model estimates parameterized in terms of the model in Equation (3.18).

second column of estimates is the AFT parameterization of the Weibull model (see 3.18), and the third column presents the proportional hazards Weibull parameterization (see 3.21). Recall that under the exponential model, the duration of peacekeeping missions is assumed to be time independent, thus yielding a flat hazard rate. However, since the exponential model is nested under the Weibull, it is easy to test this assumption. The estimates in Table 3.1 are maximum likelihood estimates, and as such, are asymptotically normal (under regularity conditions). Therefore, by testing the hypothesis that p (or σ) is equal to one, the adequacy of the duration independence assumption can be assessed with the following test statistic (using p):

$$z = \frac{p-1}{\text{s.e.}(p)}.$$

For this application, $p = .807(.10)$ and so $z = -1.93$. The probability of getting this z value by chance is about .05. This provides some evidence that the hazard rate for the U.N. Peacekeeping Missions, conditional on the covariates, exhibits time dependency. In particular, since $p < 1$ (and $\sigma > 1$), the hazard rate is decreasing over time. The interpretation of this time dependency is that the longer a peacekeeping mission lasts, the risk of it subsequently terminating decreases. Whether this interpretation is substantively interesting or not, it is clear that when compared to a model assuming a flat hazard rate, the model allowing the rate to vary is preferable on statistical grounds.

Examining the coefficients for the Weibull model, it is useful to point out the correspondence between parameter estimates of the AFT model and of the proportional hazards model. For the AFT model, which is a linear model for $\log(T)$, a positive coefficient is indicative of "longer" durations for different values of the covariate. In contrast, for the proportional hazards parameterization, because it is expressed in terms of the hazard rate, a positively signed coefficient implies that the risk of termination (or failure) increases for different values of the covariate. Further, because the parameters of one model are a simple transformation of the other, the coefficient signs for a given covariate across the two parameterizations will always be opposite. For example, we see that for the Civil War covariate, the parameter estimate for the AFT model is -1.10. To express this in the metric of the proportional hazards model, we transform the estimate as $-(-1.10)/\sigma$, which gives the proportional hazards estimate of .89. In the remainder of this section, we interpret the results of our models in terms of the accelerated failure time parameterization.

Since the parameter estimates are maximum likelihood, the interpretation of any one covariate depends on the values of the other covariates. For this reason, it is usually best to interpret the parameter estimates by computing expected duration times and median duration times for substantively interesting covariate profiles. For the U.N. Peacekeeping Missions data, we computed the expected duration time, $E(T)$ and median duration time for each type of intervention as represented by the covariates. For internationalized civil wars, we find that the expected duration of peacekeeping missions is about 82 months, with a median duration time of 46 months. In contrast, the exponential model results predicts these times to be 78 months and 54 months, respectively. For civil wars, the Weibull model predicts $E(T) = 27$ months and the median duration time to be 15 months. Finally, for interstate conflicts, these predicted duration times are $E(T) = 466$ months, and the median $= 263$ months.

We can gauge the impact a covariate has on the expected duration time since p (or σ) does not vary across observations. In this application, since the binary covariates are mutually exclusive, the value of $\exp(\hat{\beta})$ (where $\hat{\beta}$ is an estimated parameter in the AFT model) is equal to the relative expected duration time when the covariate equals 1 compared to when the covariate equals 0. Here, we see that the parameter estimate for interstate conflicts is 1.74. Consequently, interventions prompted by interstate conflicts are about 6 times longer, i.e., $\exp(1.74)$ than durations prompted by internationalized civil wars (the baseline category). Similarly, the expected duration time for missions prompted by civil wars is about 33 percent that of missions prompted by internationalized civil wars, i.e., $\exp(-1.10)$.

Additionally, substantive interpretation of event history models can be greatly facilitated by the use of graphs. For this application, we computed the estimated hazard rate for each of the covariates using the formula in equation (3.12). With covariates, λ in equation (3.12) is equal to $\exp(-\beta)$. So for the baseline category of internationalized civil wars, the estimated hazard rate, $h(t)$, is $\exp(-4.29).81(\exp(-4.29)t)^{.81-1}$, where .81 corresponds to p. The hazard rate for the other two conflict types is a simple extension of this result.

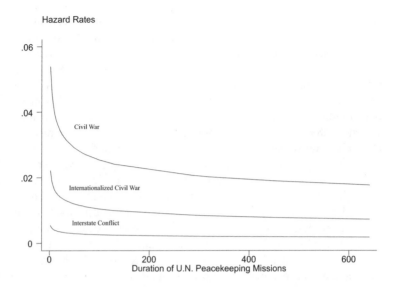

FIGURE 3.1: *This graph gives the Weibull hazard rates by the type of conflict that precipitated the U.N. Peacekeeping Mission.*

The estimated hazard rates are illustrated in Figure 3.1.[3] We see that the hazard rate for peacekeeping missions prompted by civil wars is highest, followed next by internationalized civil wars, and then by interstate conflicts. This is consonant with our results regarding the mean and median duration times for these conflict types: missions prompted by civil wars have the lowest mean and median duration times and concomitantly have the highest hazard rate.

It is also worth pointing out the proportional hazards property of the Weibull model. The three hazard rates plotted in Figure 3.1 differ in terms of the scale, λ, but are identical in terms of their shape. This is indicative of the proportional hazards property. In particular, the proportional difference in the hazard rates is constant over time and is equivalent to

$$\frac{h_i(t \mid \mathbf{x_i})}{h_j(t \mid \mathbf{x_j})} = \left[\frac{\lambda_i}{\lambda_j} \right]^p,$$

where $\lambda = \exp(-\beta)$ and the i and j subscripts denote two covariate profiles. In Figure 3.1, the ratio between the hazard rates for civil wars and internationalized civil wars is about 2.42, which is equal to $[\exp(-3.19)/\exp(-4.29)]^{.81}$. The proportionality between the other hazards can be computed in a similar

---

[3]For illustrative purposes, we have omitted computing standard errors around the estimated hazard rates given in this figure and in subsequent figures.

fashion. Again, it is important to note that the assumption of proportionality is a testable assumption. In Chapter 8, we discuss this in detail.

In this application, all of the covariates were binary variables. Frequently, researchers will also need to interpret quantitative covariates. To formally assess the impact of a continuous-level covariate, it is important to recognize that this relationship is conditional on the value of all other covariates in the model. As Beck (1998) notes, one way to assess the effect a small change in the value of a covariate has on the expected duration time is to compute the change in the expected value of T with respect to changes in the value of the covariate. This may be done by taking the following derivative:

$$\frac{\partial E(T)}{\partial x_j} = \beta_j e^{\beta' \mathbf{x}} \Gamma\left(1 + \frac{1}{p}\right)$$

$$= \beta_j E(T), \tag{3.22}$$

where $E(T)$ is the mean duration time for some set of covariates. With several covariates, $E(T)$ (as well as the median duration time) can be computed for many different covariate profiles. In terms of substantively interpreting a continuous-level covariate, then, it is often useful to compute the derivative in (3.22), the expected duration time, and the median duration time for interesting combinations of the covariates. Graphs of the survivor function and hazard rate for different constellations of covariates also nicely summarize the information produced in the event history model with quantitative covariates.

To conclude this section, we have intended to highlight and demonstrate the various ways to substantively interpret and present the results of event history models using the Weibull and exponential models. Owing to the popularity of the Weibull model in political science research, we have considered in detail this model. Nevertheless, in some settings, the assumption of monotonic hazards may be inappropriate. We turn to two alternative distributions that permit nonmonotonic hazards.

The Log-Logistic and Log-Normal Models

Two distribution functions that avoid the assumption of monotonic hazard rates are the log-logistic and log-normal. These distributions allow for nonmonotonic hazard rates. In practice, models parameterized in terms of these distributions yield very similar parameter estimates and characterizations of the hazard and survival functions; therefore, in this section, we consider the two models together.

We begin by specifying a log-linear duration model:

$$\log(T) = \beta'_j \mathbf{x} + \sigma \epsilon. \tag{3.23}$$

This parameterization is linear model for $\log(T)$. If a logistic distribution is specified for ϵ, then the log-logistic model is implied. If a standard normal

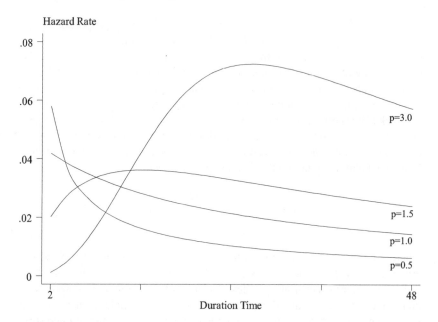

FIGURE 3.2: *This figure graphs some typically shaped hazard rates for the log-logistic model.*

distribution is specified for ϵ, then the log-normal model is implied. For each model, the distribution is scaled by the parameter σ, which is equivalent to the inverse of the shape parameter, p.[4] The hazard rate for the log-logistic can be nonmonotonic and unimodal. To see this, note that the hazard rate for the log-logistic,

$$h(t) = \frac{\lambda p (\lambda t)^{p-1}}{1 + (\lambda t)^p}, \qquad (3.24)$$

first increases and then decreases if $p > 1$, but is monotonically decreasing when $p \leq 1$. Figure 3.2 shows the forms the log-logistic hazard rate can take for various values of p. This figure illustrates the wider variety of hazard rates given by the log-logistic and log-normal models, than when compared to the Weibull.

---

[4]Note that under equation (3.18), the Weibull can be parameterized as log-linear model. Using log-linear formulation of (3.18) and (3.23), it is clear that the Weibull, log-logistic, and log-normal models are similar in one respect: they each are two-parameter distributions, i.e., σ and ϵ, for $\log(T)$. This point is important because although the log-logistic and log-normal can produce non-monotonic hazard rates, *neither* of these models are any more flexible than the Weibull model. For the log-logistic, log-normal, *and* Weibull models, once the mean and variance of the distribution are estimated, its shape is fixed. It is therefore misleading to think that a model permitting non-monotonic hazards is "more general" than the Weibull.

The survivor function for the log-logistic model is given by

$$S(t) = \frac{1}{1 + (\lambda t)^p},$$
(3.25)

while the probability density function is given by

$$f(t) = \frac{\lambda p (\lambda t)^{p-1}}{(1 + (\lambda t)^p)^2},$$
(3.26)

which is a symmetric density. Percentiles of the survival times for the log-logistic distribution can be computed by

$$t(\text{p'tile}) = \lambda^{-1} \left[\frac{100 - \text{p'tile}}{\text{p'tile}} \right]^{1/p}.$$
(3.27)

So for the median survival time, $t(50)$ is equal to λ^{-1}. The hazard rate and survivor functions for the log-logistic model can readily incorporate time-independent covariates. If the model is parameterized in terms of the log-linear model of (3.23), then $\lambda = e^{-\beta' x}$.

The logistic density is very similar to the normal density.[5] The derivation of the log-normal hazard rate is not as straightforward as it is for some of the other models we have considered. The hazard, $h(t)$, must be expressed in terms of integrals of the standard normal distribution. The survivor function for the log-normal model can be written as

$$S(t) = 1 - \Phi\left(\frac{\log(t) - \beta' x}{\sigma} \right),$$
(3.28)

where Φ is the cumulative distribution function for the standard normal distribution and $\beta' x$ are the covariates and parameter vector from (3.23). The probability density function for the log-normal model is given by

$$f(t) = \frac{1}{\sigma \sqrt{(2\pi)}} t^{-1} \exp\left[-\frac{1}{2} \left(\frac{\log(t) - \beta' x}{\sigma} \right)^2 \right],$$
(3.29)

where σ is the scale parameter of ϵ from (3.23). Given equation (2.6), the hazard rate for the log-normal is

$$h(t) = \frac{f(t)}{S(t)}.$$
(3.30)

[5]The similarity between the log-logistic and log-normal model is analogous to the similarity between the logit and probit models that are often applied to models with discrete dependent variables. A logit model is specified in terms of the logistic distribution, while the probit is specified in terms of the standard normal distribution. The similarity across distributions produces the similarity in results given by logit and probit models.

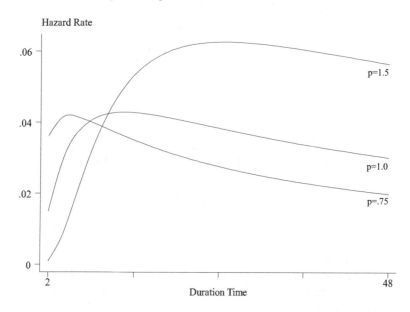

FIGURE 3.3: *This figure graphs some typically shaped hazard rates for the log-normal model.*

Noting that $\sigma = p^{-1}$, in Figure 3.3 we illustrate the nonmonotonicity of the log-normal hazard rate for various values of p. When p is small, the hazard rate rises to its peak very quickly and then falls. As Allison (1995) notes, for very small values of p, the hazard rate for the log-normal is almost indistinguishable from a decreasing Weibull hazard.

Like the log-logistic, the log-normal distribution is a symmetric distribution. The percentiles of the survival times for the log-normal may be calculated by

$$t(\text{p'tile}) = \lambda^{-1} \exp\left[\frac{-\mathbf{\Phi}^{-1} - m}{p}\right], \qquad (3.31)$$

where m corresponds to the fractional representation of the percentile of interest and $\mathbf{\Phi}^{-1}$ is the inverse of the standard normal cumulative distribution function. For the median, m in equation (3.31) is .50 and so $t(50) = \lambda^{-1}$. As in the case of the log-logistic model, time-independent covariates may be incorporated into the hazard and survivor functions of the log-normal by treating $\lambda = e^{-\beta' \mathbf{x}}$. Both the log-logistic and the log-normal distributions differ from the Weibull in one important aspect: neither of these distributions have the proportional hazards property. This can be seen by examining the hazard rates of the two models, shown in (3.24) and (3.30). Unlike the Weibull, where the differences across hazard rates are a multiple of the baseline hazard (recall

(3.19), this relationship does not hold for the log-logistic or log-normal models. Consequently, for models parameterized in terms of these distributions, not only can the scale differ in terms of λ, but the shape of the hazard rates will also differ.

Example 3.2: Models of Candidacy Winnowing

We illustrate the log-logistic and log-normal models using data on the duration of candidacies in U.S. presidential primaries for the presidential election years of 1980-1996 (see Norrander 2000a, 2000b). The dependent variable in the application is measured as the number of days starting at January 1 of the election year that a candidate stays in the race until voluntarily withdrawing from the race. Candidates not withdrawing by June 15 of the election year are treated as right-censored.[6] In all, there are 47 candidates that comprise the data set.

Several covariates are of interest in this application. Because media attention and early success in the primary season is likely to be associated with longer candidacies, we use the percentage of votes the candidate received in the New Hampshire primary, which is historically the first primary in the presidential nominee selection process. The mean for this covariate is 16.1 percent with a standard deviation of 14.9. A second covariate used in the application is a binary indicator denoting whether or not the candidate had held or is holding a visible elected position. "Visible office" is defined as having held or currently holding a seat as U.S. Senator, U.S. Representative, Governor, Vice President, or President. To measure campaign finance, we have included as a covariate the amount of money (in millions of dollars) raised by the candidate by January 1 of the election year. The mean of this covariate is 5.7 and the standard deviation is 5.7.

Also of interest in the application is assessing the impact that primary rules have on candidacy durations. The first rule of interest denotes how "frontloaded" the primary season is in terms of allocated delegates. As the number of allocated delegates is pushed closer to the start of the primary season, the duration of candidacies might become shorter. "Frontloading" is a measure of the percentage of delegates that are decided by March 31 of the election year. The mean of this covariate is 52.9 and the standard deviation is 12.1. Additionally, there is reason to assess differences in party responsiveness to this rule. The Republican party has exerted much less control over the scheduling of presidential primaries than has the Democratic party. As a result, state Republican parties have tended to move the primary date forward to garner more national media exposure. In contrast, the Democratic party has exerted much more control over the scheduling of presidential primaries.

---

[6]June 15 was chosen as the end-date of the primary season because it corresponds to the last week of the primary season.

As a result, we might expect that the duration of Republican candidacies is impacted more by frontloading rules than are Democratic candidacies. For this reason, we created an interaction between the covariate measuring the percentage of frontloaded primaries with the party of the candidate. The candidate party variable is a binary, denoted 1 if the candidate is a Republican and 0 if the candidate is a Democrat. Because the interest in this covariate is to assess how candidacy durations are influenced by changes to primary frontloading, we deviated the value of this covariate from its mean, by party, across the five elections, where 56.98 is the mean percentage of frontloaded delegates for Republican primaries and 48.56 is the mean for Democrats. This procedure produces a covariate such that increases from the average of the percentage of frontloaded delegates result in a positive deviation and decreases result in a negative deviation.

The second rule we consider is the percentage of primaries in the election cycle where delegates are allocated proportional to the number of votes the candidate received. This covariate, denoted below as "PR," indicates the percentage of primaries that use a PR allocation system. The mean for this covariate is 53.4 and the standard deviation is 21.8. Beginning in the 1980s, the Democratic party, particularly, began to tinker with P.R. rules in the primary process. In an effort to make the primary process "fairer" to all candidates, the Democratic party has exerted more control over the primary process, insisting that delegates be allocated proportional to votes, rather than as winner-take-all (Norrander 2000a). Some political scientists have argued that an implication of increasing the number of PR-based primaries is that the primary season is prolonged (Ansolabehere and King 1990). Given this assertion, we created an interaction between the PR covariate and the binary variable indicating the party affiliation of the candidate. As with the frontloading covariate, we mean-deviated the PR covariate around the mean for each party. For Republicans, the group mean is 38.62, and for Democrats, the group mean is 68.86.

The parameter estimates for the model are presented in Table 3.2. The first column of estimates correspond to the log-logistic model and the second column of estimates are for the log-normal model. Because these models are parameterized in terms of the log-linear model shown in (3.23), both of the models are AFT models. As such, a positively signed coefficient implies that the expected duration increases for changes in the values of the covariate while a negatively signed coefficient implies the expected duration decreases for changes in the values of the covariate. Looking at the scale parameter first, the value of σ is less than 1 implying that the hazard rate rises and then begins to decline at some point. We computed median survival times for Democratic candidates and Republican candidates by setting each of the other covariates to their mean, and setting the value of the "visible office" covariate to 1.

Substantively, we see that the hazard rate for these covariate profiles is higher for Republicans than Democrats. From the log-logistic estimates, we

TABLE 3.2: Log-Logistic and Log-Normal Models of Primary Exits

| | Model Parameterized As: | |
	Log-Logistic	Log-Normal
Variable	Estimate (s.e.)	Estimate (s.e.)
Constant	4.711 (.222)	4.697 (.217)
New Hampshire Vote	.028 (.006)	.027 (.006)
Campaign Finance	.016 (.018)	.006 (.017)
Republican Candidate	−.267 (.173)	−.196 (.170)
Percent P.R.	.000 (.005)	.000 (.005)
Frontloading	−.005 (.013)	−.005 (.015)
Rep. × P.R.	−.046 (.028)	−.047 (.029)
Rep. × Front.	−.023 (.018)	.016 (.020)
Visible Office	−.539 (.211)	−.436 (.199)
Scale Parameter	$\sigma = .255(.038)$	$\sigma = .451(.060)$
N	47	47
Log-Likelihood	−30.820	−31.280

find that the median duration time for Republicans is about 85 days and for Democrats, the median duration time is about 111 days. The log-normal model estimates of the median duration times are similar. We find that for Republicans, the median duration time is about 93 days and for Democrats, the median duration time is about 113 days. Despite the differences in these estimated survival times, the two models yield similar parameter estimates. For example, consider the interaction terms. Contrary to the expectations of Ansolabehere and King (1990), this model shows that the duration time of Democratic candidates is not sensitive to changes in P.R. rules in the primaries. This interaction (for Democrats) is no different from 0. This implies that despite Democratic efforts to more fairly allocate delegates, Democratic candidacy durations have remained unaffected by these changes. We find that Republicans seem to respond to changes in the rules regarding P.R. allocation. As the percentage of P.R.-based primaries increase, the duration of Republican candidacies tends to decrease slightly. This result may be indicative of other dynamics not accounted for by this model. Regarding delegate frontloading, we find no evidence that the duration of candidacies for either the Republican or Democrats is affected by changes in this rule. Regarding the influence of early success, we find that the success in the New Hampshire primary is strongly related to the duration of candidacies.

The Gompertz Model

The parametric models considered to this point are the most commonly used in the applied research of political scientists; however, duration models may be parameterized in a variety of ways apart from the Weibull, log-logistic, and log-normal. The Gompertz distribution is a popular choice for use in demographic research because the hazard rate is treated as an exponential function of the duration times, which is in contrast to the Weibull. Hazard rates produced by the Gompertz often do a good job of describing mortality data as well (Kalbfleisch and Prentice 1980). The hazard rate for the Gompertz, which is characterized as either being monotonically increasing, decreasing, or flat, is given by

$$h(t) = \exp^{\gamma t} \exp^{\lambda}, \qquad (3.32)$$

where γ is the shape parameter for the Gompertz distribution and $\lambda = \exp(\beta \mathbf{x})$. When $\gamma > 0$, the hazard rate is rising, when $\gamma < 0$, the hazard rate is decreasing, and when $\gamma = 0$, the hazard rate is flat, with respect to time. The survivor function for the Gompertz distribution is

$$S(t) = e^{-\frac{e^{\lambda}}{\gamma}(e^{\gamma t} - 1)}, \qquad (3.33)$$

while the density function is given by

$$f(t) = e^{(e^{\lambda} e^{\gamma t}) - \frac{e^{\lambda}}{\gamma}(e^{\gamma t} - 1)}. \qquad (3.34)$$

From equation (3.32), it is clear the Gompertz model is a proportional hazards model. If covariates are included in the estimation of the Gompertz model, $\lambda = e^{\beta' \mathbf{x}}$. In demography applications, the assumption of exponential growth (or decay) may be reasonable; however, in political analysis, the applicability of the Gompertz may be limited (but see Strang 1991).

Having discussed several parametric forms, the question naturally arises as to how to choose among various parametric forms. At the end of this chapter, we consider methods to adjudicate among nested and nonnested models. To illustrate these methods, we first need to consider general estimation methods for parametric models.

Estimation of Parametric Models

In this section, we provide an overview of estimation methods for fully parametric event history models (for a more detailed treatment of the issues raised here, see Kalbfleisch and Prentice 1980, Collett 1994, Blossfeld and Rohwer 2002, Klein and Moeschberger 1997, or Hosmer and Lemeshow 1999). The models presented in this chapter can all be estimated by maximum likelihood (MLE). In Chapter 2, we briefly discussed maximum likelihood in the context of censoring. In this section, we continue this presentation and illustrate how the MLE can be derived in terms of the distribution functions discussed in this chapter.

Suppose we have n observations with $t_1, t_2, \ldots t_n$ duration times. Furthermore, assume that these observed durations are independent (conditional on any covariates) realizations from the random variable T. Some duration times may be censored or uncensored; however, we assume that the censoring is non-informative. Deriving an MLE entails specifying a probability density function for the random variable T. In so doing, we assume that the probability of the t observed durations times can be derived from this probability density function. Hence, not only do we assume the observations are independent, but they are identically distributed, with the distribution being defined by the density function. Sometimes this condition is referred to as i.i.d., or "independent and identically distributed."

Specifying a probability density function therefore entails defining $f(t)$ for the data. From this, the survivor function, $S(t)$, can be retrieved. The likelihood function for event history data, as noted in Chapter 2, is a function of two components: the density of failure times, $f(t)$, and the survivor function, $S(t)$. The likelihood function is complete when the probability density function is defined for each observation. The general likelihood function for event history data is

$$\mathcal{L} = \prod_{i=1}^{n} \left\{ f(t_i) \right\}^{\delta_i} \left\{ S(t_i) \right\}^{1-\delta_i}, \tag{3.35}$$

where δ is a censoring indicator denoted 0 if the observed duration is censored and 1 if it is not. Although noted in Chapter 2, it bears repeating that censored observations only contribute to the likelihood function in (3.35) through the survivor function; such observations contribute no information regarding the failure times.

Throughout this chapter, we have defined the density function, $f(t)$, for each of the distributions discussed. In practice, deriving the likelihood implies defining $f(t)$ in terms of a distribution. So, for example, in the case of the Weibull distribution,

$$f(t) = \lambda p(\lambda t)^{p-1} \exp^{-(\lambda t)^p},$$

and the survivor function is

$$S(t) = \exp^{-(\lambda t)^p}.$$

The likelihood of the t duration times is obtained by substituting these functions into (3.35):

$$\mathcal{L} = \prod_{i=1}^{n} \left\{ \lambda p(\lambda t)^{p-1} \exp^{-(\lambda t)^p} \right\}^{\delta_i} \left\{ \exp^{-(\lambda t)^p} \right\}^{1-\delta_i}. \tag{3.36}$$

Through (3.36), it is easy to see that the likelihood of the duration times is solely a function of two parameters: λ and p. For a model like the exponential, the likelihood is a function of a single parameter, λ:

$$\mathcal{L} = \prod_{i=1}^{n} \left\{ \lambda(t) \exp^{-\lambda(t)} \right\}^{\delta_i} \left\{ \exp^{-\lambda(t)} \right\}^{1-\delta_i}, \tag{3.37}$$

which simplifies to

$$\mathcal{L} = \prod_{i=1}^{n} \lambda^{\delta_i} \exp^{-\lambda(t)}. \qquad (3.38)$$

Noting that $\lambda = e^{-\beta x}$, it is straightforward to see how covariates are included in the likelihood function. The maximum value of this function gives the parameter estimates that maximize the likelihood of the observed data. However, it is generally easier to solve the likelihood function by maximizing the log of the likelihood function. Continuing with the exponential distribution, the log-likelihood function is obtained by taking the logarithm of (7.6):

$$L = \sum_{i=1}^{n} \delta_i \log \lambda - \lambda \sum_{i=1}^{n} t_i. \qquad (3.39)$$

The maximum likelihood estimate for the model is the value of λ for which the log-likelihood function is maximized. To find this, we differentiate the log-likelihood with respect to λ, which gives

$$\frac{\partial \log L}{\partial \lambda} = \frac{\sum_{i=1}^{n} \delta_i}{\lambda} - \sum_{i=1}^{n} t_i. \qquad (3.40)$$

Setting the derivative in (3.40) to 0 and evaluating λ at this point gives

$$\hat{\lambda} = \frac{\sum_{i=1}^{n} \delta_i}{\sum_{i=1}^{n} t_i}, \qquad (3.41)$$

which is the maximum likelihood estimator of λ. When λ consists of several covariate parameters, there are as many likelihood equations to solve as there are parameters to estimate. For most problems, there is no analytical solution for these equations and so iterative procedures must be used. Kalbfleisch and Prentice (1980) and Greene (1997) provide excellent coverage of estimating algorithms typically used to solve these likelihood equations.

The method of maximum likelihood is general; the likelihood function can be expressed in terms of any of the density functions considered thus far. Under certain regularity conditions, maximum likelihood estimates are asymptotically normal, and so the usual kinds of hypothesis testing is generally possible with the estimates. Moreover, maximum likelihood estimates are consistent and asymptotically efficient, again, under certain regularity conditions (see Greene 1997, p. 134).

In the next section, we address the issue of choosing among alternative parametric forms and consider different goodness-of-fit statistics for parametric duration models.

Choosing among Parametric Distributions

One question that may naturally arise in the application of parametric duration models is how to choose among competing models? Theory should drive the choice of the parametric distribution, but like Blossfeld and Rohwer (2001) we are skeptical that social science generates such theory. In addition, the consequences of an incorrect choice are dire. As Larsen and Vaupel (1993) point out, "in the analysis of duration data, if the functional form of the hazard has the wrong shape, even the best-fitting model may not fit the data well enough to be useful" (1993, 96).

To help answer the question about which distribution to choose, we consider the generalized gamma distribution. The generalized gamma distribution function serves as an encompassing model for several of the parametric forms discussed in the preceding sections of this chapter. As such, estimation of a model parameterized in terms of the generalized gamma should permit one to adjudicate among competing nested models. The logic of using the generalized gamma to choose among nested models is easy to understand if we consider its density function, which is given by

$$f(t) = \frac{\lambda p(\lambda t)^{p\kappa-1} \exp[-(\lambda t)^p]}{\Gamma(\kappa)}, \qquad (3.42)$$

where $\lambda = e^{-\beta' \mathbf{x}}$ and p and κ are the two shape parameters of the distribution. The important difference between the generalized gamma and the other parametric models discussed in this chapter is the additional free parameter, κ, that is estimated. The Weibull, log-logistic, and log-normal densities only have one free parameter; the generalized gamma has two free parameters. This flexibility permits researchers to assess the adequacy of other (nested) parameterizations and establishes the importance of the generalized gamma for scholars using parametric distributions. The generalized gamma is "general" because, depending on the value of the shape parameters, several parametric models are implied from this distribution.

Specifically, when $\kappa = 1$, the Weibull distribution is implied; when $\kappa = p = 1$, the exponential distribution is implied; when $\kappa = 0$, the log-normal distribution is implied; and when $p = 1$, the gamma distribution is implied. The gamma distribution, which has not been explicitly considered in this chapter, is a two-parameter distribution that allows for monotonically rising or decreasing hazard rates. Like the Weibull, the gamma is a generalization of the single-parameter exponential distribution (Kalbfleisch and Prentice 1980). As such, the Weibull and gamma often produce very similar characterizations of the hazard rate. We do not discuss the gamma further, as it is nested within the generalized gamma distribution.

Typically, models specified in terms of the generalized gamma are parameterized in terms of a linear model for $\log(T)$. Thus, in equation (3.23), if ϵ is parameterized in terms of the log-gamma distribution with scale parameter σ and shape parameter κ, then the generalized gamma model is implied.

Example 3.3: Generalized Gamma Model of Cabinet Duration

In this section, we present a brief application of the generalized gamma using comparative politics data on the survival of 314 European cabinet governments. The data used in the application were originally analyzed in King, Alt, Laver, and Burns (1990). Beck (1998) provides an analysis of these data to illustrate the Weibull and exponential models. Six covariates are included in the model. The first, "investiture," is a binary variable denoting whether or not an initial confirmatory vote is required by the legislature. As King et al. (1990) note, this legal requirement is a "hurdle" that governments must overcome. Therefore, this covariate should be associated with shorter duration times. The second covariate, denoted as "polarization," measures the percentage of support for extremist parties. The idea here is that as the support for extremist parties increases, the degree of polarization in the government will increase, thus resulting in diminished cabinet durations. The mean of this covariate is 15.3 with a standard deviation of 12.8. The third covariate of interest is a binary indicator denoting whether or not the government has a numerical majority. The fourth covariate is a count of the number of attempts to form a government prior to the official formation of the government. This variable, denoted as "Formation," should be negatively associated with cabinet durations. The mean is 1.9 and the standard deviation is 1.4 for this covariate. The fifth covariate is a binary indicator denoting if the government was formed immediately after an election (denoted as "post-election" below), and the sixth covariate is a binary indicator denoting whether or not the government is serving as a "caretaker" government.

A generalized gamma model is estimated for these data and the results are presented in the first column of Table 3.3. Of primary interest for this illustration are the values of the shape and scale parameters from the model. In particular, by performing hypothesis tests on these parameters, we can test for the appropriateness of the models nested under the generalized gamma.

Testing the appropriateness of the log-normal model entails testing the hypothesis that $\kappa = 0$. A z-test or Wald test may be used as test statistics for this hypothesis. For this application, both tests suggest that κ is significantly different from 0, thus providing evidence against the log-normal model. For the case of the gamma distribution, the appropriate test is for $\sigma = 1$. For this test, we find that $z = -3.5$, and the Wald test (z^2) is 12.25. These results provide evidence against the gamma (this result also provides evidence against the exponential, which holds when $\sigma = \kappa = 1$). Finally, to test the suitability of the Weibull, we test for $\kappa = 1$. For this test, $z = -.38$ and $z^2 = .15$. The χ^2 for the Wald test on 1 degree of freedom yields a p-value of about 0.70.

TABLE 3.3: Generalized Gamma Model of Cabinet Durations

Variable	Generalized Gamma Estimate (s.e.)	Weibull Estimate (s.e.)
Constant	2.96 (.14)	2.99 (.13)
Investiture	−.30 (.11)	−.30 (.11)
Polarization	−.02 (.01)	−.02 (.01)
Majority	.47 (.10)	.46 (.10)
Formation	−.10 (.03)	−.10 (.03)
Post-Election	.68 (.11)	.68 (.10)
Caretaker	−1.33 (.21)	−1.33 (.20)
Shape Parameter	$\sigma = .79(.06)$	$1/p = 0.78(.06)$
Scale Parameter	$\kappa = .92(.21)$	
N	314	314
Log-Likelihood	−414.01	−414.07

This tells us that of the distributions nested under the generalized gamma, the Weibull distribution yields the best-fitting model.

Given this result, we estimated the Weibull model for the cabinet duration data and present the results in the second column of Table 3.3. As should be the case, the Weibull estimates and generalized gamma estimates are nearly identical. The shape parameter p for the Weibull (which is equal to $1/(1/p) = 1/0.78 = 1.28$) is greater than 1 indicating rising hazards.

The generalized gamma provides some leverage on adjudicating among the parametric models nested under it; therefore, it is advisable that if one is intent on estimating a parametric form but has little reason to prefer one (nested) distribution function over another nested distribution, then the generalized gamma should be applied. It is worth noting, however, that estimation of the generalized gamma can be nontrivial, as an additional ancillary parameter must be estimated.[7]

Assessing Model Fit

Because the models discussed in this chapter are all estimated by maximum likelihood, and because the properties of these estimators are well known, the standard battery of goodness-of-fit indices and statistics are directly applicable to the parametric modeling framework. In this section, we briefly discuss some of these approaches and consider a method to compare nonnested models.

There are three primary tests of overall model significance: the Wald, efficient score, and likelihood ratio (LR) test. Although these tests are asymptotically equivalent, the latter is generally preferred because in finite samples

---

[7]It should also be noted that an even more general distribution, the generalized F, can be specified to assess the adequacy of a wider range of duration models; however because of the complexity of this function, it is not discussed here (see Greene 1997).

the LR test is considered the most reliable (Cox and Hinkley 1974; *Guide to Statistics* 1999, 259; Therneau 1999a, 34). Further, Parmar and Machin (1995) point out that "for consistency and stability reasons in the associated methods of calculation the LR test is preferred" (1995, 140). The LR test examines the joint hypothesis that all coefficients besides the constant are zero and gives an indication of how much the explanatory variables jointly contribute to the fit of the model. The LR test is -2 times the difference in the log-likelihood between the model with no covariates and the full model. The test statistic is

$$LR = -2\log(L_0 - L_1),$$

where L_0 denotes the initial log-likelihood and L_1 denotes the log-likelihood for the full model. This statistic is distributed as a chi-square statistic. It is analogous to the F-statistic in a linear regression model. A high chi-square value does not mean, however, that the model is not satisfactory. Residual plots and diagnostics are likely to be more helpful here. This is the topic of Chapter 8.

For hypothesis tests of individual covariates, a standard z-score or Wald test may be computed. To test whether a group of covariates are contributing to the model, one can again use a likelihood ratio test (where the restricted model is that the group coefficients of interest are all zero). Testing a group of covariates is useful when assessing the statistical significance of highly correlated covariates, interactions, if there is a controversy in the literature over a group of covariates, if there are related covariates such as transformed covariates, i.e., logs or powers, or a substantively related group of variables like demographic variables or campaign related variables.

To compare the fit of competing models, the LR statistic may be used for parametrically nested models. However, given the choices available to analysts regarding the kinds of duration models that can be estimated, often one might wish to compare *nonnested* models. To assess the fit of nonnested models, the Akaike information criterion, or AIC, may be computed for different models with comparable sets of covariates. We mention the AIC primarily because analysts, in practice, may forgo estimation of the encompassing generalized gamma and wish to compare across nonnested models, for example, the log-normal and the Gompertz. The AIC is given by

$$AIC = -2(\log L) + 2(c + p + 1), \tag{3.43}$$

where c denotes the number of covariates in the model and p denotes the number of structural parameters for the model. The idea behind the AIC is to "reward" parsimonious models by penalizing the log-likelihood for each parameter that is estimated. We illustrate the use of the AIC below.

TABLE 3.4: AIC and Log-Likelihoods for Cabinet Models

Model	Log-Likelihood	AIC
Exponential	−425.91	865.82
Weibull	−414.07	844.14
Log-Logistic	−424.11	864.22
Log-Normal	−425.31	866.62
Gompertz	−418.98	853.96
Generalized Gamma	−414.01	846.02

Example 3.4: The AIC and Models of Cabinet Duration

To illustrate the AIC, we use the cabinet duration data considered earlier and estimate several parametric duration models using the form of the model shown previously in Table 3.3. In Table 3.4, we present the log-likelihood and AIC for each of these models (the coefficient estimates are not reported). Based on minimizing the AIC, the preferred model for these data is the Weibull. This is consonant with the results we presented earlier in terms of the generalized gamma. Notably, the generalized gamma model has the lowest log-likelihood; however, as we saw in the previous section, the generalized gamma model reduces to a Weibull model for these data. The difference in log-likelihoods for the Weibull and generalized gamma is trivial. In this application, both the log-likelihood and the AIC elicit essentially the same conclusions. This need not always be the case, and if not, then the analyst must judge the trade-offs between the AIC and the log-likelihood criteria.

In general, there is no single goodness-of-fit statistic that will consistently select the "best" model. Moreover, there is no statistical test for the theoretical plausibility of the model. The choice of the appropriate parametric model should be driven by theory. As we have seen, model results can differ according to the parameterization selected.

Conclusion

In this chapter, we have discussed various parametric modeling strategies for event history data. We have presented several different ways to substantively interpret the results of duration models. Nevertheless, we have repeatedly discussed the caveats associated with parametric duration models as we are skeptical of the use of parametric models in social science. Further, we have taken the perspective that duration dependency, in some sense, is a statistical nuisance. While it is certainly the case that if duration dependency exists in the data, it is preferable to account for it than to not account for it, there are alternative approaches that yield estimates of the parameters of interest, without specifying the form of the time dependency. In the next chapter, we present a model that poses an attractive alternative to the approaches taken here: the

Cox proportional hazards model. As we will argue in the next chapter, in most applications, the Cox model, or variants of the Cox model, will be preferable on both substantive and statistical grounds to parametric models. We turn now to the Cox model.

CHAPTER 4

The Cox Proportional Hazards Model

In this chapter, we present an alternative modeling strategy to the fully parametric methods discussed in the previous chapter. Specifically, we consider the Cox proportional hazards model (Cox 1972, 1975). The Cox model is an attractive alternative to fully parametric methods because the particular distributional form of the duration times is left unspecified, although estimates of the baseline hazard and baseline survivor functions can be retrieved.

Problems with Parameterizing the Baseline Hazard

The parametric models discussed in Chapter 3 are desirable if one has a good reason to expect the duration dependency to exhibit some particular form. With the exception of the restrictive exponential model, any of the distribution functions discussed in the previous chapter are "flexible" inasmuch as the hazard rate may assume a wide variety of shapes, given the constraints of the model, i.e., the Weibull or Gompertz must yield monotonic hazards. However, most theories and hypotheses of behavior are *less* focused on the notion of time-dependency, and more focused on the relationship between some outcome (the dependent variable) and covariates of theoretical interest. In our view, most research questions in social science should be chiefly concerned with getting the appropriate theoretical relationship "right" and less concerned with the specific form of the duration dependency, which can be sensitive to the form of the posited model.

Moreover, ascribing substantive interpretations to ancillary parameters (for example the p, σ, or γ terms) in fully parametric models can, in our view, be tenuous. Some have argued that the form of the duration dependency in event history models can be used to help adjudicate between or among different model specifications (Bennett 1998; see also Warwick's [1992] discussion on the interpretation of the rising hazards of cabinet durations). The argument is that duration dependency may reveal problems with model misspecification, for example, omitting an important covariate. And while this argument is generally true, it assumes that the particular distribution function that is chosen for the model is reasonable. If the data are believed to be distributed with Weibull density, then using the shape parameter of the Weibull to inform the analyst about model specification may be reasonable. However, what if the "true" distribution function is the Gompertz? In this case, using the Weibull shape parameter to inform decisions about model construction may not be reasonable. The point is, while parametric methods offer some flexibility in modeling duration data, the appeal of the kinds of models discussed in Chapter 3 is highest when there is a strong theoretical reason to expect one distribution function over another. A truly flexible duration model would be one where we could obtain estimates of the covariates of interest, and leave the particular form of the duration dependency *unspecified*. This is the basic logic underlying the so-called Cox proportional hazards model, or simply, the Cox model (Cox 1972, 1975).

The Cox Model

The Cox model gets its name from the statistician who derived it, Sir David Cox. As Allison (1995) notes, the importance of the Cox model cannot be overstated. The results from Cox's original research have been widely applied to problems in all scientific domains, and his work in this area will no doubt be regarded as one of the top statistical achievements of the 20th century. The logic of the Cox model is simple and elegant. The hazard rate for the ith individual is

$$h_i(t) = h_0(t) \exp(\beta'\mathbf{x}), \qquad (4.1)$$

where $h_0(t)$ is the baseline hazard function and $\beta'\mathbf{x}$ are the covariates and regression parameters. The hazard rate for the Cox model is proportional; indeed, it is useful to note the similarity between (4.1) and equation (3.19), which gives the Weibull hazard rate. We noted in the previous chapter that the Weibull model is also a proportional hazards model. The hazard ratio of two hazards can be written as

$$\frac{h_i(t)}{h_0(t)} = \exp(\beta'(\mathbf{x_i} - \mathbf{x_j})), \qquad (4.2)$$

which demonstrates that this ratio is a fixed proportion across time. Yet while the Weibull and Cox models are both members of the proportional hazards family of models, there is one crucial difference between the Cox model and the proportional hazards models discussed in Chapter 3. Recall that the baseline hazard rates for the Weibull and Gompertz (the two proportional hazards models discussed in the last chapter) were assumed to have a particular parametric form. This parametric form produced the smooth graphs of the Weibull hazard and Gompertz hazard rates that were presented in our applications.

TABLE 4.1: Cox Model of U.N. Peacekeeping Missions

Variable	Estimate	(s.e.)
Civil War	.73	(.38)
Interstate Conflict	−.86	(.50)
N	54	
Log-Likelihood	−127.16	

When the proportional hazards assumption holds in the Cox model, the particular form of the baseline hazard rate, $h_0(t)$ is assumed to be unknown and is left unparameterized. For this reason, the Cox model is sometimes referred to as a "semi-parametric" model: the (ordered) duration times are parameterized in terms of a set of covariates, but the particular distributional form of the duration times is not parameterized.

Because the baseline hazard rate is left unspecified, Cox regression models do not have an intercept term. To see this, note that we can express the Cox model in scalar form as

$$h_i(t) = \exp(\beta_1 x_{1i} + \beta_2 x_{2i} + \ldots + \beta_k x_{ki})h_0(t), \qquad (4.3)$$

and if we re-express the model in terms of the log of the hazard ratios, we obtain

$$\log\left\{\frac{h_i(t)}{h_0(t)}\right\} = \beta_1 x_{1i} + \beta_2 x_{2i} + \ldots + \beta_k x_{ki}. \qquad (4.4)$$

It is easy to see that the Cox model, expressed as either (4.3) or (4.4), contains no constant term β_0. This term, for the Cox model, is "absorbed" into the baseline hazard function. As we discuss below, it is possible to obtain an estimate of the baseline hazard rate from the Cox model; however, the baseline hazard is not directly estimated in the model. The absence of direct estimation of the baseline hazard has led Royston (2001) and Royston and Parmar (2002) to propose an alternative to the Cox modeling approach. In Chapter 6, we consider the models proposed by Royston (2001) and Royston and Parmar (2002). We now turn to an initial illustration of the Cox model.

Example 4.1: A Cox Model of U.N. Peacekeeping Missions

The data used in this example are the U.N. Peacekeeping data considered in Chapter 3. To provide an initial illustration of the Cox model, we estimated a model of peacekeeping mission durations as a function of the two covariates denoting the type of conflict. The first covariate denotes whether or not the mission was in response to a civil war; the second covariate denotes whether or not the mission was in response to an interstate conflict. The omitted category (when the civil war and interstate conflict equal 0 denotes an internationalized civil war). The Cox proportional hazards estimates are given in Table 4.1.

Because the coefficients are parameterized in terms of the hazard rate, a positive coefficient indicates that the hazard is increasing as a function of the covariate (and hence, the survival time is decreasing) and a negative sign indicates the hazard is decreasing as a function of the covariate. For this model, the positive coefficient of .73 suggests that missions in response to a civil war result in a higher hazard rate (and lower survival time) than either missions prompted by an interstate conflict or internationalized civil war. In contrast, the hazard for missions prompted by interstate conflict are the lowest of the three mission types. Thus, the survival time for these kinds of missions is the longest.

The absence of a constant term is immediately apparent. Because the two included covariates are binary, the omission of the constant term would seem to preclude analysis of the "baseline" category. This is not true. To explain, consider the relationship shown in equation (4.2), which illustrates the proportional hazards assumption. From this result, we can compute the hazard ratios based on the model results. First, let us consider the case of civil wars. We can compute the hazard ratio using equation (4.2) in the following way:

$$\frac{h_i(t)}{h_0(t)} = \exp \hat{\beta}_{cw}(X_{cw} - X_{ic}),$$

where the subscripts "cw" and "ic" stand for civil war and interstate conflict, respectively. Substituting in the relevant estimates and covariate values, we see that the hazard ratio between civil wars and internationalized civil wars (the omitted category) is about 2.08 (i.e. $\exp[(.73)(1 - 0)]$). In contrast, the hazard ratio between interstate conflicts and internationalized civil wars is given by

$$\frac{h_i(t)}{h_0(t)} = \exp \hat{\beta}_{ic}(X_{ic} - X_{cw}),$$

and is about .42 (i.e. $\exp[(-.86)(1 - 0)]$). Extending these results to the omitted category of internationalized civil wars, we see that the hazard ratio for this conflict type *must be exactly 1*. That is, whenever the civil war covariate and the interstate conflict covariates are 0, the hazard ratio is exactly 1. Moreover, it is easy to see how the coefficient estimates displayed in Table 4.1 can be retrieved from the hazard ratios. If we take the log of the hazard ratios, the original Cox coefficients are obtained. Thus, $\log(2.08) \approx .73$ and $\log(.42) \approx -.86$ are the parameter estimates shown above. Importantly, note that the log of the hazard ratio for internationalized civil wars is $\log(1) = 0$. Thus, the implied coefficient estimate for the baseline category is 0 and the implied hazard ratio is 1. Sometimes analysts will be interested in estimating hazard rates from the Cox model. To do this, it will be necessary to find an estimate of the baseline hazard function. Later in this chapter, we discuss how to do this.

Now that we have an initial understanding of the kind of information generated from a Cox model, we turn attention to the special issues involved in estimating the Cox model. To obtain estimates of the parameters in (4.3), Cox (1972, 1975) developed a nonparametric method he called *partial likelihood*. Estimation of the parameter values is obtained by use of maximum partial likelihood estimation, which differs from MLE in ways discussed below.

Partial Likelihood

The partial likelihood method is based on the assumption that the intervals between successive duration times (or failure times) contributes no information regarding the relationship between the covariates and the hazard rate (Collett 1994). This must be the case because the baseline hazard function for the Cox model is not directly parameterized. As such, this rate is assumed to have an arbitrary form and, as Collett (1994) notes, could actually be zero in the intervals between successive death times. Therefore, it is the *ordered failure times*, rather than interval between failure times, that contributes information to the partial likelihood function. This is in contrast to the parametric methods discussed in Chapter 3, where the actual survival times are used in the construction of the likelihood function. Because the Cox model only uses "part" of the available data ($h_0(t)$ is not estimated), the likelihood function for the Cox model is a "partial" likelihood function, hence the name.

To derive the partial likelihood function for a data set of size n with k distinct failure times, the data are first sorted by the ordered failure time, such that $t_1 < t_2 < \ldots < t_k$, where t_i denotes the failure time for the ith individual. For now, we assume that there are no "tied" events: each uncensored case experiences an event at a unique time. For censored cases, we define δ_i, as before, to be 0 if the case is right-censored, and 1 if the case is uncensored, that is, the event has been experienced. Finally, the ordered event times are modeled as a function of covariates, **x**.

The partial likelihood function is derived by taking the product of the conditional probability of a failure at time t_i, given the number of cases that are at risk of failing at time t_i. More formally, if we define $R(t_i)$ to denote the number of cases that are at risk of experiencing an event at time t_i, that is, the "risk set," then the probability that the jth case will fail at time T_i is given by

$$\Pr(t_j = T_i \mid R(t_i)) = \frac{e^{\beta' \mathbf{x_i}}}{\sum_{j \in R(t_i)} e^{\beta' \mathbf{x_j}}}, \tag{4.5}$$

where the summation operator in the denominator is summing over all individuals in the risk set. Taking the product of the conditional probabilities in (4.5)

TABLE 4.2: Data Sorted by Ordered Failure Time

Case	Duration	Censored
7	7	No
4	15	No
5	21	No
2	28	Yes
9	30	Yes
3	36	No
8	45	Yes
1	46	No
6	51	No

yields the partial likelihood function,

$$\mathcal{L}_p = \prod_{i=1}^{K} \left[\frac{e^{\beta' \mathbf{x_i}}}{\sum_{j \in R(t_i)} e^{\beta' \mathbf{x_j}}} \right]^{\delta_i}, \qquad (4.6)$$

with corresponding log-likelihood function,

$$\log L_p = \sum_{i=1}^{K} \delta_i \left[\beta' \mathbf{x_i} - \log \sum_{j \in R(t_i)} e^{\beta' \mathbf{x_j}} \right]. \qquad (4.7)$$

By maximizing the log-likelihood in (4.7), estimates of the β are obtained. This procedure is sometimes referred to as "maximum partial likelihood estimation," or MPLE. As Collett (1994) notes, the likelihood function in (4.6) is not a true likelihood. This is because the actual survival times of censored and uncensored cases are not directly incorporated into the likelihood. This is important to note because it again illustrates that the intervals between successive event times are assumed to contribute no information regarding the relationship between the covariates and the ordered event times. Nevertheless, Cox (1972, 1975) demonstrated that maximum partial likelihood estimation produces parameter estimates that have the same properties as maximum likelihood estimates (see also Collett 1994). This is convenient because under the same set of regularity conditions as maximum likelihood estimation (see Greene 1997), the parameter estimates from partial likelihood are asymptotically normal, asymptotically efficient, consistent, and invariant. So the usual kinds of hypothesis tests discussed in Chapter 3 are directly extended to the Cox model.

The logic underlying the partial likelihood method is seen by considering the data presented in Table 4.2 (this part of the presentation is directly adapted from Collett's presentation (1994)). Here, we give the survival times for nine cases. Of these nine cases, six of them experience an event, i.e., they "fail," and three of them are right-censored. It is clear that the failure times can be ordered such that $t_1 < t_2 < \ldots < t_6$. Obviously, the censored cases do not contribute a failure time. In this example, each of the nine cases is at risk of experiencing an event up to the first failure time, t_1. After the first failure in the data set, the risk set decreases in size by 1; thus, the risk set up to the second failure time, t_2, includes all cases except case 7. By the fourth failure time in the data, t_4, the risk set includes only cases 1, 6, and 8; cases 2 and 9 are right-censored before the fourth failure time is observed and do not contribute any information to this part of the likelihood function. By the last failure time, only case 6 remains in the risk set. Using the notation from Collett (1994, 64), let $\psi = \exp(\beta' \mathbf{x_i})$. Then the partial likelihood function for these data would be equivalent to

$$
\begin{aligned}
\mathcal{L}_p \;=\; & \frac{\psi(7)}{\psi(1) + \psi(2) + \psi(3) + \psi(4) + \psi(5) + \psi(6) + \psi(7) + \psi(8) + \psi(9)} \\[6pt]
& \times \frac{\psi(4)}{\psi(1) + \psi(2) + \psi(3) + \psi(4) + \psi(5) + \psi(6) + \psi(8) + \psi(9)} \\[6pt]
& \times \frac{\psi(5)}{\psi(1) + \psi(2) + \psi(3) + \psi5 + \psi(6) + \psi(8) + \psi(9)} \\[6pt]
& \times \frac{\psi(3)}{\psi(1) + \psi(3) + \psi(6) + \psi(8)} \\[6pt]
& \times \frac{\psi(1)}{\psi(1) + \psi(6)} \\[6pt]
& \times \frac{\psi(6)}{\psi(6)}.
\end{aligned}
$$

From this exercise, it is easy to see that the partial likelihood function is solely based on the ordered duration times, and not on the length of the interval between duration times. Censored observations contribute information to the "risk set" but contribute no information regarding failure times. In terms of the likelihood function in (4.6), censored observations contribute information to the denominator, but not to the numerator. Indeed, the only information contributed to the numerator in the partial likelihood function is the singular failure at time t_i.

"Ties," or coterminous event occurrences, cannot be accounted for in the partial likelihood function, as presented in (4.6). This would seem restrictive as it is not uncommon to observe events occurring at the same time. The issue of tied events is relevant for the Cox model, or indeed, for *any* continuous time model. Because of ties, the likelihood function in (4.6) must be modified to account for simultaneously occurring failure times. Indeed, the ability of the Cox model to be adapted to handle tied data is another advantage of the Cox approach over parametric approaches. Standard parametric models like those discussed in Chapter 3 are ill-equipped to handle heavily tie-laden data (Golub and Collett 2002).

Regarding the Cox model, the basic problem tied events pose for the partial likelihood function is in the determination of the composition of the risk set at each failure time and the sequencing of event occurrences. For two or more observations that fail, or experience an event at the same time, it is impossible to tell which observation failed first. Consequently, it is not possible to discern precisely the composition of the risk set at the time of the failures. In order to estimate the parameters of the Cox model with tied failure times, then, it becomes necessary to approximate the partial likelihood function in (4.6). A large body of literature has developed around this problem, and generally, there are four options to address this problem. We consider them below.

The Breslow Method

The most commonly implemented method to handle ties in duration data is the Breslow method (Breslow 1974; Peto 1972 suggested a very similar approximation). This approach is widely used because the Breslow approximation of the partial likelihood function in (4.6) is computationally simpler than other methods. The logic of the Breslow method is straightforward. Since it is impossible to determine the order of occurrence in tied events, the Breslow method assumes that the size of the risk set is the same, regardless of which event occurred first. To illustrate, suppose we have four observations with respective failure times of $t = 5, 5, 8, 14$. Two of the cases have terminal events at time 5. Since we cannot distinguish the temporal order of events between cases 1 and 2, the Breslow method would approximate the partial likelihood function for these data by assuming that case 1 and case 2 failed from the risk set consisting of all four cases. Thus, the partial likelihood for case 1 could be thought of as

$$\ell_1 = \frac{\psi 1}{\psi 1 + \psi 2 + \psi 3 + \psi 4},$$

and for case 2, the partial likelihood could be thought of as

$$\ell_2 = \frac{\psi 2}{\psi 1 + \psi 2 + \psi 3 + \psi 4}.$$

For either case, the size of the risk set is unchanged, and hence is of maximal size for either case 1 or case 2. The Breslow method approximates the partial likelihood function by assuming that the tied failure times occur sequentially (although the sequence is unknown) from a risk set consisting of all cases (including all tied cases) at risk at the failure time. The approximated likelihood function proposed by Breslow is given by

$$\mathcal{L}_{Breslow} = \prod_{i=1}^{k} \frac{e^{\beta' \mathbf{s_i}}}{\left[\sum_{j \in R(t_i)} e^{\beta' \mathbf{x_j}} \right]^{d_i}}, \tag{4.8}$$

where s_i is the sum of the covariates x for the tied cases, d_i are the number of cases that have tied event times at time t_i, and the other terms are as defined before. The Breslow approximation has proven to be adequate when the number of tied events is small at any given period (Collett 1994, Vermunt 1996); however, as the number of tied cases increases, the size of the risk set at each period gets very large and the approximation is less precise.

The Efron Method

As an alternative, Efron (1977) proposed a method of approximation that accounts for how the risk set changes depending on the sequencing of tied events. Using the data example from before, the logic of the Efron method would suggest that if case 1 failed before case 2, then the partial likelihood function for these data would be

$$
\begin{aligned}
\ell_1 &= \frac{\psi 1}{\psi 1 + \psi 2 + \psi 3 + \psi 4} \\
&\times \frac{\psi 2}{\psi 2 + \psi 3 + \psi 4};
\end{aligned}
$$

however, if case 2 failed before case 1, then the likelihood would be

$$
\begin{aligned}
\ell_2 &= \frac{\psi 2}{\psi 1 + \psi 2 + \psi 3 + \psi 4} \\
&\times \frac{\psi 1}{\psi 1 + \psi 3 + \psi 4}.
\end{aligned}
$$

The composition of the second risk set changes depending on the possible sequencing of events. Because either ℓ_1 or ℓ_2 are assumed to be equally likely, the appearance of case 1 or case 2 in the second risk set is equally likely. In this case, the probability of the second risk set would be

$$
\frac{1}{2}(\psi 1 + \psi 2) + \psi 3 + \psi 4.
$$

The logic underlying this prompted Efron to propose the following approximation to the partial likelihood function:

$$
\mathcal{L}_{Efron} = \prod_{i=1}^{K} \left(\frac{e^{\beta' s_i}}{\prod_{r=1}^{d_i} \left[\sum_{j \in R(t_i)} e^{\beta' x_j} - (r-1) d_i^{-1} \sum_{j \in D(t_i)} e^{\beta' x_j} \right]} \right),
$$

(4.9)

where r denotes the number of cases with tied event times and $D(t_i)$ is the number of cases with tied event times in the risk set at time t_i. Because this method accounts for the differing composition of the risk set at t_i, the approximation in (4.9) is more accurate than the Breslow approximation in (4.8).

Averaged Likelihood

A very accurate approximation of the partial likelihood function with tied data is the averaged likelihood method (Therneau and Grambsch 2000). The logic of the averaged likelihood method is to account for all possible orderings of tied event times. So for example, if at time t_i, there are four cases with equivalently recorded event times, this would account for each of the 24 (i.e., 4!) possible orderings of event times in its approximation of the likelihood function. The functional form of this method is cumbersome and we refer the reader to Kalbfleisch and Prentice (1980) or Therneau and Grambsch (2000). In the past, use of this method was not generally recommended as the computational resources needed to solve the approximation were formidable; however, the tradeoff between computer time and heightened accuracy is less relevant now than in years past. This approach is sometimes referred to as the "exact" method; however, the denominator patterns (i.e. the factorial) are approximated by numerical methods.

The Exact Discrete Method

An alternative approach to handling tied data is what we will call the "exact discrete" approach. As we make use of this approach extensively in Chapter 5, we describe this approach with some detail. Under the Breslow, Efron, and averaged likelihood methods, the assumption is that since the data are generated from a continuous-time process, when two or more events occur simultaneously it is important to account for the possible sequencing of the two events. For the exact discrete method, this assumption is not retained. That is, for coterminous events, the method proceeds by assuming the events *really do* occur at the same time; as such, a "discrete" view of time is taken.

The exact discrete approximation estimates the probability of event occurrences at some time t_i, conditional on the composition of the risk set at this time. The logic underlying this method can be seen by thinking of the duration data in terms of a "matched case-control" study (King and Zeng [2001a, 2001b, 2001c]).

Data in matched case-control studies are organized by some grouping in the data and analyzed in terms of this grouping. Consider the data shown in Table 4.3. The observations, which are identified in terms of an observation number, are grouped together by the time period at which they are at risk of experiencing an event. The variable "risk period" is therefore an identifier that allows us to determine which observations are in a specific risk set at any given time. The variable labeled "event occurrence" is a binary indicator denoting whether or not an event was experienced (1) or not (0). The duration time variable denotes the number of time units the observations have survived up to the timing of the first observed event in the data set. The observations are "matched" together by the risk set variable; i.e., they are grouped together by

TABLE 4.3: Matched Case-Control Duration Data

Observation Number	Risk Period	Event Occurrence	Duration
Risk Period 1			
1	1	0	5
2	1	0	5
3	1	0	5
4	1	1	5
5	1	1	5
Risk Period 2			
1	2	0	11
2	2	1	11
3	2	1	11

the risk period. For the first risk period, we see that there are five matched observations. Of these five observations, there are two "cases" and three "controls" which elicits a ratio of 2 : 3 matching. For risk period two, we see that of the remaining observations, two cases are observed and one control, for 2 : 1 matching.

Translating this language into that of event history analysis, there are two event occurrences within risk period 1 and three non-event occurrences at risk period 1, indicating two ties occur among the five observations at risk. The similarity of this data with the kind of data typically used for the estimation of Cox models is not coincidental; they are equivalent. The event occurrence indicator is analogous to the censoring indicator, δ_i, defined earlier. The difference between this variant of the Cox model and the other approximation methods is that the censoring indicator is used as the dependent variable. The implication is that the data are considered to be discrete (Therneau and Grambsch 2000).

The exact discrete approximation of the partial likelihood function proceeds by estimating the probability of a response pattern, that is, the pattern of zeroes and ones in the risk set, conditional on the composition of the risk set. To explain, consider the data shown in Table 4.3. In risk period 1, 2 observations out of the 5 at risk experience the event. Following Allison's (1995, 135) presentation, the question to ask is, given that 2 events occurred out of the 5 at risk, what is the probability that these events occurred to these 2 observations, and not some other set of 2 observations from the risk set? Estimating this probability involves a combinatorial problem. For this example, we see there are $\binom{5}{2} = 10$ possible combinations of 2 events out of the 5 observations. The probability of the response pattern for this group is estimated by computing the probability for each of the 10 possible combinations of 2 events occurring from 5 observations (or 2 cases and 3 controls). The logic of the exact discrete approximation of the partial likelihood function is to estimate the conditional likelihood for *each* risk set.

More generally, suppose there are $k = 1, 2, \ldots K$ distinct risk periods in the data set (equivalently, there are k ordered failure times observed), and $i = 1, 2, \ldots J_k$ observations at risk in the kth period. Let the response pattern of the dependent variable for the kth risk period be $\mathbf{y_k} = (y_{k1} + y_{k2} + \ldots + y_{kJ_k})$. The total number of events, n_{1k} (or "cases") observed in the kth risk period is given by

$$n_{1k} = \sum_{i=1}^{J} y_{ki},$$

and the total number of non-events or "controls" is given by

$$n_{0k} = J_k - n_{1k}.$$

The probability of the response pattern $\mathbf{y_k}$ is then estimated, conditional on n_{1k}, and is given by

$$\Pr(\mathbf{y_k} \mid \sum_{i=1}^{J} y_{ki} = n_{1k}) = \frac{\exp(\beta' \sum_{i=1}^{J} \mathbf{x_{ki}} y_{ki})}{\sum_{\mathbf{d_k} \in R_k} \exp(\beta' \sum_{i=1}^{J} \mathbf{x_{ki}} d_{ki})}, \qquad (4.10)$$

where R_k denotes all possible combinations of ones and zeroes, i.e., cases and controls, in the kth risk period, $\mathbf{d_k} = (d_{k1}, d_{k2}, \ldots, d_{kJ})$, $d_{ki} = 0$ or 1. The exact discrete approximation is estimating the probability of the response pattern $\mathbf{y_k}$ for each risk period R_k, for all possible combinations of events and non-events, i.e., 1s and 0s, observed among the J observations at risk.

It is important to point out that the approximation method shown in (4.10) is *equivalent* to a conditional logit model. When the exact discrete approximation of the Cox partial likelihood function is estimated, a conditional logit model is obtained. The conditional logit model proceeds by estimating the probability of the response pattern $\mathbf{y_k}$, for some group k. For event history data, the group is defined in terms of the risk set at time t_i. For more information regarding the conditional logit model, we refer the reader to McFadden (1974), Hosmer and Lemeshow (1989), and Hamerle and Ronning (1995). These sources also provide more details on the estimation of the conditional logit model and the recursive algorithm necessary to simplify the computation of the denominator in (4.10). This recursive algorithm is necessary because the number of terms in this denominator gets massive as J and n_{1k} increase.[1] In the next chapter we will return to this model in more detail. We now illustrate each of the approaches for handling ties discussed above with an example.

Example 4.2: Cox Models of Cabinet Durations

In this application, we estimate a Cox proportional hazards model using comparative data on the survival of European cabinet governments. These data

---

[1] The conditional logit model is also sometimes referred to as a "fixed effects" model, which is commonly used in the social sciences. In this case the "effect" that is "fixed" is the risk period.

were used in Chapter 3. Because these data have tied event times, it is necessary to approximate the partial likelihood function using one of the approaches discussed above. To illustrate the differences in parameter estimates generated from each of the three approximations, we estimate the Cox model using the Breslow, Efron, averaged likelihood, and exact discrete approximations. These results are presented in the four columns of estimates in Table 4.4.

The estimates across the parameterizations are very similar. This is obviously desirable as each of the approaches is approximating the same quantity, namely the partial likelihood. The exact discrete estimates differ most from the other three methods. The reason for this is that the coefficient estimates from the exact discrete method are based on a conditional logit estimator for matched case-control studies and the other three approaches are not. Hence, strictly speaking, the regression parameter from the exact discrete approach is a log-odds ratio parameter and not a log-relative risk parameter (Therneau and Grambsch 2000, p. 52). Nevertheless, the differences across estimates are small. In this application, the choice of which method to report would have limited bearing on the inferences made from the model. By default, most software packages report the Breslow method (historically, out of computational considerations); however, for this application, the additional time needed to compute the other methods—which as noted above are generally more accurate approximations than the Breslow method—is trivial, amounting to a few seconds. This, of course, will not always be the case in every application. But for these data, because of the accuracy of the approximation, we would choose to report the results from either the averaged likelihood method or the exact discrete method. In general, there is no reason that one should not use, at minimum, the Efron approach to handling tied data. Because the Efron and the exact methods are clearly superior to the Breslow approach, these methods are preferred. We should note that Therneau and Grambsch (2000) argue that fitting the discrete approximation to grouped duration data is "*not* [emphasis theirs] a good idea" (p. 52). Their reasoning is that since the data are not genuinely discrete, the other approximations are more appropriate and more naturally applied. In the next chapter, we return to this issue. We also note that the log-likelihoods across the three approximations are *not* comparable: the approximations are non-nested.

Interpretation of Cox Model Estimates

As discussed previously, coefficient estimates from the Cox proportional hazards model reveal information regarding the hazard rate. As such, positive coefficients imply the hazard is increasing, or "rising," with changes in the covariate, and negatively signed coefficients imply the hazard is decreasing or "falling" with changes in the covariate. Hence, positive coefficients imply shorter survival times; negative coefficients imply longer survival times.

TABLE 4.4: Cox Model of Cabinet Durations

| | Cox Model Approximated by | | | |
	Breslow	Efron	Avg. Lik.	Exact
Variable	Est. (s.e.)	Est. (s.e.)	Est. (s.e.)	Est. (s.e.)
Investiture	.38 (.14)	.39 (.14)	.39 (.14)	.41 (.14)
Polarization	.02 (.01)	.02 (.01)	.02 (.01)	.02 (.01)
Majority	−.57 (.13)	−.58 (.13)	−.58 (.13)	−.62 (.14)
Formation	.13 (.04)	.13 (.04)	.13 (.04)	.13 (.05)
Post-Election	−.83 (.14)	−.86 (.14)	−.86 (.14)	−.88 (.15)
Caretaker	1.54 (.28)	1.71 (.28)	1.74 (.29)	1.86 (.33)
N	314	314	314	314
Log-Likelihood	−1299.89	−1287.74	−918.31	−918.29

So in continuing our example using the cabinet duration data, we see that in systems that require an initial legislative confirmatory vote (denoted by the binary variable "Investiture"), the risk or hazard of government failure is higher than for governments where a confirmatory vote is not required. This is the case because the coefficient estimate is positively signed, indicating that when the value is realized, i.e., a 1 is observed, the impact of the covariate on the hazard rate is to increase the hazard, thus decreasing the survival time of governments with this attribute. In percentage terms, the Cox model (using the averaged likelihood method) suggests that the risk of termination is about 47 percent higher for governments that must overcome the hurdle of investiture, compared to governments that do not, at any time given that it has not yet terminated; i.e., $100[(\exp(.39*1) - \exp(.39*0))/\exp(.39*0)]$. The estimated impact of investiture from the Weibull model is also 47 percent (calculated in the same way). More generally, to assess the impact a covariate has on increasing or decreasing the hazard rate, the following formula is useful:

$$\%\Delta h(t) = \left[\frac{e^{\beta(x_i=X_1)} - e^{\beta(x_i=X_2)}}{e^{\beta(x_i=X_2)}}\right] * 100, \qquad (4.11)$$

where x_i is the covariate, and X_1 and X_2 denotes two distinct values of the covariate.

A natural question to ask is, how do the Cox results from this model compare with results generated from a parametric model? For comparative purposes, we estimated the model shown in Table 4.4 using a Weibull duration model (recall from the previous chapter that our generalized gamma results and the AIC suggested the Weibull was the best-fitting parametric model for these data). The side-by-side results of the Cox and Weibull models are shown in Table 4.5 (results from the averaged likelihood approximation are displayed). The Weibull proportional hazards parameterization is presented in the table to facilitate comparison with the Cox results (see equation [3.21]).

It is clear that the results from *this* Cox model produce substantive inferences that are virtually identical to the Weibull model; however, this will

TABLE 4.5: Cox and Weibull Estimates of Cabinet Duration

Variable	Cox Estimate (s.e.)	Weibull Estimate (s.e.)
Constant	−	−3.86 (.26)
Investiture	.39 (.14)	.38 (.14)
Polarization	.02 (.01)	.02 (.01)
Majority	−.58 (.13)	−.60 (.13)
Formation	.13 (.04)	.13 (.04)
Post-Election	−.86 (.14)	−.86 (.14)
Caretaker	1.74 (.29)	1.73 (.28)
Shape Parameter	−	$p = 1.29 (.06)$
N	314	314
Log-Likelihood	−918.31	−414.07

The first column gives the results from a Cox model using the averaged likelihood approximation of the partial likelihood function for tied data. The second column gives the Weibull proportional hazards estimates.

not always be the case. To illustrate, we consider data from Golub and Collett (2002).[2] Of interest in this analysis is the length of time (measured in days) that elapses between the formal initiation and adoption (or withdrawal) of a legislative proposal in the European Union (EU). There are four covariates used in the analysis. The covariate "Majority Voting" measures whether the effect of formal treaty rules that stipulate the use of qualified majority voting (QMV) increased or decreased after 1993. The baseline category is unanimous voting, and the question is whether after 1993 the emergence of a "veto culture" rendered the formal QMV voting rules less effective than before. If the post-1993 variable is statistically insignificant then we have evidence of a veto culture, where political actors behave basically the same under formal unanimity as they do under formal majority voting. The next two covariates are indicators of EU expansion. We have a dummy variable indicating the first enlargement of the EU (in 1973) and dummy variable indicating the third enlargement of the EU (in 1995). The question behind these covariates is whether or not expansion of the EU increased the time-until-adoption of EU legislation. The fourth covariate is a binary indicator denoting the years which Margaret Thatcher was Britain's Prime Minister. Golub (1999, 2002) found that the Thatcher government had an impact on decreasing the legislative efficiency of the EU during her years as prime minister. The "Thatcher effect" (Golub 1999, 2002) suggests that the length of time it takes to get legislation adopted should increase during the Thatcher years.

To compare Cox and Weibull estimates, consider Table 4.6. The first column of estimates gives the Cox model results and the second column gives the Weibull estimates. To facilitate comparison, the coefficients are expressed as hazard ratios. As each of the coefficients is less than one, the hazard rate of

---

[2]We would like to thank Jonathan Golub for graciously providing us with this example.

TABLE 4.6: Cox and Weibull Estimates of EU Legislation

	Cox	Weibull
Variable	Estimate (s.e.)	Estimate (s.e.)
Majority Voting	.05 (.09)	.23 (.09)
1st EU Enlargement	.13 (.08)	.14 (.09)
3rd EU Enlargement	.44 (.07)	.52 (.08)
Thatcher	.11 (.06)	.15 (.07)
N	1669	1669
Log-Likelihood	-8779	-2635

The first column gives the results from a Cox model. The second column gives the Weibull estimates. Coefficients are expressed as hazard ratios. This example was given to us by Jonathan Golub.

legislation adoption is decreasing (hence the time-to-adoption is increasing); however, unlike the previous example using the cabinet duration data, conclusions from the Cox model are *not* identical to conclusions from the Weibull. In particular, the majority voting covariate is not significant in the Cox model but is significant in the Weibull model. As noted above, Golub (1999) and Golub and Collett (2002) argue that the insignificance of this covariate is indicative of an EU "veto culture." For these two applications, the question naturally arises as to which model to report. As social scientists are usually interested in the relationship between covariates and the dependent variable, there is no apparent gain for the cabinet duration model in estimating the Weibull model over the Cox model. Moreover, it is always the case that a Weibull model is more restrictive in terms of the assumptions it imposes than is the Cox model. The Weibull is a proportional hazards model *and* assumes a monotonic hazard rate; the Cox model, while being a proportional hazards model, leaves the form of the duration dependency unspecified. Hence, we would choose to report the Cox results over the more restrictive Weibull results for the EU model.

In the two previous examples, the Cox estimates were expressed as nonexponentiated coefficients. As noted earlier, exponentiating Cox estimates puts the coefficients in the metric of hazard ratios. We will present a Cox model that estimates the transition to marriage. The parameter estimates in Table 4.7 are expressed in terms of hazard ratios. The data used in this illustration are based on a subset of data from the National Longitudinal Survey of Youth (NLSY).[3] The variables of interest include the respondent's racial identity (i.e., white versus nonwhite), whether the respondent is living with both biological parents at age 14, whether the father has at least some college education, whether there is parent/peer/teacher influence, whether the respondent lived in

---

[3] We thank Dan Powers for this example. The NLSY provides data designed primarily to analyze sources of variation in labor market behavior and experience. The original group for Youth were ages 14–21 in 1979. The originating agency/principal investigators(s) are the United States Bureau of Labor Statistics and Center for Human Resource Research (CHRR) at Ohio State, Disseminator.

TABLE 4.7: Cox Estimates of Transition to First Marriage for Males

Variable	Cox Estimate (s.e.)
Nonwhite	.81 (.04)
Not Living with Biological Parents	.85 (.04)
Father's Education	.81 (.04)
Influence	.62 (.03)
Urban Residence	.72 (.03)
Family Income	.99 (.00)
Test Score	1.10 (.02)
Rate of Female Head of Households	.82 (.05)
N	4687
Log-Likelihood	-14146

These results are from a Cox with Exact for handling ties. Coefficients are expressed as hazard ratios. This example is from Dan Powers.

an urban residence, family income, test scores on the Armed Services Vocational Aptitude Battery (ASVAB) test, and the county female headship rate. The results in Table 4.7 show a statistically significant coefficient for each of the included variables except for family income (the standard errors reported in the table are based on the *non*exponentiated coefficients). As noted, the results are presented in terms of the hazard ratio. As such, whenever a hazard ratio is less than one, this means that the "risk" (or hazard) decreases as the coefficient increases, thus resulting in a longer time until first marriage. In contrast, hazard ratios greater than one imply the risk (or hazard) is increasing with the covariate. This suggests the duration time until first marriage is decreasing. Hazard ratios close to one (as in the case of the family income parameter) imply that the hazard rate is essentially invariant to changes to the covariate—that is, the coefficient has no effect on increasing (or decreasing) the hazard of first marriage.

To illustrate, consider the racial identity covariate. We see that the risk of first marriage among nonwhite males is only 81 percent of the risk for white males (or about 19 percent lower). The nonexponentiated coefficient for this variable would be $-.21$ (or log[.81]). That there are substantial racial differences in marriage rates is consistent with Lloyd and South's (1996) important work. In contrast, the coefficient estimate for the ASVAB test score suggests that higher scores on this exam are associated with a higher risk of first marriage. Hence, the time until first marriage decreases in relation to increases in the value of this covariate.

Although most analysts will be primarily interested in the relationship between covariates and hazard rate, there may be applications where one is additionally interested in assessing the baseline hazard rate and baseline survivor functions. The Cox model does not provide direct estimates of these functions, but they can be retrieved. We discuss this in the next section.

Retrieving the Baseline Hazard and Survivor Functions

To retrieve estimates of the baseline hazard and baseline survivor functions, the failure times are ordered such that $t_1 < t_2 < \ldots t_k$. Following Collett's (1994) presentation, an estimate of the hazard rate for the ith case is given by

$$\hat{h}_i(t) = e^{\hat{\beta}'x_i}\hat{h}_0(t),$$

where $\hat{h}_0(t)$ is the estimated baseline hazard function. This function is not directly estimated by the partial likelihood function; however, Kalbfleisch and Prentice (1973, 1980) have derived a way to estimate this. Knowing that the event times can be ordered, it is easy to determine the size of the risk set at any given failure time (for now, we assume singular failures at t_i). Since by the definition of the risk set, cases in the risk set up to some failure time, t_i, are surviving cases. The estimated likelihood of a case being in the risk set at t_i is therefore

$$\hat{\alpha}_i = \sum_{j \in R(t_i)} e^{\beta'x_j},$$

which is the denominator in the partial likelihood function in (4.6). Kalbfleisch and Prentice (1973, 1980) show that an estimate of the baseline hazard rate at time t_i can then be obtained by

$$\hat{h}_0(t_i) = 1 - \hat{\alpha}_i. \tag{4.12}$$

If it is assumed that the hazard rate between failure times is constant (i.e., "flat"), then $\hat{\alpha}_i$ is an estimate of the probability that a case survives through the interval $t_i + t_{(i+1)}$. An estimate of the baseline survivor function can be retrieved from $\hat{\alpha}_i$, and is given by

$$\hat{S}_0(t) = \prod_{i=1}^{K} \hat{\alpha}_i, \tag{4.13}$$

which is a step-function. For $\hat{\alpha}_0$, $\hat{S}_0(t_i) = 1$, implying that the proportion of cases that are surviving in the interval before the first failure time is 1.

Once the survivor function is estimated, an estimate of the integrated hazard rate, or cumulative hazard rate, $\hat{H}_0(t)$ can be retrieved by using the result found in equation (2.11). The estimate of the integrated hazard rate is thus given by

$$\hat{H}_0(t) = -\log \hat{S}_0(t) = -\sum_{i=1}^{n} \log \hat{\alpha}_i. \tag{4.14}$$

Because of the relationship between the survival function and the integrated hazard, we can use these baseline estimates to derive the survivor function for the ith individual. Specifically, from equation (2.10), the individual-specific survivor probability is

$$\hat{S}_i(t) = \exp^{-\hat{H}_i(t)},$$

which is equivalent to

$$\hat{S}_i(t) = \hat{S}_0(t)^{\exp(\hat{\beta}'\mathbf{x})}, \tag{4.15}$$

where $\exp(\hat{\beta}'\mathbf{x})$ are the exponentiated Cox coefficients, that is, the hazard ratios.

The mathematical details regarding the estimation of these quantities have been omitted. We instead refer the reader to Kalbfleisch and Prentice (1980, pp. 84-86) or Collett (1994, pp. 95-100). We omit presentation of the likelihood necessary to estimate these components because with tied data, the approximation methods are fairly complex and beyond the scope of this book. The major point we want to stress is that if one is interested in examining the baseline functions from a Cox model, these can be retrieved from the Cox model. Furthermore, because of the connection between the hazard and survivor functions, other quantities of interest can be backed out of the Cox estimates. To illustrate the use of the baseline functions, we present an example.

Example 4.3: Baseline Functions and Cabinet Durations

To enliven the points raised in this section, we examine the baseline hazard, survivor, and integrated hazard functions using the cabinet duration results given in Table 4.5. For comparative purposes, we also compute the baseline functions from the Weibull model given in Table 4.5. As in the above example, the baseline is usually thought of as the case when all covariates assume a value of 0. This may or may not make sense given the covariates in any particular application. In the previous illustration, the two covariates had natural 0 points, but this need not be the case. If one is relying on the computer package to generate estimates of some baseline function, it is important for the analyst to understand how his or her software package actually computes these functions. If the covariates in an application do not have a natural 0 point, the estimated baseline functions will be misleading because they are computed based on data points that do not exist (i.e. when $x_i = 0$). One way to mitigate this problem when the baseline functions are of interest is to deviate or "center" each of the covariates around the mean value. Centering has the effect of producing a transformed covariate with a mean of 0 (when $x_i = 0$). Centering the covariates generally will not alter the parameter estimates, although if the model has a constant term (which the Cox model does not), this parameter will change somewhat.

To retrieve and graph the baseline functions from the Cox model and Weibull model of cabinet durations, we mean-centered the polarization and formation attempts covariates (the other covariates are dummy variables). The baseline functions were then computed based on each covariate assuming a

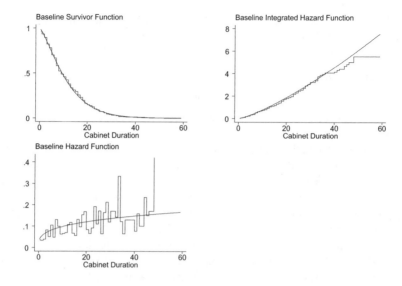

FIGURE 4.1: *This figure gives the estimated baseline survivor (top left panel), integrated hazard (top right panel) and hazard functions (bottom left panel) from the Cox Model and the Weibull Model for the cabinet duration data. The smooth function in the graphs is from the Weibull estimates; the non-smooth function in the graphs is from the Cox model.*

natural 0 point. In Figure 4.1, we graph the estimated baseline survivor function, the baseline integrated hazard function, and the hazard functions from the Cox and Weibull models. Owing to the nonparametric nature of the Cox hazard rate, the estimate of these functions are non-smooth. The estimated survivor and integrated hazards from the two models compare favorably. The Cox results suggest that the hazard of cabinet termination are increasing or "rising."

The main point we want to make through this exercise is that the same information retrievable from the Weibull (or any other parametric model) is directly estimable from the Cox model. Moreover, once the baseline functions are estimated, $\hat{S}_i(t)$ and $\hat{h}_i(t)$ can be estimated. Hence, information about the relative contribution to the survivor or hazard functions for various covariate profiles is available from Cox model estimates.

Conclusion

As we have pointed out throughout this chapter, there are few instances that we can think of where one would naturally prefer a parametric duration model over a Cox-type event history model for most kinds of social science applications.

Most importantly, the strong theory required to choose a specific distribution is almost always lacking. It *is* important to note that the Cox model's assumption of proportional hazards (which is an assumption of the Weibull and Gompertz models as well) is in fact a testable assumption (though it often goes untested). In Chapter 8, we return to the Cox model and illustrate how and why one would want to test for this assumption. Further, as Royston (2001) and Royston and Parmar (2002) lucidly show, there are occasions where analysts of survival data will be interested in the characterization of the baseline hazard functions, and in particular time dependency. In Chapter 6, we consider the alternative approaches posed by Royston (2001) and Royston and Parmar (2002).

Nevertheless, we have argued throughout this chapter that time dependency in most kinds of models proposed by social scientists *is* appropriately thought of as a nuisance. Principally, our view is that given imprecision in how time is measured coupled with the pronounced emphasis in understanding how covariates relate to the hazard rate, time dependency in and of itself should be of less interest to analysts than parameter estimates of important covariates. For this reason, the Cox model discussed in this chapter seems naturally suited for problems involving duration data in social science. We return to this issue again in Chapter 6 and in Chapter 11. In the next chapter, we consider another modeling strategy often used in the face of duration data: the discrete-time approach.

CHAPTER 5

Models for Discrete Data

The applications of event history methods discussed to this point have all presumed that the event history process is absolutely continuous. This assumes change can occur anywhere in time. Nevertheless, continuity is often belied by the data: measures of time are frequently imprecise, or are made out of practical concerns (and out of convenience). For example, although cabinet governments may fall presumably at any time, the data used in our examples treat the termination point as occurring within a month. This implies that although we have data for processes that are continuous in nature, the data themselves are discrete. As event occurrences amass at discrete intervals, it may be more practical, and perhaps substantively natural, to consider models for discrete-time processes. In this chapter, we consider some approaches for modeling event history processes where events only occur (or are only observed) at discrete intervals.

Discrete-Time Data

Event history data for discrete-time processes generally record the dependent variable as a series of binary outcomes denoting whether or not the event of interest occurred at the observation point. To illustrate, consider the public policy data in Table 5.1. These data are from a study of state adoption of restrictive abortion policy (Brace, Hall, and Langer 1999). The event of interest is whether or not a state adopted legislation that placed restrictions on abortion rights. The starting point of the analysis is the first legislative session after the *Roe v. Wade* decision (1973). The substantive question underlying these data is how long a state legislature goes before adopting restrictive legislation. Since legislation can only be adopted during a legislative session, the underlying process for policy adoption is assumed to be discrete.

The first column of data gives an identification number for each state. The second column of data is comprised of a sequence of zeroes and ones. A zero denotes that in that legislative session, no restrictive abortion legislation was

TABLE 5.1: Example of Discrete-Time Event History Data

Case I.D.	Event Occurrence	Year	Time Elapsed
1	0	1974	1
1	0	1975	2
⋮	⋮	⋮	⋮
1	0	1986	13
1	1	1987	14
5	1	1974	1
45	0	1974	1
45	0	1975	2
⋮	⋮	⋮	⋮
45	0	1992	19
45	0	1993	20

adopted—i.e., no event occurrence is observed. A one denotes the adoption of restrictive abortion legislation—i.e., the event occurs. For discrete-time data, this is generally the form of the dependent variable used in an event history model. Finally, the third column gives the year of the legislative session in which the policy was adopted. For discrete-time data, the dependent variable, although different in form from the actual duration time, *conveys the same information as the duration time* (Petersen 1995; see also Yamaguchi 1990, 1992). To see this, consider case 1. We see that this state "enters" the process in 1974 (as do all states) and progresses through 14 legislative sessions until in the 1987 session, it adopts restrictive abortion legislation: the event occurs. Now, if we look at the column measuring the time that elapses from *Roe vs. Wade* until policy adoption, we see that at year 14, the state adopts restrictive legislation; again, the event occurs. *Both* measures of time lead to the same conclusion: at $t = 14$, state 1 adopted restrictive abortion legislation. The only difference between the two forms of the dependent variable is that in the case of the discrete-time formulation, the history is "disaggregated" into discrete intervals. In this case, the intervals correspond to legislative sessions, which are measured in terms of years (see Berry and Berry [1990, 1992, 1994], Mintrom [1997], Mintrom and Vergari [1998] for examples of this kind of coding).

The point is, even though the dependent variable is a sequence of zeroes and ones, the information conveyed by this sequence is equivalent to that conveyed by the actual duration time. One convenient aspect of recording the dependent variable as a series of binary outcomes is that this form of the dependent variable naturally leads to models familiar to social scientists. In particular, a discrete-time event history model can be estimated by a logit or probit model, two models widely used in social science. To get there from here, however, we need to consider some mathematical concepts underlying the discrete-time model.

$S(t)$, $f(t)$, and $h(t)$ for the Discrete-Time Model

To fix ideas, let the random variable T denote a discrete random variable indicating the time of an event occurrence. Since we assume events are observable at specific, discretely defined points, t_i, the probability mass function for a discrete random variable is

$$f(t) = \Pr(T = t_i) \tag{5.1}$$

and denotes the probability of an event occurring at time t_i. Through (5.1), it is clear that there can be multiple failures occurring at the same time. The survivor function for the discrete random variable T is given by

$$S(t) = \Pr(T \geq t_i) = \sum_{j \geq i} f(t_j), \tag{5.2}$$

where j denotes a failure time. Using the result shown in equation (2.6) for the continuous case, the hazard rate for the discrete-time case is given by

$$h(t) = \frac{f(t)}{S(t)}, \tag{5.3}$$

which demonstrates that the risk of an event occurrence is equivalent to the ratio of the probability of failure to the probability of survival. The ratio in equation (5.3) can be reexpressed in terms of the conditional probability of failure given survival; hence the hazard probability for the discrete-time case can be written as

$$h(t) = \Pr(T = t_i \mid T \geq t_i). \tag{5.4}$$

Conversely, suppose that the conditional probability of *survival* is

$$\Pr(T > t_i \mid T \geq t_i) = 1 - h(t). \tag{5.5}$$

Then the probability of failure, which is given by $f(t)$, can be written as

$$
\begin{aligned}
\Pr(T = t_i) \quad = \quad & \Pr(T = t_i \mid T \geq t_i) \times \Pr(T > t_{i-1} \mid T \geq t_{i-1}) \times \ldots \times \\
& \Pr(T > t_2 \mid T \geq t_2) \times \Pr(T > t_1 \mid T \geq t_1),
\end{aligned} \tag{5.6}
$$

where the subscripts 1 and 2 index the first and second time periods. If we express (5.6) in terms of the hazard probability in (5.4) and in terms of the conditional survival probability in (5.5), then

$$
\begin{aligned}
f(t) \quad = \quad & h(t_i) \times (1 - h(t_{i-1})) \times \ldots \times (1 - h(t_2)) \times (1 - h(t_1)) \\
= \quad & h(t_i) \prod_{i=1}^{t-1} (1 - h(t_i)),
\end{aligned} \tag{5.7}
$$

thus demonstrating that the probability mass function is equal to the hazard probability times the product of the conditional survivor functions. Furthermore, since by equation (5.3), it must be the case that $f(t) = S(t)h(t)$, then it is easy to see that the survivor function must be equal to

$$
\begin{aligned}
\Pr(T > t_i) &= (1 - h(t)) \times (1 - h(t_{i-1})) \times \ldots \times (1 - h(t_2)) \times (1 - h(t_1)) \\
&= \prod_{i=1}^{t} (1 - h(t_i)),
\end{aligned} \tag{5.8}
$$

which illustrates the intuition that the probability of survival beyond time t_i is equal to the conditional probability of surviving through each of the t previous periods.

Suppose that we have an event history data set consisting of n cases observed over t periods. For each observation in the data set, the dependent variable, which we denote as y_{it}, is a binary indicator coded 1 if an event occurs and 0 if an event does not occur at time t. If the event never occurs, the observation is right-censored and contributes to the data set a vector of zeroes. Using the results shown in (5.7) and (5.8), it is clear that the likelihood of such a data set is

$$
\mathcal{L} = \prod_{i}^{n} \left[h(t_i) \prod_{i=1}^{t-1} (1 - h(t_i)) \right]^{y_{it}} \left[\prod_{i=1}^{t} (1 - h(t_i)) \right]^{1 - y_{it}},
$$

which is equivalent to

$$
\mathcal{L} = \prod_{i=1}^{n} \left\{ f(t) \right\}^{y_{it}} \left\{ S(t) \right\}^{1 - y_{it}}. \tag{5.9}
$$

For the likelihoods discussed in Chapters 2 and 3, it was necessary to define a right-censoring indicator, which we called δ_i; for the discrete-time case with a dependent variable measured in terms of a series of binary outcomes, failure times are implicitly indexed when the dependent variable assumes the value of 1. For all other instances, the dependent variable is coded as 0. Given the likelihood function in (5.9), it is clear that *only* cases experiencing an event contribute information regarding the probability of failure, i.e., $f(t)$, and cases not experiencing an event contribute information only regarding the probability of survival, i.e., $S(t)$. Thus, for the discrete-time case, the dependent variable is also an implicit indicator of right-censoring. We now turn attention toward models for discrete-time data.

Models for Discrete-Time Processes

Given the structure of discrete-time data and the form of the dependent variable, a wide variety of models are available. Inclusion of covariates into (5.4) is straightforward, and is accomplished by treating the probability of failure as conditional on survival as well as covariates:

$$h(t) = \Pr(T = t_i \mid T \geq t_i, \mathbf{x}). \tag{5.10}$$

For discrete-time event history data, where the dependent variable is binary, constructing models relating this variable to the covariates involves selecting one function from a variety of suitable distribution functions for binary data. As such, two commonly applied functions are the logistic distribution (which gives rise to the familiar logit model) and the standard normal distribution (which gives rise to the probit model). In the discrete-time formulation of the event history model, we are interested in modeling the risk, or the probability an event will occur. The hazard probability conveniently conveys this notion of risk, as it reflects the probability of an event's occurrence, conditional on survival and covariates, to some time t_i. To simplify the presentation of the models discussed in this section, we denote the probability of an event's occurrence as $\Pr(y_{it} = 1) = \lambda_i$, and the probability of a nonoccurrence as $\Pr(y_{it} = 0) = 1 - \lambda_i$. It is assumed that this probability is a function of covariates, $\mathbf{x}$. To derive a discrete-time model, we first need to specify a distribution function for the following model:

$$\lambda_{it} = \beta_0 + \beta_1 x_{1i} + \beta_2 x_{2i} + \ldots + \beta_k x_{ki}.$$

A commonly used function for this model is the logit function, which has the following form:

$$\log\left(\frac{\lambda_i}{1 - \lambda_i}\right) = \beta_0 + \beta_1 x_{1i} + \beta_2 x_{2i} + \ldots + \beta_k x_{ki}. \tag{5.11}$$

This function specifies λ_i in terms of the log-odds ratio of the probability of an event occurrence to the probability of a nonoccurrence. The logit coefficients, β_k, are therefore interpreted in terms of their relationship to the log-odds of an event occurrence. When $\beta_k > 0$, the log of the odds ratio in (5.11) is increasing as the covariate increases, and decreasing when $\beta_k < 0$. Because log-odds ratios are not always obvious to interpret substantively, the predicted probability of an event occurrence, that is $\hat{\lambda}_i$, can be retrieved from the logit model by reexpressing (5.11) directly in terms of the probability,

$$\hat{\lambda}_i = \frac{e^{\beta' \mathbf{x}}}{1 + e^{\beta' \mathbf{x}}},$$

where $\exp(\beta' \mathbf{x})$ represents the exponentiated logit parameters for a given covariate profile.

An alternative function that can be specified for binary event history data is the probit function, which has the form

$$\Phi^{-1}[\lambda_i] = \beta_0 + \beta_1 x_{1i} + \beta_2 x_{2i} + \ldots + \beta_k x_{ki}, \tag{5.12}$$

where Φ is the standard normal cumulative distribution function. The probability λ_i can be directly estimated by reparameterizing (5.12) as

$$\hat{\lambda}_i = \Phi(\beta'\mathbf{x}),$$

and computing the probability of an event for different covariate profiles. The logit and probit models for discrete-time event history data are appealing because social scientists have considerable familiarity with these models. The choice between the logit and probit models is usually trivial and in practice, the two models produce nearly equivalent results (recall the similarity between the log-normal and the log-logistic models discussed in Chapter 3).

A third model sometimes used with discrete duration data is the complementary log-log function. This function produces an event history model taking the form

$$\log[-\log(1 - \lambda_i)] = \beta_0 + \beta_1 x_{1i} + \beta_2 x_{2i} + \ldots + \beta_k x_{ki}. \qquad (5.13)$$

Estimates from the complementary log-log model can depart substantially from those obtained by the logit or probit models. For logit and probit, the response curve is symmetric about $\lambda_i = .5$, whereas for the complementary log-log model, the response curve departs "slowly" from $\lambda_i = 0$ and approaches $\pi = 1$ very rapidly (Agresti 1990). The implication of this is that estimated event probabilities could markedly differ, depending on which model is reported. This probability, λ_i, can be computed for the complementary log-log model by reexpressing (5.13) as

$$\hat{\lambda}_i = 1 - \exp[-\exp(\beta'\mathbf{x})].$$

The complementary log-log model has not been widely used in social science applications. Typically, of the models discussed to this point, the logit model has most commonly been applied, perhaps owing to the prevalence of its use in the non-duration modeling setting. Nevertheless, the complementary log-log model provides an alternative to the logit or probit distribution functions. Moreover, as the complementary log-log function is asymmetric, in data sets where there are relatively few failures (i.e. ones), results may differ between the logit model and the complementary log-log model.

Incorporating Duration in the Discrete-Time Framework

When event history data are in the form of a discrete-time process and the dependent variable is binary, some well known models may be used to estimate the covariate parameters. What is less obvious from the presentation is how one accounts for duration dependency in the context of these models. Unlike the Cox model, where the baseline hazard is not directly estimated, the discrete-time model is most analogous to a parametric model using the exponential distribution. Recall that under the exponential, the hazard rate is flat with respect to time. Similarly, a logit discrete-time model will lead one to the same conclusion. To see this, consider the logit model again. Suppose one estimates the following model:

$$\log\left(\frac{\lambda_i}{1 - \lambda_i}\right) = \beta_0 + \beta_1 x_{1i} + \beta_2 x_{2i},$$

where x_{ki} are two covariates of interest that have a mean of 0 and β_0 is the constant term. The "baseline" hazard under this model would be equivalent to

$$\hat{\lambda}_i = h_0(t) = e^{\beta_0},$$

which is a constant. Hence, the hazard probability is flat with respect to time. Just as the parametric exponential model is often inappropriate for social science data, assuming a flat baseline hazard for the discrete-time model is equally problematic. In general, it is often desirable to make some attempt to account for duration dependency in the discrete-time model. The reason for this is straightforward. Each individual case in a discrete-time event history data set contributes multiple records (or lines of data). The repeated measures on the ith case *can* exhibit temporal dependence, or duration dependency. Below, we discuss approaches to account for time-dependency within discrete duration data.

Temporal Dummy Variables and Transformations

The most general way to account for duration dependency is by the inclusion of temporal dummy variables. Suppose that in a data set, there are $j = 1, 2, \ldots, k$ time points at which events can occur. The inclusion of $k - 1$ temporal dummy variables would allow a very general way to directly model the duration dependency in the data. This approach, while having the attractiveness of generality, has two drawbacks. First, and most obviously, if the number of time points in the data set is large, then the number of temporal dummies included in the model will also be substantial. The temporal dummies can quickly consume many degrees of freedom. Second, if one is interested in ascribing substantive interpretation to temporal dependence, then interpreting the coefficients of many dummy variables can become unwieldy, particularly if the pattern of the coefficients is very noisy.

    Transforming the values of the duration time can sometimes lead to a better (and more parsimonious) characterization of the time dependency in the hazard. For example, through the use of the natural log transformation or polynomials, different forms (or "shapes") of the baseline hazard can be captured. Indeed, there are numerous kinds of mathematical transformations of the duration time that could be applied, and the choice of which one (or if one is even necessary) should routinely be tested against a null model of temporal independence. In this sense, the choice of the appropriate transformation is an empirical matter.

Smoothing Functions

Smoothing functions for discrete duration data by the use of spline functions (see also Gray 1992) and locally weighted smoothing functions (lowess) are discussed in Cleveland (1979, 1981), Hastie and Tibshirani (1990), as well as Beck and Jackman (1998) and Beck, Katz, and Tucker (1998). The basic idea behind the use of spline functions or lowess is to estimate a function that provides a smooth characterization of the survival times. Beck and Jackman (1998) consider the use of lowess in the context of generalized additive models (GAMs) and demonstrate how these models can be fit with duration data. Recently, Royston (2001) and Royston and Parmar (2002) have proposed a very general spline-based duration model. The use of these kinds of models will be considered in the next chapter. For now, we discuss the use of smoothing functions as a method to account for duration dependency.

At issue in the consideration of spline functions is the determination of the location of so-called *knot* points—that is, the point at which two segments of T are joined together. The choice of knot placement as well as the number of knots used in the spline function can be an issue. It is common that knots are placed at given percentiles of T, or that cubic spline functions are implemented. What makes the use of splines (as well as other smoothing methods) appealing is that they provide a very general way to characterize duration dependency. Moreover, few assumptions regarding duration dependency need to be made, as the shape of the function is empirically determined (conditional on the location and number of knot point placements). This flexibility is desirable insofar as it avoids having to make (perhaps wrong) assumptions about the shape of the baseline hazard rate or having to make (perhaps arbitrary) decisions regarding transformations of T.

Lowess proceeds by estimating the relationship between y_i and x_i at several target points over the range of x (Beck and Jackman 1998, p. 603). For each value of y_i, a smoothed value of y_i is estimated. The resulting smoothed function, in the context of the discrete-time duration model, can be used to characterize the baseline hazard function. As with the use of spline functions, there are important issues that must be considered when implementing lowess. Among them is the "bandwidth" decision. Bandwidth denotes the fraction or proportion of the data that is used in smoothing each point. The larger the bandwidth, the greater the data reduction (and the more smooth the function becomes); the smaller the bandwidth, the closer the lowess function follows the actual data. Beck and Jackman (1998) provide more details on issues related to lowess, and more generally, GAMs. In Figure 5.1, we illustrate a baseline hazard function using a spline and lowess function. The baseline hazard estimates

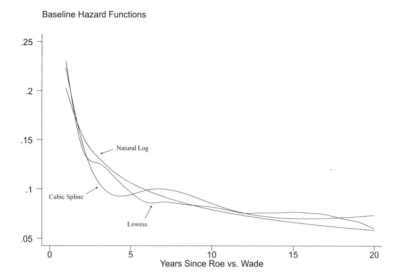

Baseline Hazard Functions

FIGURE 5.1: *This figure illustrates a cubic spline function, lowess, and natural log transformation of the baseline hazard function from a model of restrictive abortion policy adoption.*

in this figure are based on the Brace, Hall, and Langer (1999) data. The event of interest is a state's adoption of restrictive abortion policies since the *Roe v. Wade* decision. For these data, a cubic spline function was estimated as well as a lowess function. For comparison purposes, the natural log transformation of T is also presented. Both the cubic spline function and the lowess function provide a smoothed and easy-to-visualize characterization of the baseline hazard function. Though both are quite similar to the log transformation of T (which in any given application will, of course, not always be the case), the spline and lowess functions are more bumpy. This is to be expected. The log transformation simply rescales the duration times, which results in a smooth, monotonic transformation. The smoothed functions given by the spline function and lowess are estimated empirically. As such, fewer assumptions need to be made regarding the shape of the baseline hazard than when compared to the mathematical transformations discussed earlier.

Interpretation of Discrete-Time Model Estimates

The statistical models discussed in this chapter all proceed by essentially estimating the likelihood an event occurs. Because data on both survival and failures are accounted for by the dependent variable—which explicitly records survival and failure—results from the discrete-time model can be appropriately interpreted in terms of the hazard function, or more precisely, the hazard probability. To illustrate the discrete-time models considered thus far, we present an application.

Example 5.1: Discrete-Time Models of U.S. House Member Careers

In this application, we use data on the career paths of U.S. House of Representative incumbents. The data are comprised of information pertaining to the career path for every House member elected in each freshman class from 1950 to 1976.[1] Each member of the House was tracked from his or her first reelection bid until the last term served in office. For this example, the event of interest is electoral defeat (defeat is denoted as one). At each election cycle, members are observed as either winning or losing an election. One covariate is included in the models below and it measures the party affiliation of the incumbent. The variable is scored a 0 if the incumbent was a Democrat and 1 if the incumbent was a Republican. The first set of models we discuss are based on logit estimates.

Because the data set has multiple observations of the same member of Congress over time, it is desirable to account for any duration dependency that may be exhibited in the data. To test for different specifications of duration dependency, we estimated several models and tested the fit against a null model where no duration dependency was assumed (which gives rise to the exponential assumption discussed earlier). Specifically, five functional forms for the baseline duration dependency were tested: linear, natural log transformation, quadratic transformation, cubic spline, and lowess.[2] To assess which of these characterizations of duration dependency best fit the data, we computed the likelihood ratio test against the null model. The log-likelihoods from each logit model are presented in Table 5.2. Additionally, the estimate of the party identification coefficient is also presented for each model.

Using the likelihood ratio statistic,

$$LR = -2\log(L_0 - L_1),$$

where L_0 corresponds to the null model of no duration dependency, we find that each of the models provides a superior fit to the data than when compared to the null model. This suggests that models accounting, in some way, for duration dependency will be preferable to models ignoring the dependency. Of the five methods used to account for duration dependency, we find that the cubic spline and the lowess functions seem to provide a better fit than do the

---

[1] The core data set used is the *Roster of U.S. Congressional Officeholders*. Additional data were collected by Jones (1994).

[2] The lowess estimate was derived by first estimating the lowess function of the failure variable (denoting winning or losing an election) on the duration times. This estimated function was output as a new variable and included as a covariate in the models estimated and shown in Table 5.2.

TABLE 5.2: Likelihood Ratios Duration Specification

Duration Dependency	Logit Model	Party Identification Estimate
None	−1352.15	.19 (.11)
Linear	−1343.01	.16 (.11)
Natural Log	−1335.54	.16 (.11)
Quadratic	−1337.76	.17 (.11)
Cubic Spline	−1329.46	.17 (.11)
Lowess t	−1331.34	.16 (.11)

transformations or the linear characterization. The χ^2 from the likelihood ratio test for the cubic spline was 45.37 on 4 degrees of freedom; the χ^2 from the likelihood ratio test for the lowess function was 41.61 on 1 degree of freedom. Based on the χ^2 value, we might slightly prefer the cubic spline model over the lowess model. In Figure 5.2, we plot the estimated baseline hazard functions from the logit model for both the cubic spline and lowess functions. The party identification variable is set to 0; hence the baseline category represents the hazard for Democrats. Both estimates show a precipitous drop in the hazard very early in the congressional career. After this sharp decline, the hazard tends to "flatten" out over the remainder of the congressional career. For this simple example, both the cubic spline and the lowess functions yield fairly similar conclusions. Given the slightly better fit of the cubic spline model, we would choose to present these results over the lowess model. Regarding the estimated coefficient for party identification, we see that the coefficient estimate from the cubic spline model is about .17. The positive coefficient in the context of the logit duration model suggests that the risk of electoral defeat is slightly higher for Republican incumbents than for Democratic incumbents. The coefficients from the logit model are expressed in terms of log-odds ratios. If we exponentiate the coefficient, we can compute the predicted increase in the odds of a Republican losing office over a Democrat. We find that the increased risk of electoral defeat associated with being a Republican amounts to about 19 percent. Put another way, at each election cycle, Republicans are about 19 percent more likely to lose electorally than are Democrats. Of course as we can see from the estimated baseline hazard, this relative increase in the hazard *still* yields a fairly low probability of electoral defeat.

This example illustrates how the discrete-time formulation of the event history model can be implemented and interpreted. Further, this example illustrates how one can test for differing specifications of duration dependency in the discrete-time model. In the next section, we present an alternative modeling strategy for discrete data using the Cox model. Specifically, we reconsider the exact discrete approximation presented in Chapter 4.

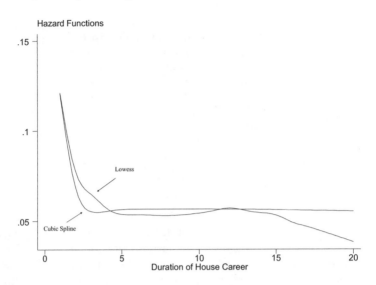

FIGURE 5.2: *The lines represent the estimated baseline hazard from the discrete-time logit model of House career paths. The cubic spline and lowess functions are presented.*

Conditional Logit and the Cox Model

As with the parametric models discussed in Chapter 3, considerable attention needs to be paid to the form of duration dependency in the discrete-time models. However, if one believes that duration dependency is best thought of as a nuisance—the residual effects of time after accounting for covariates—then a modeling strategy where the functional form of the duration dependency is left unspecified might be desirable. In Chapter 4, we discussed the problem that tied events pose for the Cox regression model. We discussed three commonly used approximations for handling ties: the Breslow method, the Efron method, and the averaged likelihood method. We also discussed a fourth approach to handling tied data, which we called the exact discrete method. We mentioned in Chapter 4 that this approximation of the partial likelihood function was equivalent to a logit model for matched case-control studies. This kind of logit model is frequently referred to as the *conditional logit* model.

The conditional logit model differs from the standard logit model (discussed above) in that the data are grouped according to some attribute and the likelihood is estimated *conditional* on each grouping. Sometimes, the conditional logit model is referred to as a fixed effects model. The reason for this is simple. Suppose that in a discrete choice model, observations are grouped by some unit (for example, individuals, firms, countries, dyads, and so on). Any factor that remains constant within the grouping is perfectly collinear with the group. For example, in studies of international conflict using the familiar dyad data, Green, Kim, and Yoon (2001) have advocated the use of fixed effects models. For this conditional logit model, the grouping is in terms of the country dyad. An implication of this is that any covariates that are constant within the dyad cannot be estimated (and covariates having limited variance within a dyad cannot be estimated well [Beck and Katz, 2001]). In some applications, this could be problematic.

In the context of duration data, however, the fixed effects approach is not problematic. For the conditional logit Cox model, observations are grouped (or "matched") by the risk set at the ordered failure times. Coefficient estimates for covariates of interest are then estimated conditional on the composition of the risk sets. Any covariate constant within a time interval cannot be estimated (for example time dummy variables would not be estimable), but other covariates of interest can be estimated. From these estimates, inferences about the hazard rate and survivor function can be made. Moreover, as the exact discrete approximation—or the conditional logit model—does not require estimation of the baseline hazard, the form of the duration dependency in the data need not be directly specified. As with other Cox models, this dependency is assumed to have an arbitrary form. We now present an application to illustrate the exact discrete method. In the application, we provide some comparisons of this method to the other discrete-time models discussed above.

Example 5.2: Militarized Interventions

In this application, we consider data on militarized interventions. The dependent variable in these models is binary, indicating whether or not an intervention has terminated (1) or is on-going (0). Recorded in this way, the dependent variable is equivalent to the censoring indicator, δ_i, that has been discussed throughout this book. The duration of militarized interventions is treated as a function of six covariates. The first is a measure of the relative material capabilities of the intervenor state to the target state. The measure is a ratio using the correlates of war (COW) composite capabilities index. In the table, this variable is referred to as "relative capabilities." Scores on the variable closer to 1 indicate a materials capabilities imbalance in favor of the intervenor state, and scores closer to 0 indicate an imbalance in favor of the target state. The mean on this variable is .70 with a median of .77. The second covariate is a binary indicator of territorial contiguity. This variable is coded 1 if the intervenor and target are territorially contiguous and 0 otherwise. The third covariate is a binary indicator denoting whether or not the target and intervenor are joined in any formal alliance or security treaty. The fourth and fifth covariates are a measure of the level of democracy in the intervenor and target states. The democracy measure ranges from -10 (least democratic, most autocratic) to 10 (most democratic). It is based on the Polity IIId democracy index minus the

TABLE 5.3: Models of Militarized Interventions

	Conditional Logit	Logit	Weibull
Variable	Estimate (s.e.)	Estimate (s.e.)	Estimate (s.e.)
Constant	−	−4.07 (.13)	−1.76 (.12)
Relative Capabilities	−.50 (.15)	−.43 (.16)	−.50 (.15)
Territorial Contiguity	−.26 (.11)	−.25 (.11)	−.28 (.10)
Intervenor Allied to Target	.24 (.10)	.22 (.10)	.26 (.10)
Intervenor Democracy	.01 (.01)	.01 (.01)	.01 (.01)
Target Democracy	.02 (.01)	.02 (.01)	.02 (.01)
Breakdown of Authority	−.46 (.21)	−.43 (.20)	−.44 (.20)
Duration Dependency	−	16.20 (.95)	.66 (.02)
N	9374	9374	9374
Log-Likelihood	−1591.41	−1779.31	−1004.86

The duration dependency parameter for the logit model (second column) is a lowess function of the baseline hazard rate. For the Weibull model (third column), the duration dependency parameter is the Weibull shape parameter p. Data are from *International Military Interventions, 1946-1988* (ICPSR 6035) compiled by Pearson and Baumann. Supplementary data are from McLaughlin et al. (1998) *Polity III* project and various correlates of war (COW) data collections.

Polity IIId autocracy index (McLaughlin, Gates, Hegre, Gissinger, and Gleditsch 1998). The mean and median democracy scores for intervenors are .25 and −3 and for targets are −2.22 and −6. The sixth covariate is a binary indicator denoting whether or not institutional authority patterns in the target state have broken down. The source of this variable is from Jaggers and Gurr (1995).

Of interest in this application is to illustrate the use of the exact discrete approximation and compare estimates from this model with a logit model as well as a Weibull model. The results from the three models are shown in Table 5.3. The first column of estimates give the results from the Cox model based on the exact discrete approximation; the second column of estimates are from a logit model; and the third column gives the Weibull estimates. For the logit model, a lowess function was used to characterize the baseline hazard rate. The scale of the coefficients for the duration dependency parameter in these models are large because the individual estimates for smoothed t are quite small in scale.

Looking across the models at the coefficient estimates, there are no appreciable differences in the magnitude of any of the covariates. For these models, a positively signed coefficient implies the hazard rate is increasing as a function of changes to the covariate; a negatively signed coefficient implies the hazard is decreasing. Thus, we see that democratization is positively related to the risk of intervention termination; that is, the risk of an intervention terminating increases as the level of democratization in a state increases. More generally, substantive conclusions regarding the relationship between the covariates and the risk of an intervention terminating would be similar across the three models (though this may not always be the case; recall the Cox vs. Weibull results using the EU data from Chapter 3). The principal difference between the Cox estimates and the other models is the absence of a duration dependency parameter for the Cox model. However, as noted in Chapter 4, the baseline hazard function can be generated from Cox estimates.

The major point of this application is to illustrate how the discrete-time formulation of the Cox model can be used to generate estimates from an otherwise continuous-time process. At least in this application, substantive conclusions about the covariates would be quite similar across the three models. The similarity in results, of course, raises the issue of which is the most "appropriate" model. We turn to this question in the next chapter.

Conclusion

To conclude, there are two points we want to stress. First, the distinction between purely discrete and purely continuous-time processes is not so clear-cut in practice. "Discrete-time" models like the logit can be used to estimate the parameters of models for underlying continuous time processes (see also Beck, Katz, and Tucker 1998). In contrast, the Cox model, parameterized as a conditional logit model, can be used to estimate parameters of interest, even in the face of highly discretized data. Second, much of the data social scientists work with are highly discrete in nature. By this we mean that our measurements of time are often not well defined and so events amass, or occur in discrete "clumps." The discrete version of the Cox model discussed in this application is an acceptable modeling strategy for many problems in social science. In the next chapter, we consider the issue of modeling strategies more directly.

CHAPTER 6

Issues in Model Selection

A wide variety of models for duration data have been discussed. Each of the approaches has certain advantages and disadvantages. The principal argument we have made is that in most social science settings, the Cox model should generally be preferred over its alternatives, for example the parametric models or some of the discrete models discussed in the last chapter. In this chapter, we revisit some of the models proposed and discuss some of the desirable and undesirable features inherent in the implementation of them. Following this discussion, we consider another class of models that create, in a sense, a "middle ground" between the Cox and parametric alternatives. The basic models discussed in this section are proposed by Royston (2001) and Royston and Parmar (2002).

Advantages and Disadvantages of Modeling Strategies

In this section, we discuss some of the advantages and disadvantages of the parametric models, discrete-time models, and the Cox models. We consider the standard parametric models first.

Parametric Models Revisited

The principal advantage of parametric duration models is the ability of the model to provide parameter estimates while simultaneously producing a relatively simple and easy-to-interpret characterization of the baseline hazard rate. Further, the parametric approach is flexible insofar as one simply needs to specify one of any number of suitable distribution functions. Commonly (and often by default), the Weibull distribution function is the distribution of choice in many applications; but there are numerous other functions that can be applied to duration data (each having concomitant assumptions regarding $h_0(t)$). The parametric models are relatively easy to implement, as most statistical software packages offer a wide variety of distribution functions suitable for estimating models on duration data. Finally, because many of the parametric models can be parameterized as linear models for $\log(T)$ (i.e. log-linear models), estimated coefficients "look like" familiar regression slope coefficients, as they reveal information about predicted survival times (though appropriate interpretation of model estimates usually requires analysis of ancillary parameters).

The main drawback to the parametric approach is the potential for arbitrary decisions regarding the nature of the baseline hazard rate. Unfortunately, much of the applied work using parametric models in the social sciences indicates that little attention is paid to model selection across different parametric forms. If a parametric modeling strategy is opted for, some of the model selection procedures discussed in Chapter 3 should routinely be applied. In some instances, estimation of the generalized gamma model may be feasible. Recall that the generalized gamma is an encompassing distribution having nested under it the exponential, Weibull, log-normal, and gamma distributions. From the ancillary parameters of the generalized gamma, one may be able to adjudicate which of these distributions best fits the data. For non-nested models, the Akaike information criterion (AIC) may be applied. Finally, analysis of residuals may be useful in judging the adequacy of different parametric forms. In Chapter 8, we discuss event history residuals and demonstrate how residual plots can be used to evaluate the goodness-of-fit.

A useful question to ask is, in what context is a parametric duration model naturally preferred over its alternatives, chiefly the Cox model? The simple answer to this question centers on the extent to which the analyst is interested in: 1) making explicit inferences regarding duration dependency; and 2) the degree to which the researcher believes time dependency is substantively meaningful (as opposed to thinking of it as a nuisance). Indeed, one clear advantage of using parametric models is predicting or forecasting what will happen beyond the ''follow-up'' period of the data—that is, making out-of-sample predictions. For example, in public policy studies of when states enact a particular law, it may be useful to predict which states are likely to enact the legislation beyond the time frame of the observation period. Schmidt and Witte (1988) point out that criminal justice decision-makers are keenly interested in prediction because they may base their decisions on the prediction of likely future actions by the individuals, say charged with a crime, in front of them. In contrast, Cox models cannot be easily used to extrapolate beyond the last observed failure time in a data set (*Guide to Statistics* 1999, 326); the parametric form can be extrapolated beyond the data. Parametric models elicit smooth baseline functions, which can make graphical displays of the hazard rate easier to visualize (of course a disadvantage is that the posited model can be the wrong model and therefore the functions, while smoothed, are incorrect).

Yet if one believes duration dependency is a nuisance and if interest centers primarily on the relationship between covariates and the hazard rate, then it is difficult to find settings where a parametric model would be preferred over a Cox model. Furthermore, in practice, discrimination between a Cox and Weibull model may be difficult, particularly if there are a lot of failures (Collett 1994). In some instances, a Cox model may be useful in helping to determine a parametric form. In Chapter 4, we discussed how the baseline hazard estimates from a Cox model can be derived. These estimates can be used to help select a distribution function. For example, if the shape of the Cox baseline hazard function is monotonically increasing or decreasing, the Weibull model may be suitable. In this situation, if the Weibull model is fit and the coefficient estimates are comparable between the Weibull and a Cox model, the standard errors can be compared (Collett 1994). In this case, the effect of the covariates may be roughly similar, but the standard errors for the Weibull *may* be slightly smaller than those for the Cox model due to efficiency gains (the Weibull uses the full information on the duration times; the Cox model only uses the ordered failure time).

In fact, simulation evidence shows that the gains will be small because the Cox is approximately 95 percent as efficient as the Weibull (Peace and Flora 1978). The precision of the MPLE parameter estimates compared to those of MLE can be less when the sample size is small because the MPLE method only uses information about the relative order of durations. If one has a very small sample, the parametric model may be useful. But one should be wary of applying any of these models in a very small data set, particularly when covariates are estimated. To conclude, if duration dependency is thought of as a nuisance—and very often it will be—then the Cox model will be preferred over a parametric model. However, if one is interested in prediction (and therefore is assuming the time path is substantively meaningful), then the parametric models may be preferable to the Cox model.

Discrete-Time Models Revisited

The principal advantage of discrete-time models is that they are widely used and well understood by social scientists. However, there are some ostensible disadvantages of discrete-time models. First, the form of the duration dependency must be explicitly accounted for (or tested for). As such, some of the problems mentioned in the context of the parametric models are relevant in this setting. If little attention is paid to the functional form of the time dependency (or if it is ignored), then the characterization of the baseline hazard may be misleading. Second, if the underlying time process is continuous, then discrete-time methods may be inappropriately applied.

Regarding the issue of otherwise continuous-time processes modeled as if they are discrete-time processes, Sueyoshi's (1995) important work is relevant. He demonstrated the close connection between grouped duration data and binary response models, showing that such models can be used to estimate the underlying hazard rate. Further, Beck, Katz, and Tucker's (1998) analysis, building on Sueyoshi's work, also makes the same point (as do we, in Chapter 5). In our view, there is little use in starkly demarcating discrete-time from continuous-time processes in the construction of duration models.

The disadvantage of having to specify the nature of the duration dependency may or may not be a serious issue to wrestle with, in practice. *Ignoring* duration dependency in grouped binary data is undoubtedly problematic. Because in such data sets, there are multiple observations of the same unit over time, it is likely that observations will be temporally correlated. As noted in Chapter 5, accounting for this time dependency, in most instances, will yield models preferable to ones ignoring it. And to that end, there are a variety of approaches to account for this kind of duration dependency, and these approaches were covered at length in Chapter 5.

Yet as with the parametric models, the issue of time dependency emerges. If an analyst is particularly intent on making claims about duration dependency and believes such dependency is substantively important, then serious attention needs to be paid to the characterization of the duration dependency found in the data. In such situations, use of smoothing functions like splines or lowess to characterize duration dependency will most likely yield better fitting models than some standard (or arbitrary) transformation of the duration times.

However, if duration dependency is regarded as a nuisance, then the question naturally arises as to the appropriateness of discrete-time models like the logit model, when compared to the Cox alternative. In Chapters 4 and 5, we showed that the conditional logit model is a special case of the Cox model for discrete grouped duration data. As such, the model *is* a model for discrete data. But as is the case with Cox models, the form of the duration dependency need not be directly modeled. Hence, the approaches for handling time dependency discussed in Chapter 5 can be ignored if one regards the duration dependency as chiefly a nuisance. Put another way, there is no reason we can think of why one would naturally prefer a standard logit model over the conditional logit Cox model *if duration dependency is assumed to be a nuisance parameter.* By implication, if one thought of duration dependency as indicating something substantively meaningful, then discrete-time models that account for duration dependency might be preferred to the Cox model. Again, this issue hinges on the analyst's view of duration dependency.

The Cox Model Revisited

The primary advantage of the Cox model is simple: the relationship between covariates and the hazard rate can be estimated without having to make any assumptions whatsoever about the nature and shape of the baseline hazard rate. This advantage makes the Cox model the first choice among modeling strategies for many applied problems. Nevertheless, some cautions apply. In instances where inference on the baseline functions (and derivations of these functions) is of interest, the Cox model has some undesirable properties. As

Gelfand et al. (2000) and Royston and Parmar (2002) point out, the baseline hazard function is a "high dimensional, very overfitted estimate" (Royston and Parmar, 2002). It is easy to see why the estimate is "overfitted." The baseline hazard is closely adapted to the observed data. As such, the estimate of $\hat{h}_0(t)$ is often a very noisy function, one that is highly sensitive to outlying event times.

Hjort (1992) takes the argument one step further noting that "the success of Cox regression has perhaps had the unintended side-effect that practitioners too seldomly invest efforts in studying the baseline hazard" (Hjort 1992 [quoted in Royston and Parmar, 2002]). Royston and Parmar (2002) further note than in some research settings, the form of the underlying time dependency will be of central interest. This is particularly relevant, they argue, in medical studies of illness progression. They note that understanding the form of the baseline hazard is crucial in understanding the time path that an illness may take. And because the Cox estimate of the baseline hazard is so closely tied to the observed data, it is difficult to generalize these estimates to other settings. To remedy this problem, Royston and Parmar (2002) propose a generalized hazard model that relies on splines to characterize the duration dependency. Their approach is conceptually similar to that advocated by Beck and Jackman (1998) and Beck, Katz, and Tucker (1998), in the political methodology literature. We turn to the Royston-Parmar models in the next section.

Flexible Parametric Models

We consider in more detail a class of models proposed by Royston and Parmar (2002). The Royston and Parmar approach differs from the standard parametric approach in that the distribution of the integrated hazard (from which the hazard rate can be retrieved) is not assumed to follow a specific distribution function such as the Weibull, log-logistic, or log-normal. Instead, the baseline function is modeled with the use of splines. The models proposed by Royston and Parmar (2002) make use of the link function originally proposed by Aranda-Ordaz (1981):

$$g(x; \theta) = \log \frac{x^{-1} - 1}{\theta}, \qquad (6.1)$$

where when $\theta = 1$, the proportional odds model is obtained, when $\theta \to 0$, the proportional hazards model is obtained, and when $g(x) = -\Phi^{-1}(x)$, the inverse standard normal model is obtained (Royston and Parmar, 2002). In language more familiar to social scientists, a "link function" is terminology used in the context of generalized linear model. It is so-named because the function "links" the systematic part of a model (usually thought of as $\beta'\mathbf{x}$) to the response or outcome variable. As such, the link function given by Aranda-Ordaz (1981) has nested within it three familiar duration models, the proportional odds, the proportional hazards model, and the inverse standard normal model. In the parametric duration modeling context, the proportional odds model gives rise to the log-logistic model, the proportional hazards model gives rise to the familiar Weibull, and the inverse standard normal gives rise to the log-normal model.

However, the Royston-Parmar model differs substantially from the standard Weibull or log-logistic model in that the duration dependency is modeled as a function of splines. Hence, the basic models they propose are given by

$$\log H(t; \mathbf{x}) = \log H_0(t) + \beta' \mathbf{x} = s(x) + \beta' \mathbf{x} \qquad (6.2)$$

and

$$\log O(t; \mathbf{x}) = \log O_0(t) + \beta' \mathbf{x} = s(x) + \beta' \mathbf{x}, \qquad (6.3)$$

where $\log H_0(t)$ is the log integrated hazard and $\log O_0(t)$ is the log of the cumulative proportional odds (Royston 2001; see also Royston and Parmar 2002). The baseline functions in equations (6.2) and (6.3), which are denoted as $s(x)$ are approximated by a spline function. Interestingly, if equations (6.2) and (6.3) are modeled as a linear function (that is, splines are not used to specify $s(x)$), then the Weibull model is obtained for the proportional hazards model, the log-logistic model is obtained for the proportional odds model, and the log-normal model is obtained from inverse normal model. Hence, the Royston-Parmar approach can be viewed as a generalization of some of the standard parametric models considered in Chapter 3.

For analysts explicitly interested in making inferences based on the time dependency in the data, the Royston-Parmar approach provides an attractive middle ground between the standard parametric models and the Cox model. Unlike the standard parametric models, the shape of the time dependency is not determined by the distribution function (unless equations (6.2) and (6.3) are estimated linearly). Instead, the time dependency is estimated by splines, which permit greater flexibility in the characterization of the dependency. Unlike the Cox model, the smoothed estimate of the baseline hazard is generally easier to interpret than the overfitted Cox estimate. If one is interested in making out-of-sample predictions regarding the hazard rate (or survival times), then a more parsimonious depiction of the duration dependency would seem to be desirable. To illustrate the Royston-Parmar approach, we present an application.

Example 6.1: Adoption of Restrictive Abortion Legislation

In this application, we consider the public policy issue of states' adoption of restrictive abortion legislation in the wake of the *Roe vs. Wade* decision of 1973. The motivation for an event history model stems from the interest in assessing how a landmark Supreme Court decision is related to subsequent statehouse policy making. Rosenberg (1991) contends that the influence of

TABLE 6.1: Models of Adoption of Restrictive Abortion Legislation

Variable	Cox Model Estimate (s.e.)	Royston-Parmar Model Estimate (s.e.)	Weibull Model Estimate (s.e.)
Pre-Roe	−.22 (.09)	−.21 (.08)	−.22 (.08)
Shape Parameter	−	−	.98 (.12)
Spline 1	−	1.86 (.44)	−
Spline 2	−	.62 (.33)	−
Spline 3	−	−.32 (.22)	−
Constant	−	−2.39 (.39)	−2.10 (.32)
N	50	50	50
Log-Likelihood	−96.60	−74.16	−77.36

Data are from Brace, Hall, and Langer (1999).

Court decisions on such things as interest group membership, public opinion, and Congressional legislation is very limited. However, because states are often charged with the implementation and enforcement of Supreme Court decisions, it is natural to ask if state legislatures are responsive to landmark Court decisions.

Using the data discussed in the context of Table 5.1 from Chapter 5, we estimated the time-until-adoption using the Royston-Parmar model, a Cox model (using the exact discrete approximation) and a Weibull model. The dependent variable in this application is the time (in years) until state adoption of restrictive abortion legislation. We include as a covariate, one time-independent covariate. This covariate is the Mooney index of pre-*Roe* abortion permissiveness (Mooney and Lee 1995). This covariate ranges from 0 to 5, where 5 indicates the state was most permissive of abortion prior to the *Roe* decision, and 0 denotes the state was least permissive. We mean-centered this covariate (mean=2.18) to compute baseline hazards. Data for this application are from Brace, Hall, and Langer (1999). The results are shown in Table 6.1.

Regarding the covariate of interest, the Mooney index of pre-*Roe* abortion permissiveness, we find that the three models produce essentially equivalent results. We find that states which were more permissive regarding abortion rights prior to the 1973 Supreme Court decision had a much lower risk of subsequently adopting restrictive abortion legislation after the broadly written *Roe vs. Wade* decision. The inferences generated from any of these three models would be nearly identical regarding this covariate.

But what about time dependency? Assuming one was interested in studying the time path of policy adoption following a landmark Supreme Court decision, the baseline hazard estimates may be a quantity of interest. Comparing the Royston-Parmar spline model to the Weibull, we see that it fits the data slightly better than the Weibull model (coincidentally, given the shape parameter is no different from one, the Weibull reduces to the exponential model). To see how the three models characterize duration dependency, we computed the

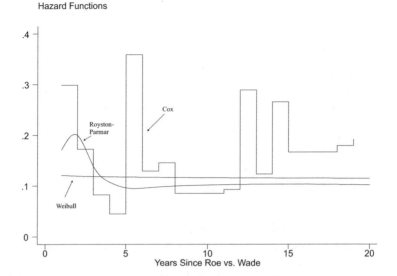

FIGURE 6.1: *Each line is the estimated baseline hazard function from the model of state adoption of restrictive abortion legislation. The three models are: Cox, Royston-Parmar, and Weibull.*

baseline hazard from each model and plotted with respect to time. The results are shown in Figure 6.1.

Here, we see clear differences across the estimates of the baseline hazards. The Weibull estimate is flat (as suggested by the exponential model), while the Royston-Parmar spline estimates suggest that the baseline hazard rose in the wake of the *Roe v. Wade* but soon declined to an essentially constant rate. The Cox estimates are more complicated to interpret owing to the fact that the Cox baseline hazard is closely adapted to the observed data. Again, if the analyst were interested in the underlying duration dependency, then in this setting, the Royston-Parmar model would be preferable over both the Weibull and the Cox models. Next, we consider the issue of model selection in light of our consideration of the Royston-Parmar models.

Do All Roads Lead to the Cox Model?

The spline-based approach outlined by Royston and Parmar (2002) provides a nice alternative to the standard parametric models *and* the Cox models in research settings where there is strong substantive interest in duration dependency. More generally, when interest centers on making claims about the underlying time path of a process, the approaches utilizing smoothing functions on the baseline hazard seem quite attractive. Of these approaches, we have discussed the Royston and Parmar approach primarily. However there are other methodological approaches as well. Beck and Jackman's (1998) use of lowess functions to characterize the baseline hazard (which were discussed in Chapter 4) is also a useful approach to account for duration dependency. Ultimately, the most attractive feature of these kinds of modeling strategies is that they parsimoniously describe the underlying time dependency without having to rely on distributional assumptions that may or may not hold. The Royston-Parmar approach is particularly useful as their models reduce to three standard parametric forms under the condition of linearity (the Weibull, log-normal, and log-logistic). It *is* important to note that these models do come with a price. The issue of knot selection in spline functions is a perennial and controversial issue. Further, with lowess smoothing, the computational burden can become very high with large data sets and many observations on t. Yet if one is interested in interpreting the baseline hazard rate (and derivations of this rate), then these approaches constitute natural modeling strategies. In this sense, all roads *do not* lead to the Cox model.

Conclusion

In this chapter we have pointed out some of the advantages and disadvantages associated with the three dominant kinds of duration models discussed in this book. We also introduced a "middle-ground" approach, the Royston-Parmar model, that is attractive when one is interested in time dependency. In general, our recommendation on model selection essentially boils down to one's conception of time dependency and the baseline hazard rate. If the baseline hazard is not of central interest, then the Cox model is strongly recommended; if the baseline hazard is of central importance, then the Cox model can be improved upon (in terms of characterizing t). It is instructive to point out that in the examples discussed in this chapter, in no instance would one's substantive conclusions regarding the covariates have changed had one used a Cox model or its alternative. The only differences we saw were in terms of the baseline hazards. If interest in this function is low, then there are not many compelling reasons why a Cox model should *not* be estimated.

CHAPTER 7

Inclusion of Time-Varying Covariates

One of the strengths of the event history model over the traditional regression model is the ability of the event history model to account for covariates that change values across the span of the observation period. In principle, inclusion of TVCs in the event history model is straightforward. However, the use of TVCs can raise special problems, both substantively and statistically, for event history analysis. And while these problems are not exclusive to duration models, the problems sometimes manifest themselves differently in the context of duration analysis. In this chapter, we consider some of these problems and note that the "solutions" to these problems are in large part theoretical, and not statistical. Additionally, we illustrate how TVCs can be readily included in each of the models discussed to this point.

Incorporating Exogenous TVCs into the Duration Model

Several researchers have variously categorized the different kinds of TVCs used in event history analysis. Kalbfleisch and Prentice (1980) provide the most thorough and widely used categorization scheme. They distinguish TVCs as either being *external* or *internal*. Further, they subcategorize external covariates as being "fixed," "defined," or "ancillary" (Kalbfleisch and Prentice 1980, 123). A fixed external covariate is equivalent to a time-independent covariate; i.e., one having values that are known in advance and do not change over the course of the study. Defined covariates have values that can change over time, but the time path is known in advance. An example of such a covariate is an individual's age or treatments to be given at different points in an experiment. Defined covariates, in this sense, are non-stochastic: their values can be determined in advance. Ancillary covariates are stochastic, but the process affecting change in the covariate values is not influenced by the event history process under study.

A second distinction is whether the TVCs are exogenous or endogenous (Lancaster 1990). Generally, an exogenous covariate is any covariate having a value that is determined outside the system under study. Exogeneity implies that the values of the covariates may influence, but are not themselves influenced by, the process under study. Most statistical models assume that the covariates on the right-hand side of the model are exogenous, hence the oft-used phrase, "independent" variables. The suitability of exogeneity assumptions has been a widely researched topic, and the same issues that emerge regarding exogeneity assumptions and endogeneity problems for traditional linear models affect the event history model.

If a covariate is truly exogenously determined, then inclusion of TVCs into a likelihood function (partial or maximum) and estimation of covariate parameters raises no special problems (Petersen 1995). Estimation of these parameters is less trivial than in the case of time independent covariates (or no covariates), and data management with exogenous TVCs puts a greater burden on the analyst, but in principle, such TVCs can be readily handled within the duration modeling framework. However, before directly addressing this issue, a more basic question must be answered: How does one know if a TVC is truly exogenous? This question is obviously relevant to any statistical modeling endeavor, and the answer centers on determining if the covariate not only influences the dependent variable, but is itself influenced by the dependent variable.

Lancaster (1990), in the context of the duration model framework, provides a formal definition of exogeneity (1990, 28). He argues that a covariate is exogenous if and only if the values it can take are independent of the duration that an observation survives. Formally, Lancaster (1990) states this as

$$\Pr(X(t, t + \Delta t) \mid T \geq t + \Delta t, X(t)) = \Pr(X(t, t + \Delta t) \mid X(t)), \quad (7.1)$$

which illustrates that the additional survival time shown in the left-hand term does not affect the probability that a covariate will assume some particular value. Yet despite the apparent clarity of (7.1), the determinance of exogeneity is less clear-cut. Despite the clarity of the Lancaster definition of exogeneity, the determination of this condition is largely a theoretical issue. Absolutely determining the veracity of the exogeneity assumption is, to say the least, difficult; we stress that this determination, given the nonexperimental nature of most data social scientists work with, must be done with a thorough understanding of the underlying social process; this determination is generally *not* a statistical issue.[1] Nevertheless, the Lancaster definition provides some analytical leverage in thinking about exogeneity.

If we can assume that the covariates are exogenous in the sense of (7.1), then the derivation of the survival function is reasonably straightforward. If we recognize that the covariates can only change values at discrete times, then we can assume that the interval between these measurement times results in

---

[1] Sobel 1995 provides a lucid overview of the problems and pitfalls of causal inference, which of course is directly relevant to the issue of exogeneity (see also Sobel 1996).

a constant value for the covariate. Petersen (1995) refers to this condition as a "jump process": a TVC remains constant from t_j until t_{j+1}, at which time its value can change, or "jump" to another value. The logic of constructing the survivor function in the face of TVCs is to evaluate the function in the duration intervals in which the TVCs remain constant. In this sense, we divide the observed duration time into successive intervals, with each interval corresponding to different values of the exogenous TVCs.

The survivor function for this kind of process has the form

$$S(t_k) = \prod_{j=1}^{k} \Pr(T > t_j \mid T \geq t_{j-1}), \tag{7.2}$$

where each of the terms on the right-hand side of (7.2) is equal to

$$\Pr(T > t_j \mid T \geq t_{j-1}) = \exp\left(-\int_{t_{j-1}}^{t_j} h(u \mid \mathbf{x}_j) du \right) \tag{7.3}$$

and where $h(u \mid \mathbf{x}_j)$ is the hazard rate conditional on the covariate having the value $\mathbf{x}_j$, which is constant in the interval t_{j-1} to t_j.[2] It is also useful to point out that the integral in (7.3) is equivalent to

$$\int_{t_{j-1}}^{t_j} h(u \mid \mathbf{x}_j) du = H(t_k),$$

which is the integrated or cumulative hazard rate in the integrable interval, t_{j-1} to t_j. From equations (7.2) and (7.3), it is easy see that when the survival times are treated as a function of exogenous TVCs, the survivor function is expressed as the product of the successive survivor functions defined for each interval in which the TVCs remain constant. Given the functional relationship between the survivor function, hazard rate, and density function, once we have defined the survivor function (as we have in (7.2)), the other two functions are determined. Thus, the mathematical relationships between the survivor function, hazard rate, and the probability density function shown in Chapter 2 require only the modification that the duration time is evaluated in terms of the k successive intervals corresponding to the path the TVC takes.

The data requirements necessary to account for TVCs are more demanding than the simpler case of time-independent covariates. Since we assume the TVC changes values as a step-function of time (or as a jump process), then each time a TVC changes value, another record of data is required for the interval in which the TVC remains constant. In the next section, we consider what duration data "look like" with TVCs by introducing the counting process

---

[2]Notationally, we could have expressed this conditionality in terms of $\mathbf{x}_{j-1}$ because it is assumed that the covariate is constant within the integrable interval. Thus, the covariate at either end of the interval would have the same value.

concept. As we note in Chapter 10, compiling data in the form of a "counting process" will be essential toward estimating more complicated event history models (Fleming and Harrington 1991). Because of the relevance of counting processes in the use of TVCs, and because the counting process approach will become useful to us later, we discuss this kind of process in more detail in the next section.

Counting Processes and Duration Data with TVCs

A key extension of the Cox model and of the parametric models has been the introduction and use of the counting process formulation of Andersen and Gill (1982) (see also Fleming and Harrington 1991). Indeed, the introduction of the counting process formulation has been regarded as "one of the most significant advances in failure time data analysis" (Lin, Wei, and Ying 1998, 605) and has led to theoretical and computational breakthroughs with the use of martingale theory. To understand the intuition, think of an observation as the realization of a *very slow* Poisson process (Therneau 1997a, 52). Censored data are then part of a Poisson process where the event has not yet occurred, or as Therneau and Grambsch (2000) put it, "the geiger counter just has not clicked yet" (p. 68).

For example, suppose we were studying the duration that a political party held control of a state legislature. In this example, the event is defined as a switch in party control. If there were two events observed for Ohio in the time frame of the data set, then in the counting process framework, there will be three observations for Ohio. The first observation starts at the same time as the study and ends at the time of the first event. The second observation starts at the end of the first event and ends at the time of the second event. The third observation starts at the end of the second event and ends at the completion of the study, at which point it is censored. Because of the data setup, counting process formulations are also referred to as "start stop data."

The start-stop nature of duration data is easy to see. The individual enters the risk period (or "starts" the process) at time t_0 and is observed to time t at which point the individual is observed as either failing or surviving (or being right-censored). Letting δ denote whether or not the observation has failed or is right-censored, then, as Gutierrez (2001) notes, the observed survival time is fully described by the triple (t_0, t, δ). Hence, the individual is observed from $(t_0, t]$ and either fails ($\delta = 1$) or survives ($\delta = 0$).

Incorporating TVCs into the counting process framework is straightforward and involves three pieces of information, each readily available to the researcher. First, the analyst must know when the observation entered the risk period (i.e. t_0); second, the analyst must know at what time the TVC changes values; and third, the analyst must know when (or if) the observation failed (i.e. δ). With TVCs, the process starts at t_0 at which time the TVC assumes some value. This value remains constant in the interval $(t_0, t]$ where at t, the TVC changes value. In the subsequent interval, $(t, t_k]$, the TVC again remains constant. Within each interval, the individual is observed as either failing or surviving. Described in this way, it is clear that TVCs produce a step function.

To illustrate the counting process setup we consider two examples. First, we consider the well known data of Oneal and Russett (1997) in counting process form and second, we consider Box-Steffensmeier's (1996) data on campaign warchests. A portion of the Oneal and Russett data is reproduced in Table 7.1. Due to the yearly economic growth data, this is an example of yearly counting process notation because there is a new interval at every measurement period. The full data set consists of 20,990 observations on 827 "politically relevant" dyads between 1950 and 1985. Because economic growth is a TVC that changes yearly, there is an observation for each year. In contrast, contiguity is not a TVC and so its value does not change. Note that the "start stop" interval only starts over when there is a new dyad being studied. The censoring indicator tells whether or not a dispute occurred; it is equal to one when a dispute occurred and zero when an observation is censored. In the TVC counting process setup, an observation is censored in each line unless an event occurs. So for example, the last observation for dyad 2020 (U.S. and Canada) is for 1985 (when the data set ends) and is censored, since we do not know if the spell ended in 1986, 1987, or is still ongoing. The first observation for dyad 2041 (U.S. and Haiti) does not begin until 1961 and starts with the interval (0, 1].

Discontinuous intervals of risk can be easily incorporated into the counting process formulation. Discontinuous intervals of risk can occur if an observation is not at risk for an event during a particular time frame. For example, if one were studying the duration of domestic peace across a number of countries, there could be discontinuous intervals of risk due to internal conflict. That is, during an internal conflict that lasts for three years, the country is not considered at risk for further internal conflict and so the start-stop data skip from (2, 3] to (5, 6]. Another example arises due to institutional constraints. When studying the duration of executive branch confirmations by the U.S. Senate, there are discontinuous risk intervals when the Senate is in recess. Table 7.2 shows the data setup with discontinuous intervals of risk for a conflict that began in 1953 and was over in 1956; i.e., years 1954 and 1955 are not in the table. The censoring variable is equal to one, indicating an event began in 1953. Similarly, if one looks closely at Table 7.1 one will see that 1975 is missing for observation 2020 and the interval skips from (23, 24] to (25, 26]. This is another example of a discontinuous risk interval that is due to an on-going dispute that began in 1974; a dyad is not at risk for a dispute to begin if they are already in a dispute! The counting process notation is required for most of the applications presented in this chapter as well as for the models laid out in Chapter 10.

TABLE 7.1: Example of Counting Process Data with a Yearly TVC

Year	Dyad Id.	Interval (Start, Stop]	Censoring Indicator	Economic Growth	Contiguity Status
1951	2020	(0, 1]	0	0.01	1
1952	2020	(1, 2]	0	0.03	1
1953	2020	(2, 3]	0	0.02	1
1954	2020	(3, 4]	0	0.01	1
1955	2020	(4, 5]	0	0.01	1
1956	2020	(5, 6]	0	0.01	1
1957	2020	(6, 7]	0	0.02	1
1958	2020	(7, 8]	0	−0.01	1
1959	2020	(8, 9]	0	0.00	1
1960	2020	(9, 10]	0	0.00	1
1961	2020	(10, 11]	0	0.00	1
1962	2020	(11, 12]	0	0.01	1
1963	2020	(12, 13]	0	0.02	1
1964	2020	(13, 14]	0	0.04	1
1965	2020	(14, 15]	0	0.04	1
1966	2020	(15, 16]	0	0.04	1
1967	2020	(16, 17]	0	0.04	1
1968	2020	(17, 18]	0	0.03	1
1969	2020	(18, 19]	0	0.02	1
1970	2020	(19, 20]	0	0.01	1
1971	2020	(20, 21]	0	0.01	1
1972	2020	(21, 22]	0	0.01	1
1973	2020	(22, 23]	0	0.03	1
1974	2020	(23, 24]	1	0.01	1
1976	2020	(25, 26]	0	0.00	1
1977	2020	(26, 27]	0	0.02	1
1978	2020	(27, 28]	0	0.04	1
1979	2020	(28, 29]	1	0.03	1
1980	2020	(29, 30]	0	0.00	1
1981	2020	(30, 31]	0	0.00	1
1982	2020	(31, 32]	0	−0.01	1
1983	2020	(32, 33]	0	0.00	1
1984	2020	(33, 34]	0	0.02	1
1985	2020	(34, 35]	0	0.04	1
1961	2041	(0, 1]	0	−0.05	0
1962	2041	(1, 2]	0	−0.01	0
1963	2041	(2, 3]	1	−0.01	0
1964	2041	(3, 4]	0	0.00	0

Of course when the TVCs assume unique values at every observation (in the above example, changes are observed each year), it is easy to see how TVCs can be incorporated into the data set: each period has a unique record of data. However, in many instances, analysts will be interested in TVCs that

TABLE 7.2: Example of Counting Process Data with a Yearly TVC and Discontinuous Risk Intervals

Year	Country	Interval: (Start, Stop]	Censoring Indicator	Per Capita Income	Contiguity Status
1951	1	(0, 1]	0	$3,051	1
1952	1	(1, 2]	0	$3,067	1
1953	1	(2, 3]	1	$3,165	1
1956	1	(5, 6]	0	$3,240	1
1957	1	(6, 7]	0	$3,300	1
1958	1	(7, 8]	0	$3,345	1

change intermittently across time. To illustrate what event history data look like with this kind of TVC, we reproduce in Table 7.3 a portion of the Box-Steffensmeier (1996) data set on challenger deterrence and "war chests" in the 1990 U.S. House elections. This data set records the duration (in weeks) that passes from the start of a campaign cycle until the emergence of a high quality challenger against the incumbent. If no high quality challenger emerges by the primary date, the campaign is treated as right-censored. In the first column of the reproduced data, we have included an identification variable for each campaign; in the second column, we record the weeks until the event occurs (or is right-censored); in the third column, we record whether or not the congressional district is in the South (1 if in the South, 0 if not); in the fourth column we record the party affiliation of the incumbent such that 1 denotes a Democrat and 0 denotes a Republican; in the fifth column, we record the incumbent's vote share in the 1988 election; in the sixth column, we record the amount of money raised in the campaign (the "war chest"); and in the seventh column, we record whether the race is right-censored (0) or not (1).

The time-dependent war chest variable is critical for the argument that war chests deter challengers. That is, we need to incorporate the campaign finance dynamics over the course of the election cycle, not just at the beginning of the two-year election cycle. Federal Election Commission (FEC) regulations require candidates to periodically file campaign finance reports. At each reporting period, the amount of money in the war chest may change value, producing a TVC. Note that the value of the TVC in this example does not change with each "click of the clock," as in the case of the economic growth measure considered above. The other variables in the table are time-independent—their values do not change within the observation plan. Because of the presence of the war chest covariate, we have multiple records of data for each congressional race. Consider the first case, which has the identification number of 100. Case 100 contributes two records to this data set because the value of the war chest covariate changes values once prior to a high quality challenger entering. For case 100, the campaign goes from week 0 to week 26 with the war

TABLE 7.3: Example of Event History Data Set with TVCs

Case I.D.	Weeks to Event	Southern District	Incumbent's Party	1988 Vote	"War Chest" (in Millions)	Censoring Indicator
100	26	0	0	.62	.003442	0
100	50	0	0	.62	.010986	1
201	26	1	0	.59	.142588	0
201	53	1	0	.59	.158570	0
201	65	1	0	.59	.202871	0
201	75	1	0	.59	.217207	0
516	26	0	1	.79	.167969	0
516	53	0	1	.79	.147037	0
516	65	0	1	.79	.164970	0
516	72	0	1	.79	.198608	1
706	26	0	0	.66	.139028	0
706	53	0	0	.66	.225633	0
706	65	0	0	.66	.225817	0
706	78	0	0	.66	.342801	0
706	83	0	0	.66	.262563	1
905	26	1	0	1.00	.211122	0
905	53	1	0	1.00	.270816	0
905	65	1	0	1.00	.262153	0

Data are from Box-Steffensmeier (1996).

chest variable having the value of .003442. After week 26, the value of this covariate changes to .010986, and remains at this value until week 50, when a high-quality challenger emerges. We can illustrate this more compactly in the following way using the counting process notation:

Interval	South	Party	Vote	War Chest	Censoring
(0, 26]	0	0	.62	.003442	0
(26, 50]	0	0	.62	.010986	1

The full duration time, which is 50 weeks, is split into multiple time periods, or episodes, that correspond to the values the TVC takes within the reporting interval. The censoring indicator also reveals some additional insight into event history processes. Note that with TVCs, the data are constructed such that they have the form of a series of discrete intervals. Within each interval for which we have measures of the covariates, we can observe, or "count" the number of events that occur within the interval. As the event of interest in these data is the emergence of a quality challenger, and since this event can occur (in practice) but once, we either observe the event in the interval, or we do not observe the event. In this sense, the event history can be equivalently thought of as a series of zeroes and ones, where a one denotes the occurrence of an event, and a zero denotes the nonoccurrence of the event (i.e. it is censored). This is the information conveyed by the "censoring" variable. Indeed, as we saw in Chapter 5, this indicator constitutes the dependent variable for discrete-time approaches.

The importance of counting process theory cannot be overstated. Indeed, the extension of the Cox model to the counting process formulation is credited with allowing time varying covariates, time dependent strata, discontinuous risk intervals, left truncation, alternate time scales, extensive use of residuals, multiple events per subject, repeated events models for correlated data, and various forms of case-cohort and matched case-control models (Aalen 1978; Andersen and Gill 1982; Fleming and Harrington 1991; Andersen, Borgan, Gill, and Keiding 1992; Therneau 1997a; Therneau and Hamilton 1997; Fahrmeir and Klinger 1998; Therneau 1999; Therneau and Grambsch 2000).

Having now introduced the counting process framework, we consider the implementation of TVCs into several different kinds of duration models. In later chapters, we will make use of the counting process framework to consider model diagnostics and models for complicated event structures. We begin with the Cox model.

TVCs and the Cox Model

Inclusion of TVCs into the Cox model entails a fairly straightforward extension of the partial likelihood function shown in equation (4.6). Let $\mathbf{x}$ denote the covariates (as before), some of which may be time-varying, which are indexed by (t). The likelihood function for the Cox model with TVCs is given by

$$\mathcal{L}_p = \prod_{i=1}^{K} \left[\frac{e^{\beta' \mathbf{x_i}(t_i)}}{\sum_{j \in R(t_i)} e^{\beta' \mathbf{x_j}(t_i)}} \right]^{\delta_i}, \tag{7.4}$$

and the corresponding log-likelihood function is given by

$$\log L_p = \sum_{i=1}^{K} \delta_i \left[\beta' \mathbf{x_i}(t_i) - \log \sum_{j \in R(t_i)} e^{\beta' \mathbf{x_j}(t_i)} \right]. \tag{7.5}$$

Maximizing the log-likelihood function gives estimates of the β parameters that are, under regularity conditions, asymptotically normal. This presentation again presumes there are no tied cases. This condition is likely not to hold and so the methods for tied data discussed earlier, must be used to approximate the partial likelihood function with TVCs. We do not present the likelihood functions for these methods, but note that the extension to the case of TVCs is relatively straightforward.

The Cox model is particularly well suited to include TVCs because the partial likelihood function is determined by the ordered failure times, but not by the actual duration times. Because of this, calculations of the hazard ratio are only made at failure times. Hence, the Cox regression coefficients for the

TABLE 7.4: Cox Model of Challenger Deterrence

Variable	Estimate (s.e.)	Percent Change in Hazard Rate
South	−.44 (.42)	−35.5
Party	.23 (.32)	26.4
Prior Vote	−6.97 (1.66)	−6.7
War Chest	−3.01 (1.39)	−26.0
N	1376	
Log-Likelihood	−197.39	

TVCs can be interpreted as the change in the log-hazard ratio for observations having a unit change in the value of the covariate at time t compared to the value of the covariate for the remaining observations in the risk set at time t. In this sense, the estimated covariate tells us by how much the risk of an event "jumps" due to a change in the value of the TVC. We now turn to an illustration.

Example 7.1: Challenger Deterrence in U.S. House Elections

The Cox model with time varying covariates is applied to the problem of challenger entry. The issue is whether war chests (campaign finance reserves) deter challenger entry in U.S. House elections.[3] The data used in the application are the same data discussed above in the context of Table 7.3. There are 1,376 records in the data set. Time varying covariates are critical because they allow the temporal dynamics of war chests to be incorporated into the model.

Table 7.4 shows the estimation results of a Cox regression model. The event is defined as the entry of a high quality challenger. The definition of "high quality" is whether or not the challenger had held prior elective office (Jacobson 1997). The signs of the coefficients tell us that incumbents from the South are more likely to enjoy a race without a high quality challenger for a longer time period. Republican incumbents are also more likely to not face a high quality challenger early on; however, note that standard errors for these estimates are very large indicating that the relationship between these covariates and the risk of challenger emergence is no different from 0. Of most interest in the application, we find that having a large war chest and doing well in the previous election helps deter high quality challengers. Indeed, only the war chest and prior vote covariates are statistically significant. The subsequent discussion focuses on the interpretation of these two covariates.

In the third column of Table 7.4 we have computed the percentage change in the hazard rate attributable to a change in the value of the covariates. This was done using the procedure shown in (4.11). The results suggest that for a

---

[3]This application is taken directly from Box-Steffensmeier (1996).

1 percent increase in the value of the prior vote covariate, the hazard rate decreases by almost 7 percent. That is, the percentage change in the hazard of challenger entry at any time t for two incumbents who differ by 1 percent in prior vote and who have the same values for the other covariates is approximately 7 percent. A one standard deviation increase in the prior vote, which is 14.2 percent, decreases the hazard rate by 62.9 percent. A 5 and 10 percent increase results in a 29.4 and 50.2 percent decrease, respectively.

With regard to the incumbent's war chest, each $100,000 increase in an incumbent's war chest decreases the hazard of a high quality challenger entering by 26 percent. That is, the percentage change in the hazard of challenger entry at any time t for two incumbents whose war chests differ by $100,000 and who have the same values for the other independent variables is 26 percent. A one standard deviation increase in an incumbent's war chest, which is $239,000, results in a 51.3 percent decrease in the hazard rate. The effect of the increase in the war chest is nonlinear. For example, if the increase is $100,000, the hazard rate decreases 26 percent; if the increase is $200,000, the hazard rate decreases by 45 percent. So this $100,000 differential increase ($200,000−$100,000) results in a decrease of 19 percent ($-45.0\% - (-26.0\%)$). In contrast, a $100,000 differential increase between $900,000 and $1,000,000 results in a decrease of only 1.8 percent ($-95.1\% - (-93.3\%)$). Thus, there are diminishing returns.

To conclude this application, incorporating the dynamics of war chests through the use of the Cox model with TVCs allows us to answer an important question in the field of legislative electoral research. The exercise also helps illustrate how continuous TVCs can be readily incorporated and interpreted in a Cox model. We next turn attention to inclusion of TVCs in parametric models.

TVCs and Parametric Models

Inclusion of TVCs into parametric models presents no special problems. The principal issue analysts typically face is compiling their data in a way that allows episodes to be split into successive intervals that correspond to changes in the value of the TVC (recall Table 7.3). Additionally, computation of the likelihood function will be more complicated as the likelihood function, with TVCs, is evaluated in terms of k successive intervals, where the intervals correspond to the distinct episodes.

To illustrate what a likelihood function would look like for a parametric duration model with exogenous TVCs, consider the simplest case of the exponential model. The hazard rate for the Weibull with exogenous TVCs is given by

$$h[t \mid \mathbf{x}(t^-)] = \exp^{-\beta' \mathbf{x}(t^-)} p \ [\exp^{-\beta' \mathbf{x}(t^-)} t]^{p-1},$$

where the notation t^- denotes that the change in the covariate is observed prior to t (Petersen 1995). If $\lambda = \exp^{-\beta' \mathbf{x}(t^-)}$, the survivor function for the Weibull

TABLE 7.5: Weibull Model of Challenger Deterrence

Variable	Estimate (s.e.)
South	−.53 (.42)
Party	.23 (.32)
Prior Vote	−6.44 (1.66)
War Chest	−2.58 (1.38)
Shape Parameter	2.43 (.35)
N	1376
Log-Likelihood	−118.84

model with exogenous TVCs is

$$S[t \mid \mathbf{x}(\mathbf{t}^-)] = \exp^{-(\lambda t)^p},$$

and the density function for the Weibull is therefore

$$f[t \mid \mathbf{x}(\mathbf{t}^-)] = \lambda p (\lambda t)^{p-1} \exp^{-(\lambda t)^p}.$$

From $f(t)$ and $S(t)$, we can construct a likelihood function for the t duration times and the TVCs in the manner discussed in Chapter 3; specifically, this likelihood is

$$\mathcal{L} = \prod_{j=}^{k} \left\{ \lambda p (\lambda t)^{p-1} \exp^{-(\lambda t)^p} \right\}^{\delta_i} \left\{ \exp^{-(\lambda t)^p} \right\}^{1-\delta_i}, \qquad (7.6)$$

which aside from the modification that the likelihood is defined for the k intervals on which the covariates are measured, equation (7.6) is equivalent to equation (3.36), which was presented in terms of time independent covariates. For TVCs, the coefficients provide information on how the hazard rate changes for a unit change in the TVC. As with the Cox model, this incremental change results in a jump process. Below, we present an illustration using the campaign war chest data.

Example 7.2: Use of TVCs in a Weibull Model

In this application, we reestimated the model in Example 7.1 using a Weibull model. Of interest in this application is illustrating the interpretation of a TVC in the context of a parametric model. The Weibull estimates (parameterized as log-relative hazards) are presented in Table 7.5. The war chest covariate has an estimated coefficient of −2.58, implying that the risk of a quality challenger entering a race is decreasing as the amount of money in an incumbent's war chest increases.

The interpretation of the TVC in terms of hazard ratios suggests that for a $100,000 increase in the incumbent's war chest, the risk of the event occurring decreases by about 23 percent. This can be seen by exponentiating the

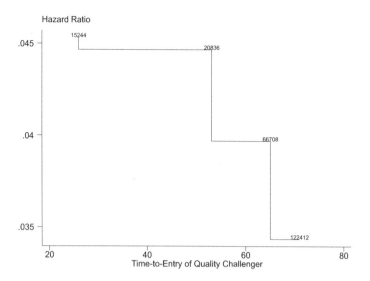

FIGURE 7.1: *This figure plots the estimated hazard ratios of quality challenger entry for a selected incumbent. The change in the hazard ratios are a function of changes in the value of the TVC.*

coefficient estimate. So for two incumbents, one having \$200,000 on hand and another having \$100,000 on hand, the risk of facing a quality challenger is about 23 percent lower for the first incumbent; that is, $\exp[(\hat{\beta}_{WC} * .2) - \exp(\hat{\beta}_{WC} * .1)]/\exp(\hat{\beta}_{WC} * .1)$. Since an incumbent's war chest changes value over the course an election, the covariate can be analogously interpreted as representing the change in the risk the incumbent incurs as the war chest changes in value. To illustrate this pedagogically, we computed the hazard ratio for a specific incumbent in the data set and graph this incumbent's risk profile in Figure 7.1. For this incumbent, the covariate profile is a non-southern Democrat who received 51 percent of the vote in the previous election. The only covariate that changes is the war chest covariate.

We see that the incumbent enters the process with an estimated war chest of about \$15,244. The estimated hazard ratio for this incumbent is about .045. This ratio, as a function of this covariate profile, is assumed to remain constant within the interval over which the TVC is unchanged, that is, $(0, 26]$. However, in the interval $(26, 53]$, the war chest is recorded as increasing to \$20,836. The estimated hazard ratio decreases ever slightly to about .044. Again, this risk level is assumed unchanged over the interval. In the interval $(53, 65]$, the war chest increases to \$66,708, resulting in a predicted hazard ratio of about .039. Finally, in the interval $(65, 71]$, the war chest increases to \$122,412 resulting in an estimated hazard ratio of .034.

The jump process concept is easy to visualize with this case: rates are constant within the interval with which the TVC remains constant. When the TVC changes, the estimated hazard "jumps" to a new level. We present Figure 7.1 principally for illustrative purposes. It is usually *not* wise to interpret but a single observation from a data set! In order to facilitate interpretation of the TVC, we recommend computing predicted hazard for various covariate profiles, or conversely, estimating predicted survival times for various covariate profiles. To isolate the effect of the TVC, it is usually helpful to hold other covariates at some natural level (like the mean, median, or 1 or 0 point for binary variables) then estimate the change in the hazard (or survivor time) for changes in the TVC. For parametric models, it is important to account for the duration dependency parameter in calculations of the hazard rate or survivor function. The baseline functions will take a particular shape depending on the estimated value of any ancillary parameters and so in making comparative evaluations across covariate profiles, estimates of the hazard will be highly sensitive to "where in time" a particular covariate profile is observed.

TVCs and Discrete-Time Models

We have considered the use and interpretation of TVCs in the context of the Cox and parametric models. Inclusion of TVCs in discrete-time models like those discussed in Chapter 5 present no special problems. Indeed, the ease with which, say, the logit model can accommodate TVCs has sometimes been touted as an advantage of the discrete-time approach. It is easy to see why discrete-time models are so readily adapted to TVCs. In such models, the outcome variable is equivalent to the binary censoring variable that we have discussed in various places. When the indicator is a 0, the observation is assumed to be at-risk; when the indicator is 1, the observation is assumed to have failed. Because in an event history data set, there will be as many 0s and 1s as there are periods of survival, each observation contributes multiple records. For each observation, then, the value of the TVC can be recorded. For the logit model, the estimated coefficient for a TVC reveals information in how the log-odds of an event occurring increases or decreases for a unit change in the TVC. In terms of the hazard probability, a coefficient for a TVC provides information on how the probability or risk of an event occurrence changes for a unit change in a covariate. To illustrate, we provide a brief application.

Example 7.3: House Careers and TVCs

In this illustration, we use the data on congressional career paths discussed first in Chapter 5. Of interest in this application is modeling the length of time (where t denotes the number of terms served) a member of the House of Representatives "survives" until he or she loses office. In the model, there

TABLE 7.6: Logit Model of House Careers

Variable	Estimate (s.e.)
Party Identification	−.15 (.11)
Redistricting	1.15 (.30)
Leadership	−.91 (.49)
Scandal	2.65 (.31)
Prior Margin	−.04 (.005)
Duration Dependency	5.61 (2.92)
N	5399
Log-Likelihood	−1169.09

are five covariates, three of which are binary TVCs. The first TVC indicates whether or not the incumbent's district was substantially redistricted; the second TVC indicates whether or not the incumbent had a leadership position in the House; the third TVC indicates whether or not the incumbent was involved in a scandal (see Jones 1994 for more details). The fourth TVC measures the percentage of votes the incumbent (or his or her party) received in his or her previous election. The fifth covariate is time-independent and denotes party identification (0 denotes Democrats, 1 denotes Republicans). The event of interest is electoral defeat. A logit model was applied to these data and duration dependency was accounted for using a lowess function of time (see Chapter 5 for more details; see also Beck and Jackman 1998). The results from the logit model are presented in Table 7.6.

The interpretation of a covariate in this model is that it gives the change in the log-odds of an event for a unit change in the covariate. It is useful to convert the logit estimates to odds ratios by exponentiating them. In so doing, we see that the odds of defeat for incumbents who are redistricted are about 3 times higher than for non-redistricted incumbents. For incumbents beleaguered by scandal, the odds of defeat are about 13 times greater than for non-scandal plagued incumbents. For incumbents entering the leadership, the associated risk of electoral defeat is about .40 that of incumbents not in the leadership (that is, about 60 percent lower). Finally, for the prior margin covariate, we see that the for every 1 percent increase in the incumbent's prior margin of victory, the odds of defeat decrease by about 3.7 percent.

More generally, it is important to note that when some TVCs change continuously in time, then the hazard probability will always change from period-to-period. Consequently, it is usually helpful to compute odds ratios (or first differences in these ratios) for each of the covariates to help get a sense of how the risk changes as a function of changes in the TVC. Moreover, computing probability estimates based on interesting covariate profiles may be helpful in illustrating the relationship between a TVC and the hazard rate.

As we have demonstrated, inclusion and interpretation of TVCs in the duration modeling framework is relatively straightforward for all of the models considered to this point. Yet despite the relative ease with which the event history model can accommodate TVCs, there are important issues that need to be considered when incorporating TVCs into a model. We consider some of these issues in the rest of this chapter.

Temporal Ordering of TVCs and Events

In this section, we discuss the issue of temporal ordering of TVCs and event occurrences. Earlier, we noted that if one is conditioning the hazard rate or survival function on TVCs (as well as on time), then special care needs to be taken to ensure that changes to the value of the TVCs do not occur coterminously with the occurrence of the event of interest. Even worse, special care needs to be taken to ensure that the change to the value of the TVC does not occur *after* the occurrence of the event. The basis of the first problem stems from the fact that the "cause" and the "effect" change at the same time, thus making it difficult to claim any semblance of "causality" between the covariate and the dependent variable. The basis of the second problem is that the "cause" proceeds the "effect," rendering the usual kinds of causal claims problematic. That we should avoid such problems is obvious, but the problems are not so obviously avoided.

Suppose that we were interested in modeling the duration of time some process lasted until it terminated with an event occurrence. Furthermore, suppose that we believed some exogenous covariate Z was related to the event occurrence and that the precise timing of the event was impossible to determine so we approximated the timing of the event using a relatively crude measure of time. The potential for measurement error in assessing when events occur, coupled with the use of TVCs, even exogenous TVCs, can present problems. These are illustrated in Figure 7.2, where we depict three scenarios.

The x-axis in the figure corresponds to time (measured in discrete units, $t = 1, 2, 3, 4$), and the end points to each of the lines correspond to the measured duration time until the event occurs. Case 1 illustrates the problem that although there is no measurement error in recording the event time, the event occurs simultaneously with the change in the TVC. Since we hypothesize that changes to the TVC are associated with changes in the risk of an event occurrence, this simultaneity makes it difficult to sustain the causal inference. Case 2 illustrates an instance where, despite the measurement error in recording event times, the actual event occurrence temporally follows the TVC change. In this case, we "get lucky" because the true event occurrence is proximal to our measured event time: the cause precedes the effect. In Case 3, owing to the crudeness in our time measure, we record the event as occurring at Time 4, when in "reality," the event occurred sometime just prior to Time 1. With regard to our

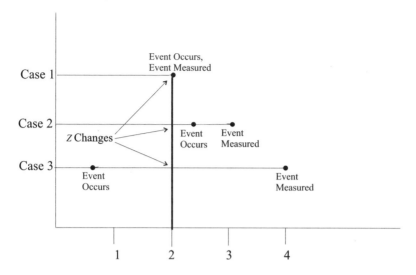

FIGURE 7.2: *This figure represents some problems that can occur when event times are imprecisely measured and TVCs are included in the analysis. In Case 1, the event occurs and the TVC changes at the same point; in Case 2, the event, although imprecisely measured, occurs after the change to the TVC; in Case 3, the event actually occurs before the TVC changes value.*

time-varying covariate, Z, we see that it is measured as changing values, or jumping to a different value, at Time 2. Assuming that our TVC is measured with some degree of accuracy, Case 3 poses a real dilemma for making unambiguous causal claims: the cause proceeds the effect. Unfortunately, given the measurement error in recording event occurrences, this problem would not be noticeable to the analyst, despite the fact that conclusions about the relationship between Z and the failure time may be highly questionable.

Regarding the problem of Case 1, Petersen (1995) demonstrates that if one conditions on a TVC at t instead of conditioning at t^-, then the resulting survivor (and by extension hazard) function is fundamentally different for these two cases (1995, 471-72). It is for this reason that when one incorporates exogenous TVCs into a duration model, it is generally recommended that one record a *lagged* value of the TVC into the data set to ensure that simultaneity between the event occurrence and the TVC change does not exist. In addition to avoiding simultaneity problems, incorporating lagged values of the TVC may also help to avoid the type of problem found in Case 3 in Figure 7.2. The issues associated with temporal ordering are relevant to any statistical design, especially time-serial or longitudinal designs. However these problems, which seem easily avoided in principle, are more likely to arise in duration data, where one is measuring potentially many observations longitudinally. These problems should be most apparent when event occurrences are not precisely measurable.

Unfortunately, temporal ordering is not the only problem that emerges with TVCs. In the next section, we consider the problem of endogeneity and event history analysis.

Endogeneity of TVCs

We referred to the idea of simultaneity as denoting the situation where the value of TVC changes at the moment an event is observed. Under this condition, the usual interpretations afforded covariates in the event history model do not hold. Another kind of simultaneity occurs when a TVC and the duration time exhibit a "simultaneous" relationship. That is, not only does information regarding the TVC help to predict duration times, but information on the duration time can help predict the path that the TVC will take. Under this condition, the Lancaster definition of exogeneity given in (7.1) will not hold because the probability that a TVC will take some value is, in the absence of exogeneity, conditional on the duration time. When the TVC influences the dependent variable and is itself influenced by the TVC, we can think of the TVC as being endogenous: its path is partially determined within the system under study.

As discussed earlier, social scientists have a long tradition of exploring the substantive implications of endogeneity in both methodological work and in applied work. Endogeneity is troublesome because it precludes the usual kinds of causal statements social scientists like to make. In the context of event history analysis, a simple example of endogeneity might be the relationship between the duration of a war and the number of casualties amassing during the war. As the number of casualties increase, this may have some relationship to the subsequent duration of the war; conversely, as a war increases in duration, the number of casualties will increase. In this sense, the duration, which is meant to only be influenced by the TVC, would do a reasonably good job of predicting the path of the TVC. Endogeneity in this example is obvious.

As another example, suppose we were modeling the duration of time a national political leader survives and thought that the national economy had some bearing on the hazard rate of the leader losing his or her seat. If we believed the macroeconomy was exogenous, i.e., akin to Kalbfleisch and Prentice's (1980) idea of an ancillary TVC, to political survival, we could proceed in ways discussed in this chapter. However, suppose that national leaders could influence the economy in some way, perhaps by influencing national bankers or the legislature into taking action that would affect the economy. Would covariates measuring the state of the macroeconomy, under this condition, be endogenous? Endogeneity in this example is not obvious.

Determination of endogeneity, or conversely, exogeneity, is a theoretical issue and one that cannot be satisfactorily resolved with statistical methods. Unfortunately, if one constructs a likelihood function for the duration data using an endogenous TVC, then the natural interpretations afforded the survival function, which is a part of the likelihood function, cannot hold (Lancaster 1990, Petersen 1995). To illustrate the problem, we can define endogeneity, at least conceptually, by reexpressing the Lancaster definition of exogeneity as

$$\Pr(X(t, t + \Delta t) \mid T \geq t + \Delta t, X(t)) \neq \Pr(X(t, t + \Delta t) \mid X(t)), \quad (7.7)$$

which denotes that the probability of a TVC taking on some value is dependent upon the survival time of the observation. The problems with endogenous TVCs emerge because the survivor function, which can be written as (adapting the notation from Petersen 1995, equation 9.46)

$$\Pr[T \geq t_k \mid \mathbf{X}(t_k)] = \exp\left\{ -\sum_{j=1}^{k} \int_{t_{j-1}}^{t_j} h(u \mid \mathbf{x}_j) du \right\}, \quad (7.8)$$

no longer can be interpreted as a true survival function. The expression in (7.8), although written in slightly different form, is equivalent to the survivor function presented in (7.2). With an endogenous TVC, the probability of survival is conditional on a covariate that is itself, assuming values that are conditional on the survival time. Thus, the right-hand side of (7.8) does not give rise to the standard interpretation for a survival function. By extension, incorporation of (7.8) into a likelihood function renders the usual interpretation of the likelihood function problematic. The basic problem is that since the conditioning factor $\mathbf{X}(t_k)$ is *also* a function of t, its value changes when t changes (Lancaster 1990).

The advice here is to be careful in making exogeneity assumptions when they may or may not hold. Methods to explicitly account for endogeneity or selection bias in the context of the duration modeling framework are nascent (although sporadic efforts to address this problem have been published over the years; see Gail 1972; Kalbfleisch and Prentice 1980; Aitken, Laird, and Francis 1983; Lancaster and Chesher 1984; and Firth, Payne, and Payne 1999). The problem of endogeneity for event history models is similar to other statistical models: when endogeneity is present, the standard interpretations given by any statistical model generally do not hold, or must be tempered. And like other areas of statistical modeling, the statistical solutions to the endogeneity problem are not entirely satisfactory.

Clearly, there are important issues analysts need to consider when incorporating TVCs into event history models. Issues pertaining to simultaneity and endogeneity are two of them. But perhaps a more important point needs to be stressed: *not* using TVCs when TVCs are theoretically important induces substantial problems in the event history model. Apart from estimating the wrong theoretical model, event history parameters will be biased due to obvious problems with model misspecification. Put differently, if one estimates a model and treats a TVC *as if* it were time invariant (i.e., the analyst set the TVC to a constant value for the cases in the data), the conclusions one would draw would be far different than from a model where TVCs were included (Golub and Collett 2002). Hence, the problems with including TVCs discussed in this chapter should be weighed against the equally serious problems that ensue by ignoring TVCs when TVCs are theoretically relevant.

Temporal Dependence among Observations

The use of TVCs also introduces another kind of problem. Because TVCs generally require the use of multiple records of data per observation, the assumption that the observations are (conditionally) independent in such a data set may not be sustainable. If not, then it is likely that the observations of a unit will be serially dependent. In our discussion of discrete-time models, we addressed this problem explicitly by making an attempt to account for the grouped nature of the data through the introduction of a time dependency parameter. More generally, it is usually advisable *not* to start with the assumption of temporal independence. If the assumption is wrong, then the estimated standard errors will be incorrect and inferences based on them could be misleading.

There has been considerable work done in the statistics and econometrics literature to address the problem of accounting for temporal dependence among observations, particularly in the context of the linear model (cf. Huber [1967], White [1980, 1982]; see also Beck and Katz [1995] for the case of pooled cross-section data; also, see Zorn [2001]). In the context of the duration model, specifically the Cox model, Lin and Wei's (1989) important work has addressed the problem (among other problems) of serial dependence in failure time data. The methods developed in these and other similar works are sometimes called "robust" estimators because they lead to statistical estimates that are "robust" to violations of the common assumptions that are made.

Specifically, in the case of serially dependent data, robust estimation involves relaxing the assumption that the observations are independent. Practically, robust estimation entails reestimation of the traditional estimator of the variance to account for the grouping or clustering of observations within a data set. The standard (i.e. non-robust) variance estimator is given by

$$I^{-1} = \frac{-\partial^2 \log(L)(\beta)}{\partial \beta \partial \beta'}.$$

However, the assumption of independence among the observations is assumed to hold. Lin and Wei (1989) proposed a modification to the standard variance estimator. When observations are clustered among m groups, then the Lin and

Wei (1989) robust covariance matrix estimator is given by

$$V = I^{-1}G'GI^{-1},$$

where V is the robust covariance matrix and G is an $m \times p$ matrix of the group efficient score residuals (and p is the vector of coefficients; Cleves 1999, 31 [score residuals are defined in the next chapter]). Note that with repeated observations (which occurs when TVCs are utilized), the m groups will be comprised of the repeated observations on each of the i individuals. The resulting standard errors from the robust estimator are "correct" insofar as the assumption of independence among observations need no longer be maintained. Commonly, use of robust estimators typically (though not always) produces estimates of standard errors that are larger than standard errors estimated from models assuming independence. This is the case because positive serial dependency among repeated observations will tend to attenuate, or understate, the standard errors produced from standard estimation methods. That is, in assuming independent observations we assume we have more information than we really do. Finally, it is worth noting that the Lin and Wei (1989) estimator is similar to the "sandwich" estimator developed by Huber (1967). Indeed, robust variance estimation in the case of the parametric models relies on Huber's estimator. To illustrate the implications of ignoring temporal dependence in duration data, we present a brief example using the Cox model.

Example 7.4: Robust Variance Estimation

For this application, we use a data set on regime changes in 19 Latin American countries.[4] Specifically, we are interested in modeling the hazard that a country will make the transition from an authoritarian regime to a less authoritarian (i.e. more democratic) regime. Several covariates are used to model regime transition. They are: real per capita income (in $1000s of dollars); the annual percentage change in the gross domestic product (GDP); and a measure of trade dependence. The trade dependence covariate is measured as "the sum of country's imports and exports divided by its gross domestic product" (Gasiorowski 1995, p. 886). The higher the score on this variable, the more dependent its economy is on trade (Gasiorowski 1995). Gasiorowski hypothesized that per capita income, declines in a country's GDP, and trade dependency were positively related to the likelihood of democratic transitions (see Gasiorowski [1995] for more details). To illustrate the use of a robust variance estimator, we first applied a standard Cox model to these data and then applied a Cox model using the Lin and Wei robust variance estimator. Because the data consist of repeated observations of the same country over time, it is reasonable to expect observations within each country may be temporally dependent. The results from each of these models are shown in Table 7.7. The

---

[4]These data were compiled by Sal Peralta for this application. Part of this data set comes from the data used by Gasiorowski (1995).

TABLE 7.7: Robust Variance Estimation Using Lin-Wei Estimator

Variable	Standard Variance Estimate (s.e.)	Robust Variance Estimate (s.e)
P.C. Income	.627 (.146)	.627 (.148)
ΔGDP	$-.122$ (.056)	$-.122$ (.064)
Trade Dependency	.009 (.011)	.009 (.015)
Log-Likelihood	-37.96	-37.96
N	430	430

first column corresponds to the standard Cox model and the second column corresponds to the robust estimates. Two things are worth noting. First, note that the coefficient estimates themselves are unchanged. Robust variance estimation only affects the standard errors. Second, note that the standard errors from the model using robust estimation are larger than the standard errors from the "non-robust" Cox model. While the differences are small, they could have some bearing on the inferences an analyst might like to draw. For example, the z statistic for the GDP covariate from the standard Cox model is -2.18 ($p = .029$). For the Cox model with robust variance estimation, the z statistic is -1.92 ($p = .055$). This application illustrates the basic problem often caused by temporal dependence: standard errors will usually be smaller when clustering is not accounted for. The recommendation is simple: use robust variance estimation. Most software packages routinely make such estimation a standard option and so implementation of the Lin and Wei or Huber methods is now very easily done. In Chapter 10, we will revisit the issue of temporal dependence.

Conclusion

One of the primary motivations for the use of event history type methods is the ability to readily incorporate information on time-varying covariates. Although use of TVCs is not without problems—many of which we have addressed in this chapter—properly handled, TVCs can reveal information on how the risk of an event occurring is sensitive to changes in the value of important covariates. Moreover, not incorporating TVCs when such covariates are theoretically relevant induces far more serious problems in the form of model misspecification. Any of the models considered in this book can readily incorporate TVCs into the specification. The principal issue the analyst needs to be aware of is understanding how to properly interpret TVCs. The "jump process" idea is useful in this regard. Moreover, use of TVCs also may induce temporal dependence in the data, as spells are "split" to account for changes in the value of a TVC. Hence, the use of TVCs typically requires multiple records of data per observation. Robust variance estimation techniques should be applied in this setting. Ultimately, because most statistical software packages now readily (and easily) permit the use of TVCs in duration models, it is up to the analyst to make sure careful interpretation is made regarding the relationship between TVCs and the hazard rate or survival function.

Now that we have an understanding of how to implement and interpret the event history model, we next turn attention toward evaluating the fit of the model, the functional form of covariates, and testing important assumptions residing in some of the models considered thus far.

CHAPTER 8

Diagnostic Methods for the Event History Model

In this chapter, we consider some important issues regarding model selection, assessment, and diagnostic methods through the use of residuals. The issues discussed in this chapter have a direct analog to methods of model selection and to model diagnostics in the context of the traditional linear model. For example, issues pertaining to functional form, influential observations, and similar other topics are directly relevant to the duration model. Because most of the methods of specification analysis discussed in this chapter make use of residuals, in the next section, we consider the different kinds of residuals that are retrievable from a typical duration model. Following this, we present several illustrations using residual analysis to assess various facets of the duration model. Most of the discussion in this chapter is presented in terms of the Cox model; however, diagnostic methods for parametric models are considered at the end of the chapter.

Residuals in Event History Models

The basic idea of a residual is to compare predicted and observed durations. In OLS regression, residuals are deviations of the observed values of the dependent variable from the values estimated or predicted value under the regression model, that is $y_i - \hat{y}_i$. In event history analysis, defining a residual is more difficult because of censoring and because of issues relevant to estimation methods like maximum likelihood (in the case of parametric models) or maximum partial likelihood (in the case of the Cox model). Moreover, several types of residuals may be defined on an event history model, each suitable for examining different features of a model's fit and specification. In the remainder of this section, we present the basic definition and intuition of the different residuals used to evaluate the adequacy of the chosen model.[1] Following this, we provide several illustrations using residual analysis.

Cox-Snell Residuals

If an analyst is interested in assessing the overall fit of a posited model, the residuals most commonly used for such analysis are the Cox-Snell residuals (Cox and Snell 1968; see also Klein and Moeschberger 1997). If the Cox model, given by

$$h_i(t) = h_0(t)e^{\beta'\mathbf{x}},$$

holds, then estimates of survival times from the posited model, that is $\hat{S}_i(t)$, should be very similar to the true value of $S_i(t)$ (Collett, 1994, p. 151; see also Klein and Moeschberger, 1997, p. 329). To evaluate this, Cox-Snell residuals may be calculated. The Cox-Snell residual is given by

$$r_{CS_i} = \exp(\hat{\beta}'\mathbf{x_i})\hat{H}_o(t_i), \quad\quad\quad (8.1)$$

where $\hat{H}_o(t_i)$ is the estimated integrated baseline hazard (or cumulative hazard), which was given in (4.14). An important result demonstrated by Cox and Snell (1968), Collett (1994) and Klein and Moeschberger (1997) is that if the correct model has been fit to the data, then the r_{CS_i} will have a unit exponential distribution with a hazard ratio of 1. Thus, the Cox-Snell residuals can be thought of as a sample of observations from the unit exponential distribution (or a censored sample if there exists right-censoring).[2] To test whether or not the Cox-Snell residuals are approximately unit exponentially distributed, a residual plot can be constructed. The logic of this approach is straightforward. If the Cox-Snell residuals are in fact distributed as unit exponential, then an estimate of the integrated hazard rate *based on* r_{CS_i} when plotted against r_{CS_i} should yield a straight line with a slope equal to 1. That is, a plot of $H_r(r_{CS_i})$ vs. r_{CS_i} should yield a straight line through the origin with slope 1 if the posited model fits the data. In this case, $H_r(r_{CS_i})$ can be thought of as the integrated hazard rate for the Cox-Snell residuals. Below, we illustrate the use of this kind of residual plot.

Schoenfeld Residuals

The next set of residuals we consider are Schoenfeld residuals. These residuals are fundamental in testing the critical proportional hazards assumption.[3] To explain, assume that there are p covariates and n independent observations

---

[1] Additional recommended sources on the development and use of event history residuals are: Andersen, Borgan, Gill, and Keiding 1993; Fleming and Harrington 1991; Grambsch, Therneau, and Fleming 1995; McCullagh and Nelder 1989; Schoenfeld 1982; Therneau et. al. 1990.

[2] Collett, 1994, p. 151, provides the proof of this result.

[3] We draw extensively upon Hosmer and Lemeshow (1999) for this section.

of time, covariates, and censoring, which are represented as (t_i, x_i, c_i), where $i = 1, 2, ..., n$, and $c_i = 1$ for uncensored observations and zero otherwise. Schoenfeld residuals "are based on the individual contributions to the derivative of the log partial likelihood" (Hosmer and Lemeshow 1999, 198). To derive the Schoenfeld residuals, one takes the derivative for the kth covariate,

$$
\begin{aligned}
\frac{\partial L_p(\beta)}{\partial \beta_k} &= \sum_{i=1}^{n} c_i \left\{ x_{ik} - \frac{\sum_{j \in R(t_i)} x_{jk} e^{x_j' \beta}}{\sum_{j \in R(t_i)} e^{x_j' \beta}} \right\} \\
&= \sum_{i=1}^{n} c_i \left\{ x_{ik} - \bar{x}_{w_i k} \right\},
\end{aligned}
\tag{8.2}
$$

where

$$
\bar{x}_{w_i k} = \frac{\sum_{j \in R(t_i)} x_{jk} e^{x_j' \beta}}{\sum_{j \in R(t_i)} e^{x_j' \beta}}.
$$

The estimator of the Schoenfeld residual for the ith subject on the kth covariate are then obtained by substituting the partial likelihood estimator of the coefficient, $\hat{\beta}$:

$$
\hat{r}_{S_i k} = c_i (x_{ik} - \hat{\bar{x}}_{w_i k}),
\tag{8.3}
$$

where

$$
\hat{\bar{x}}_{w_i k} = \frac{\sum_{j \in R(t_i)} x_{jk} e^{x_j' \beta}}{\sum_{j \in R(t_i)} e^{x_j' \beta}}.
$$

The Schoenfeld residual given in (8.3) can essentially be thought of as the observed minus the expected values of the covariates at each failure time. Hence, Schoenfeld residuals are useful for assessing the proportional hazards property because plots of these residuals against time can reveal whether or not a covariate coefficient is time-dependent (that is, are the $\hat{r}_{S,k}$ changing values with respect to time). The sum of the Schoenfeld residuals is zero because the partial likelihood estimator of the coefficient, $\hat{\beta}$, is the solution to the equations when (8.2) is set equal to zero (Hosmer and Lemeshow 1999, 199).

Martingale Residuals

Another, arguably more intuitive, approach that has been used to motivate the study of residuals for event history diagnostics is through the counting process approach. When using a counting process approach, we intuitively think about following one observation until the event of interest occurs. The counting process representation of the Cox model is a linear-like model that counts whether the event occurs at time t,

$$
\delta_i(t) = H_i(t) + M_i(t),
\tag{8.4}
$$

where $\delta_i(t)$ is the "count" that represents the observed part of the model, $H_i(t)$ is the "systematic component" of the model, and $M_i(t)$ is the "error component." The count component of the model is observed and is equal to zero until the exact time that the event occurs and is equal to one thereafter. So, this count is actually equal to the value of the censoring indicator variable. The systematic component of the model is equal to the integrated hazard at time t as long as the observation is part of the study, and is equal to zero thereafter. Finally, the error component in the counting process is also referred to as a *martingale* and has the same properties that error components in other models have, such as the mean equalling zero and the covariance between observations equalling zero (Therneau and Grambsch 2000; Collett 1994, 153); that is,

$$E(M_i) = 0,$$

and

$$\text{cov}(M_i, M_j) = 0.$$

By rearranging, we see that the martingale residual, $M_i(t)$, is defined as the difference between the "observed" event indicator, given by the censoring indicator $\delta_i(t)$, and the "expected" number of events, which is given by the integrated hazard $H_i(t)$, that is:

$$M_i(t) = \delta_i(t) - H_i(t). \tag{8.5}$$

It is useful to note that the result in (8.5) is *equivalent* to

$$M_i(t) = \delta_i(t) - r_{CS_i}, \tag{8.6}$$

where r_{CS_i} are the Cox-Snell residuals discussed previously. Hence, by (8.5), the Cox-Snell residuals can be equivalently thought of as *the expected number of events in a given time interval*. In this way, the Cox-Snell residual is really an expected *count*. Thus, martingale residuals have the form of a residual because it resembles the difference between an observed outcome and a predicted outcome (Hosmer and Lemeshow 1999, 204). The martingale residual is used later in this chapter to assess the functional form of the covariates in the chosen model. In contrast to martingale residuals, some other event history residuals considered below are covariate specific.

Deviance Residuals

Although the residuals in linear models are symmetrically distributed around zero, martingale residuals are not (Collett 1994, 153). In fact, the domain of martingale residuals is $(-\infty, 1)$ implying that $M_i(t)$ will be highly skewed. To obtain symmetry, *deviance residuals* are sometimes used. Deviance residuals are simply a normalizing transformation of the martingale residuals such that they are symmetric about zero when the correct model is estimated. The deviance residual is given by

$$D_i = \text{sign}(M_i(t))\{-2[M_i(t) + \delta \log(\delta_i - M_i(t))]\}^{1/2}, \quad (8.7)$$

where $M_i(t)$ is the martingale residual for the ith observation. When $M_i(t)$ is 0, the deviance residual is 0. The log transformation has the effect of inflating $M_i(t)$ that are close to 1 and deflating $M_i(t)$ that are negative. This produces a residual that is roughly symmetrical when an appropriate model is fit (Collett 1994; Klein and Moeschberger 1997). The normalization of martingale residuals to get deviance residuals is useful when assessing graphical plots because of the added symmetry.[4] Below, we provide an illustration using deviance residuals.

Score Residuals

To assess covariate-specific residuals, score residuals are useful to consider. The score residual for the ith subject on the kth covariate can be obtained by using the martingale residual representation:

$$L_i = \int_0^\infty [X_i(t) - \bar{X}_i(t)]d\hat{M}_i(t). \quad (8.8)$$

Here $\bar{X}(t)$ is the weighted mean of covariate X over the observations still in the risk set at time t, with weights corresponding to $\exp(X\beta)$ and $d\hat{M}_i(t)$ is the change in martingale residuals for the ith subject at time t. The score residuals equal zero when summed by observations within each covariate. The score residuals can be used to identify influential observations and we illustrate this later in the chapter. In passing, it is useful to note that we have now come full circle back to the Schoenfeld residuals, which can also be defined through the counting process framework. Specifically, the Schoenfeld residuals are the cross-observation sums of the score residuals (Hosmer and Lemeshow 1999, 203):

$$s_{kt} = \sum L_i(t). \quad (8.9)$$

This summation gives us one value for the whole model at each time point and is used to diagnose violations of the important proportional hazards assumption.

We now turn more explicitly to using these various residuals for assessing different aspects of an event history model. Our first set of illustrations are based on use of the Cox model. Following this, we consider in much less detail, residual analysis for parametric models.

---

[4]Therneau and Grambsch 2000 point out that the deviance residual is essentially equivalent to the Pearson residual used commonly for assessing goodness-of-fit in generalized linear models; see also Collett (1994).

Residual Analysis and the Cox Model

We first turn attention to assessing the adequacy of the Cox model using Cox-Snell residuals. Following this, we consider issues pertaining to functional form of a covariate. In this application, we make use of martingale residuals. We also provide applications assessing influential observations and outliers using score residuals and deviance residuals. Finally, we consider the issue of assessing the adequacy of the proportional hazards assumption made by the Cox model. Here, we will make use of Schoenfeld residuals (and tests derived from these residuals).

Adequacy of the Cox Model

A natural question to ask is "how adequate is the Cox specification?" A useful diagnostic approach to help answer this question is through the use of Cox-Snell residuals. Recall from our discussion of Cox-Snell residuals that a residual plot can be constructed to judge the assumption that the r_{CS_i} follow a unit exponential distribution with hazard ratio 1. If this assumption holds, then a plot of the integrated hazard rate *based on* the r_{CS_i} when plotted against the r_{CS_i} should yield a straight line through the origin with a slope equal to 1. To illustrate this, we turn to an example.

Example 8.1: Application Using Cox-Snell Residuals

For this illustration, we use the data on cabinet durations introduced in Chapters 3 and 4. We estimated a Cox model using the same covariates shown in Table 4.4. The exact method was used to handle tied cases (see column three of the estimates from Table 4.4). For this model, the Cox-Snell residuals were estimated. To evaluate whether the r_{CS_i} are distributed as unit exponential with hazard rate 1, we computed an estimate of $S_i(t)$ using the Kaplan-Meier estimate based on the r_{CS_i}; that is, the Cox-Snell residuals were treated as "the data" and the estimated survivor function from the Kaplan-Meier estimate was computed. Recall from (2.11) that $\hat{H}_o(t_i) = -\log \hat{S}_i(t)$. This implies that the negative log of the estimated survivor function is equal to the integrated hazard function. For these data, we computed the integrated hazard based on using the r_{CS_i} and obtained $H_r(r_{CS_i})$. We graphed $H_r(r_{CS_i})$ versus r_{CS_i} to evaluate whether or not the Cox-Snell residuals are distributed as unit exponential. The graph is shown in Figure 8.1.

In general, the residual plot suggests that the model fits the data reasonably well. At the upper end of the cumulative hazard rate, the line lies above the 45°; however, it is in the tail where variability due to estimation uncertainty is the greatest and so these deviations are not a major concern. In general, systematic deviations from the reference line provides some evidence against the adequacy of the Cox model that is posited. Such deviations may suggest an

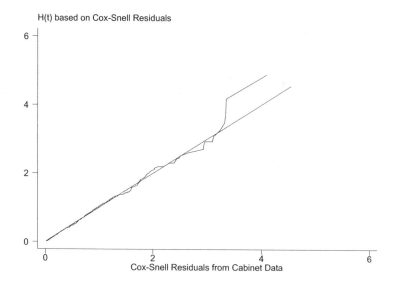

FIGURE 8.1: *Cox-Snell residual plot using data on cabinet durations. The 45-degree line through the origin is a reference line. If Cox model holds, Estimated $H_r(r_{CS_i})$ versus r_{CS_i} should fall roughly on the line.*

important covariate is omitted or the functional form of some covariates are incorrect. Cox-Snell residual plots are useful devices to quickly gauge the adequacy of the posited model; however, they are far from foolproof. Deviations from the assumption that the residuals are distributed as unit exponential could simply be a function of uncertainty in the data. For small samples, this could particularly be a problem. Moreover, the Cox-Snell residual plot may provide *some* evidence that the model holds even if other problems plague the model. For this reason, such residual plots should be a first step toward specification analysis of the model. In the next few sections, we consider other facets of the Cox model that require attention.

Functional Form of a Covariate

It is natural to consider the functional form of the covariates **x**. For example, should a given covariate X be entered linearly, as a quadratic, or one of the many other possibilities? There are two approaches to using martingale residuals to answer this question, each relying on plots of the smoothed residuals against a covariate of interest. Plots of martingale residuals against individual covariates from a model can reveal information regarding functional form.

In the first approach, one estimates a Cox model of interest and then computes the martingale residuals. The smoothed residuals are then plotted against each of the covariates. The logic of these martingale plots is straightforward. Since the martingale residuals have an expected value of 0, systematic deviations from the 0 reference might indicate incorrect functional form. The analogy to traditional regression analysis is in the use of residual plots versus the independent variables to assess functional form. If the relationship is centered around 0 with slope 0 then the functional form is not adjusted. However, if the plot of the residuals against the values of a particular covariate is nonlinear, the covariate might be replaced by its square root, a log transformation, a quadratic, or some higher-order polynomial.

An alternative but complementary second approach to assessment of functional form is advocated by Klein and Moeschberger (1997), Therneau and Grambsch (2000) [see also Therneau, Grambsch, and Fleming (1990)]. They suggest a two-step process. First, assuming there are m covariates in a model, estimate a Cox model based on $m-1$ covariates. From this model, compute the martingale residuals. Second, plot the smoothed martingale residuals against the omitted covariate. If the smoothed plot is linear, no transformation on the omitted covariate is necessary; however, departures from linearity will help to reveal the functional form of the omitted covariate. Again, transformations like those discussed in the previous paragraph may be in order. Below, we illustrate each of these approaches.

Example 8.2: Application Using Martingale Residuals

In this application, we use the data on cabinet durations considered in the previous application. To demonstrate the use of martingale residuals, we estimate a simplified model of cabinet government duration where interest centers on two covariates: polarization and the number of formation attempts (see Chapter 3 for variable explanations). To illustrate the first approach to assessing functional form outlined above, we first estimated a Cox model using the two covariates of interest, polarization and formation attempts. From this model, we computed the martingale residuals and plotted the smoothed residuals against the polarization covariate and the formation attempts covariate. We used lowess (locally weighted scatterplot smoothing) to smooth the martingale residuals.[5] The top two panels of Figure 8.2 show these plots (labeled "Approach 1"). The plots for both covariates illustrate a relatively flat line (slope 0) centered around 0. This provides evidence that no adjustments need to be made to the functional form.

To illustrate the approach suggested by Klein and Moeschberger (1997) and Therneau and Grambsch (2000), we first estimated a Cox model using formation attempts as the singular covariate. The martingale residuals from this model were computed and plotted against the polarization covariate. This

---

[5]Lowess functions are typically advocated for use for these kinds of residual plots (Therneau and Grambsch 2000).

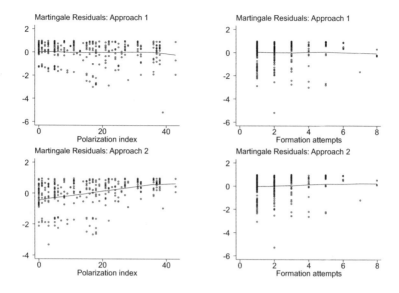

FIGURE 8.2: *The top two panels show the smoothed martingale residual plots for the first approach discussed in the text. The bottom two panels show the smoothed martingale residual plots for the second approach discussed in the text. The plots are complementary and lead to the same conclusion that no adjustments are necessary for the functional form of these covariates.*

plot is shown in the bottom left panel of Figure 8.2. Next, we estimated a Cox model using the polarization covariate as the singular covariate and computed the martingale residuals from this model. The smoothed residuals were plotted against the formation attempts covariate and the results are shown in the bottom right panel of Figure 8.2. Both plots suggest that no adjustments are needed for the covariates; both graphs show no substantial deviations from linearity. In short, this approach is complementary to the approach discussed above. In our view, either approach is suitable for evaluating issues pertinent to functional form. We now turn attention to assessing the presence of influential observations in the duration model.

Influential Observations

It is important in any statistical model to identify influential observations. For example, we want to make sure that in a study of the time to democratic transition there is not one country, which if removed from the data, would result in the relative hazard increasing or decreasing by a substantial amount. Moreover, influence diagnostics are often useful in determining the presence of coding error. One approach to examining the influence of individual observations on parameter estimates is to consecutively drop one observation from the data set and reestimate the model, repeating the exercise for each i observation. This approach is not attractive in many instances as it requires the estimation and reestimation of a Cox model $n + 1$ times (the first iteration is the model with the full sample and the remaining iterations are estimated deleting the ith observation). An alternative to this is through the use of score residuals. As Klein and Moeschberger (1997) and Therneau and Grambsch (2000) demonstrate, score residuals can be used in conjunction with the variance-covariance matrix of parameter estimates to approximate the iterative deletion process just discussed.

Through the score residuals, we can plot the scaled change in a coefficient that would occur if observation i was dropped from the model. In this sense, using the score residuals to evaluate the influence of the ith observation on the jth covariate is analogous to the computation of dfbeta in the traditional regression setting. In the Cox model, the score residuals are a decomposition of the first partial derivative of the log-likelihood. Large absolute values of the score residuals indicate an observation point with high leverage on the value of the coefficient. An analog to dfbeta may be constructed from Cox model estimates by computing the matrix of score residuals, the variance-covariance matrix of the $\hat{\beta}$ and multiplying the two matrices together. The resultant "influence" matrix will be an $n \times m$ matrix with each element in the matrix corresponding to the (scaled) change in parameter estimate for the ith observation (m denotes the covariate). Klein and Moeschberger (1997, pp. 362-365) provide more mathematical detail. We illustrate the procedure with an example.

Example 8.3: Influence Diagnostics Using Score Residuals

In this application, we consider the data on militarized interventions first discussed in Chapter 2 and analyzed in Chapter 5. A Cox model was estimated treating the hazard as a function of six covariates: relative capabilities, the democracy score for the intervening state, the democracy score for the target state, territorial contiguity, alliance status, and breakdown-of-authority. Of interest in the application is to assess whether or not any observations are exerting influence on the estimated regression coefficients. After estimating the Cox model, we created a matrix of score residuals and scaled them by multiplying this matrix by the variance-covariance matrix that was generated by the Cox model. The elements in this influence matrix allow us to evaluate by how much a given observation is increasing or decreasing the parameter estimates given by the Cox model. Because the score residuals are scaled by the variance-covariance matrix of the estimates, the change in coefficients (sometimes referred to as dfbeta) can be interpreted in terms of standard deviation changes to an estimate attributable to the ith observation.

For this model, we graphed the scaled change to the estimates (i.e. the dfbeta) by the observation number and checked for aberrant observations. The

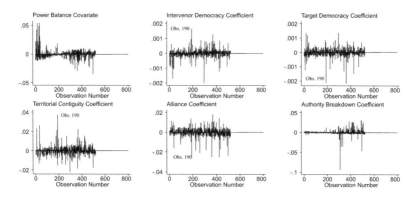

FIGURE 8.3: *The panels in this figure give the scaled change in the coefficient estimates across each covariate for each observation. The vertical lines represent the change attributable to the ith observation. The y-axis denotes the value of the scaled change, that is, the dfbeta.*

residual plots for each covariate in the model are presented in Figure 8.3. The vertical lines extending to the reference line at 0 correspond to the effect the ith observation has on changes to the jth covariate. The y-axis represents the scaled change to the coefficient, that is, the dfbeta. In general, there are no observations that we find to be exerting substantial leverage on the Cox estimates. As the scaled change is interpretable in terms of standard deviations, even the most aberrant observation (observation 312, which corresponds to the largest residual for the breakdown-in-authority covariate [see the bottom right panel in Figure 8.3]) only decreases the coefficient estimate by slightly less than one-tenth of one standard deviation.

Nevertheless, to illustrate further interpretation, we have identified one observation that may merit further attention, observation 190. This observation is labeled in the plots corresponding to the intervenor democracy covariate, the target democracy covariate, the territorial contiguity coefficient and the alliance coefficient. Compared to the other observations, this observation seems to exert (slight) leverage on these covariates. In looking at this case more carefully, we see that the covariate profile for this observation is slightly unusual. It represents a relatively rare case where an autocratic state engages in an intervention into a strongly democratic state (intervenor score is -2 and the target score is 10). Moreover, these states are territorially contiguous and are non-allied. Although the influence is decidedly small, such a case may merit further analysis to evaluate if coding error is present or if this case is unusual in other respects that might help the analyst understand the substantive problem better.

Influential observations, if found, are problematic in event history models because they directly influence the claims a researcher can make about estimated survival times. A high-leverage observation may increase a parameter estimate. In the context of the Cox model, this has the deleterious effect of producing possibly misleading conclusions about the hazard rate and the survival times. If a covariate is found to be positively related to $h(t)$, but is being highly influenced by an observation, then $\hat{S}(t)$ will be understated. As such, influence diagnostics for the duration model, just as with the linear regression model, are important to undertake. Checking for coding errors, assessing whether the observation really belongs in the data set, and evaluating if results differ with and without the observation are some remedies should influence be deemed a problem. Next we consider the issue of poorly predicted observations.

Poorly Predicted Observations

Poorly predicted observations, or outliers, can affect the claims made by an analyst. For example, if many observations yield large martingale residuals, then conclusions regarding the hazard rate or survival times may be misleading. As such, it is useful to evaluate the model in terms of the overall fit for the ith observation. The residual commonly used to evaluate outlying observations is the deviance residual. Recall that the deviance residual is simply a martingale residual rescaled to have approximate symmetry around 0. Plots of deviance residuals against the duration time or against the observation number can assist the researcher in identifying aberrant observations or clusters of observations. We illustrate the approach with an example.

Example 8.4: Assessing Poorly Predicted Observations

In this application, we use the data on military interventions considered in the previous section. To evaluate the presence or absence of outliers, we use results from the Cox model discussed previously. From the model, the deviance residuals were calculated. We first plot the deviance residuals against the observation number. This plot is given in Figure 8.4. To facilitate visualization of the deviance residuals, we also plotted the smoothed residuals (using lowess). The residuals in this plot seem to be uniformly distributed around 0; however, there are a few observations with quite large negative residuals that might merit further attention. In the context of the deviance residual, a negative residual implies that the predicted failure time is less than the actual failure time. This, of course, means that for these observations, the estimated hazard rate is overestimated (that is, the interventions last longer than "they should" given the Cox

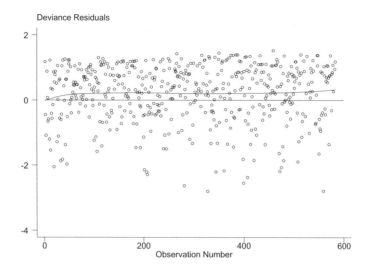

FIGURE 8.4: *The points in the plot correspond to the deviance residuals. The x-axis corresponds to the observation number. The smoothed line corresponds to the lowess residuals.*

estimates). In addition to plotting the deviance residuals by the observation number, we can plot the residuals by the duration time. In so doing, we can get a partial snapshot of the adequacy of the Cox model. To explain, consider Figure 8.5. Here, the deviance residuals are plotted against the observed duration time (with the lowess residuals overlayed) and we see immediately some problems associated with observations having very long survival times. It is clear from Figure 8.5 that interventions that persist for a very long time tend to have large negative residuals. As discussed above, for these observations, the probability of an intervention terminating is overestimated by the Cox model. Conversely, for observations having positive deviance residuals, we see that the Cox model slightly *underestimates* the probability of failure (that these interventions end sooner than "they should" given the Cox estimates). For these data, however, the largest deviance residuals are negative. Given Figure 8.5, it might be wise to examine in more detail these interventions and consider whether or not the model could be improved to better account for these poorly predicted observations.

The Adequacy of the Proportional Hazards Assumption

Whether the proportional hazard assumption holds is arguably the primary concern when fitting a Cox model. As noted in Chapter 4, the term "proportional hazards" refers to the effect of any covariate having a proportional and

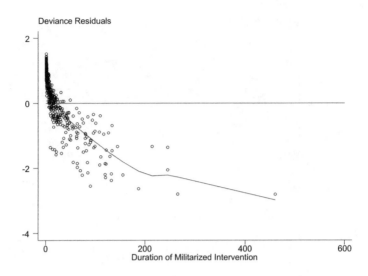

FIGURE 8.5: *The points in the plot correspond to the deviance residuals. The x-axis corresponds to the duration time. The smoothed line corresponds to the lowess residuals.*

constant effect that is invariant to when in the process the value of the covariate changes. That is, each observation's hazard function follows exactly the same pattern over time (but there is no restriction on what this pattern can be). Theoretically, one would be suspicious of the proportional hazards assumption if there was reason to suspect that the effect of a covariate changes over time.

Misspecified proportional hazards models will overestimate the impact of variables whose associated hazards are increasing, while coefficient estimates for covariates in which the hazards are converging will be biased towards zero (Kalbfleisch and Prentice 1980). If a covariate, x, affects survival only to time t, then there are nonproportional hazards. Estimating a Cox model in this case would result in underestimation of the effect prior to t and overestimation of the effect subsequent to t. Because of the consequences from a violation of the assumption, the restrictive proportional hazards assumption should be tested, and if needed, the violation adjusted for in one's model.

Box-Steffensmeier and Zorn (2002) point out that there are three general classes of tests for nonproportional hazards: 1) piecewise regressions to detect changes in parameter values; 2) residual based tests that are both graphical and statistical; 3) explicit tests of the coefficients for the interaction of covariates and time. This class of tests also provides a means of explicitly modeling time dependent covariate effects into the model. We advocate that statistical residual tests be used and corrections implemented with interaction effects (see

Collett 1994 and Collett and Golub 2002 as well). We illustrate proportional hazards testing with two examples.

Example 8.5: Testing the PH Assumption

The first class of tests mentioned above focuses on piecewise regressions. To implement this approach, one estimates separate event history regression models for observations whose survival times fall above and below some predetermined value and assesses if the estimated covariate effects are consistent across the separate models. While better tests are now available for testing proportional hazards in the Cox model (i.e., the residual based methods discussed shortly), if one uses a parametric model, the piecewise regression model is the best that one can do in terms of testing the proportional hazards assumption. In Tables 8.1 and 8.2, we present the results for a series of event history models of Supreme Court retirements.[1] The covariates used in the analysis are: critical nominations, where justices receive a one for this variable if their appointment causes the partisan balance on the Court to shift, or if their appointment moves the Court from a 6-3 to a 5-4 margin or vice versa; partisan agreement (coded one for party agreement, zero otherwise; labeled "Partisan Agreement" in tables), whether the justice in question is of the same political party as his or her appointing President; age of the justice at his or her nomination; 20th century, which denotes whether a justice was appointed in the 20th century (coded one) or not (coded zero; labeled "20th. C. Appoint." in tables); Republican justice, which denotes the political party of the justice (coded one for Republicans and zero for Democrats); and indicator variables for Chief Justices and justices appointed from the South.

In Table 8.1, we present the Cox model for the full data set (shown in the first column of estimates). In columns 2 and 3 of Table 8.1, the results of the piecewise model are presented. Here the data are divided by the median survival time ($T = 15$), but any division of the data can be used, such as quartiles. The data may also be divided into other time periods as suggested by theory. For example, natural breakpoints in political science may include periods of realignment, congressional redistricting, elections, coups, policy eras, or international treaties. Regarding the Supreme Court retirement data, we see that the model does a better job of explaining retirements for justices serving longer terms. Three coefficients show substantial variation and thus potential nonproportional hazards: age, critical nominations, and South.

In Table 8.2, we present the results from three stratified Cox models. A benefit of stratification is that it allows, like piecewise Cox regressions, straightforward comparisons of model fit and parameter sensitivity. Importantly, stratification allows for separate baseline hazard rates, e.g., nonproportional hazards between different levels of the stratified variable. However, a

TABLE 8.1: Cox and Piecewise Cox Models of Supreme Court Retirement

	Cox	Piecewise	
Rep. Justice	.56 (.33)	.56 (.50)	.29 (.46)
Partisan Agreement	.39 (.47)	1.11 (1.08)	.17 (.57)
Age	.08 (.03)	.02 (.04)	.12 (.05)
Chief Justice	−.40 (.47)	−.26 (.63)	−.31 (.81)
Southern Justice	.08 (.37)	1.19 (.53)	−.25 (.56)
20th C. Appoint.	.53 (.32)	.70 (.45)	.74 (.50)
Critical Nom.	−.58 (.40)	.56 (.81)	−.43 (.50)
N	107	52	55
Log-Likelihood	−181.71	−73.16	−75.72
χ^2	26.87 ($p < 0.001$)	7.72 (n.s)	26.35 ($p < .001$)

major drawback is that the impact of the stratification variable cannot be estimated, which is a problem since theoretically this variable was included because it was expected to affect the duration of the justices' tenure. Table 8.2 shows that the age stratification model (column 1) does not fit as well as models which include age as an explanatory variable. While part of this may be due to the loss of information when the age variable is dichotomized, it also suggests that, rather than simply acting on the baseline hazard, age is better modeled as directly influencing the hazard rate itself.

The models with stratification on the southern justice covariate (column 2) and the critical nominations covariate (column 3) provide better fits to the data than the model stratified on age. But it is also the case that we see a greater degree of coefficient variability across these models relative to the basic Cox regression (shown in column 1 of Table 8.1). The variable for critical nominations is marginally statistically significant in both stratified models it is included in, but other coefficients (notably that for political party) show relatively wide swings in value across the different models. Consistent with Schemper (1992), we see that stratification provides only minimal information about the nature of nonproportional hazards. But again, if one uses a parametric model, the methods for detecting a violation of proportional hazards are confined to the piecewise and stratified regressions.

An alternative way to assess the proportional hazards assumption for the Cox model is to plot Schoenfeld residuals against survival time. Linearity implies no violation. The major drawback for the use of these plots is that linearity is often "in the eye of the beholder." Violations of proportionality can innocently be hidden. If there are even only two "outliers" (a particularly large and small rescaled Schoenfeld residual), the y-axis on the graph will be shifted to accommodate them and the slope of the line will be minimized. Hence, if one looks at the proportional hazards assumption graphically and *finds* a problem, one can be pretty confident there *is* a problem; however, if there is not an obvious slope in the graph, one would still want to check the statistical tests

TABLE 8.2: Stratified Cox Models of Supreme Court Retirement

	Stratified Cox		
Rep. Justice	.51 (.32)	.73 (.36)	.60 (.32)
Partisan Agreement	.33 (.48)	.55 (.50)	.33 (.49)
Age	n/a	.08 (.03)	.08 (.03)
Chief Justice	−.22 (.46)	−.24 (.48)	.40 (.47)
Southern Justice	.13 (.38)	n/a	.11 (.37)
20th C. Appoint.	.75 (.32)	.49 (.32)	.48 (.33)
Critical Nom.	−.69 (.41)	−.54 (.40)	n/a
N	107	107	107
Log-Likelihood	−152.94	−151.95	−161.90
χ^2	12.11 ($p = 0.06$)	26.16 ($p < 0.001$)	23.68 ($p < 0.001$)

since figures can be deceiving. Thus, using the statistical tests saves an unnecessary step. For this reason, we place more emphasis on the Harrell (1986) and Grambsch and Therneau (1994) statistical tests for nonproportionality, which also use the Schoenfeld residuals.[6] We illustrate the use of this test with the Supreme Court data.

At the bottom of Table 8.3 a global test for nonproportional hazards is shown (Grambsch and Therneau 1994; Therneau, Grambsch, and Fleming 1990). The Grambsch and Therneau global test uses the maximum of the absolute cumulative summed Schoenfeld residuals and asks whether the model as a whole shows evidence of nonproportional hazards. The global test is marginally statistically significant, suggesting one or more variables in the model are nonproportional. Thus, we examine particular covariates to isolate the proportional hazards violation(s). Harrell's rho is a statistical test for proportional hazards based on the Schoenfeld residuals for *each* covariate. Specifically, Harrell's rho is based on the correlation between the Schoenfeld residuals for a particular covariate and the rank of the survival time (Harrell 1986). Statistical significance is based on the chi-square distribution. In Table 8.3, columns 1, 2, and 3 present rho, the associated chi-square statistic, and the p-value for each covariate. The southern justice covariate is most clearly the offending covariate, but age and Republican justice are also possibilities due to the p-values of 0.14 and 0.13, respectively.

We also illustrate the nonproportionality tests using a subset of the data on the transition to first marriage by males in the National Longitudinal Survey of Youth (NLSY).[7] The results in Table 8.4 suggest that the model as a

---

[6]Technically, the global test uses rescaled Schoenfeld residuals that correct for correlation among the covariates (Grambsch and Therneau 1994).

[7]We thank Dan Powers for this example; see the Cox model in Chapter 4 as well. The NLSY provides data designed primarily to analyze sources of variation in labor market behavior and experience. The original group for Youth were ages 14–21 in 1979. The originating agency/principal investigators(s) are the United States Bureau of Labor Statistics and Center for Human Resource Research (CHRR) at Ohio State, Disseminator.

TABLE 8.3: Nonproportionality Tests of Supreme Court Retirements

Variable	Estimated ρ	χ^2 statistic	p-value
Rep. Justice	−.213	2.24	.13
Partisan Agreement	−.117	.71	.40
Age	.195	2.16	.14
Chief Justice	−.064	.23	.63
Southern Justice	−.281	4.86	.03
20th C. Appoint.	−.009	.01	.94
Critical Nom.	.142	1.01	.31
Global Proportionality Test	−	13.20	.07

TABLE 8.4: Nonproportionality Tests for First Transition to Marriage

Variable	Estimated ρ	χ^2 statistic	p-value
Nonwhite	.039	3.78	.05
Not Living with Biological Parents	−.028	1.84	.18
Father's Education	.032	2.47	.12
Influence	.233	129.66	.00
Urban Residence	.289	2.01	.16
Family Income	−.007	.11	.74
Test Score	.044	4.52	.034
Rate of Female Head of Households	−.013	.38	.54
Global Proportionality Test	−	153.98	.00

whole shows evidence of nonproportional hazards. That is, the global tests are statistically significant. Harrell's rho reveals that the offending covariates include the indicator for nonwhite respondents; influence by a parent, peer, or teacher; and standardized test score on the ASVAB, which is the Armed Services Vocational Aptitude Battery.

If evidence of potential nonproportional hazards is found, as in the previous example, one would estimate the event history model with the addition of an interaction effect between the offending covariate and some function of time.[8] The most straightforward example of a model with the interaction term is to include the new covariate x_2, where $x_2 = x_1 \times \log(t)$ and x_1 is a covariate already in the model.[9] Using the covariate interactions with time should prove to be particularly valuable in light of Willett, Singer, and Martin's (1998) conclusion that interactions with time are the rule rather than the exception.

[8]It is important to use the statistical tests prior to including the interaction terms because otherwise nonproportional hazards are introduced and the model should naturally fail the test.

[9]Other forms of the interaction are possible, such as $x_1 \times (t)$ or $x_1 \times (t)^2$, which reflect diversity in the shape of the nonproportionality. However, most applied treatments favor the $\log(t)$ (e.g., Kalbfleisch and Prentice 1980; Collett 1994).

In sum, when assessing the proportional hazards assumption, we recommend Grambsch and Therneau's global proportional hazards test statistic and Harrell's rho should be calculated. If there is evidence of nonproportional hazards, interaction terms should then be added to the model to account for nonproportional hazards. In the study of transition to first marriage, an interaction between test scores and time would address this issue.

Residual Analysis and Parametric Models

The principal venue of statistical research on residual analysis has been done in the context of the Cox model; however, Cox-like residuals are becoming available for parametric duration models and should be applied using the methods discussed in the previous several sections. In the remainder of this section, we apply some diagnostic methods to parametric models that can assist the researcher in possibly adjudicating among possible parametric forms.

Cox-Snell Residuals Applied to Parametric Models

The basic theory underlying the Cox-Snell residual in the context of the Cox model extends directly to the parametric setting. Specifically, suppose that a given parametric model is estimated, and the integrated hazard rate is

$$\hat{H}_o(t_i) = \hat{g}(\cdot),$$

where $g(\cdot)$ is a function of the scale and shape parameters for a given distribution function. For example, in the case of the Weibull, $\hat{g}(\cdot) = \hat{\lambda} t^{\hat{p}}$. The Cox-Snell residuals are defined similar to equation (8.1),

$$r_{CS_i} = \exp(\hat{\beta}'\mathbf{x_i})\hat{g}(\cdot), \tag{8.10}$$

with the only difference being the substitution of the appropriate integrated hazard function for $\hat{g}(\cdot)$. As with the Cox-Snell models, the r_{CS_i} are assumed to have a unit exponential distribution with hazard rate 1 if the appropriate model has been fit. Consequently, to assess the adequacy of a parametric form, one can obtain an estimate of the integrated hazard function based on the r_{CS_i} and graph this function with respect to the Cox-Snell residuals. If the model holds, the resulting residual plot should approximate a straight line through the origin with a slope of one. We now illustrate the use of the Cox-Snell residuals in assisting with model assessment over different parametric forms.

Example 8.6: Using Cox-Snell Residuals to Assess Parametric Forms

For this application, we use the data on cabinet durations considered earlier in this chapter and in previous chapters. Of interest in the illustration is to demonstrate how residual plots based on Cox-Snell residuals can be used to

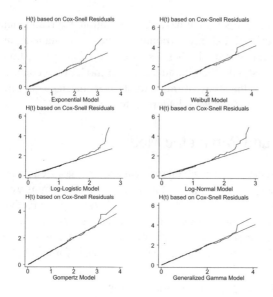

FIGURE 8.6: *Cox-Snell residual plot using data on cabinet durations. The 45-degree line through the origin is a reference line. If a parametric model holds, Estimated $H_r(r_{CS_i})$ versus r_{CS_i} should fall roughly on the line.*

help adjudicate among competing parametric forms. To proceed, we first estimate a parametric duration model using the same set of covariates shown in Table 3.3 from Chapter 3. Five parameterizations were selected: exponential, Weibull, log-logistic, log-normal, and the Gompertz (coefficient estimates are not reported here). From each model, the Cox-Snell residuals were computed and then based on these residuals, the integrated hazard rate was estimated from Kaplan-Meier estimates (i.e. $-\log(\hat{S}_i(t))$). The integrated hazard was then plotted with respect to the Cox-Snell residuals for each parametric model. These residual plots are shown in Figure 8.6 (for now, ignore the bottom right panel).

From the residual plots, we see that two distribution functions, the Weibull and the Gompertz, each seem to fit the data, while the other distribution functions provide a less adequate fit. To tie this analysis in with our discussion in Chapter 3 concerning choosing among parametric forms, we also estimated a generalized gamma model. From this model, the Cox-Snell residual plot was constructed. This plot is given in the bottom right panel of Figure 8.6. The generalized gamma model seems to fit the data about as well as the Weibull or the Gompertz, at least given the evaluative criteria of this kind of residual plot. Recall from Chapter 3 that the generalized gamma distribution is an encompassing distribution having nested under it the Weibull (and exponential), the log-normal, and the gamma distribution. In fitting the generalized gamma to the cabinet duration data (see Chapter 3), we found that the Weibull model best fit the data. Hence, the results from the Cox-Snell residual plots confirm, as they should, the statistical evidence provided by the generalized gamma estimates shown in Chapter 3; the residual plot is a complementary evaluative method. What makes the use of Cox-Snell residuals appealing for parametric models is that they can help the analyst adjudicate among non-nested parametric forms. In Figure 8.6, we see that the log-logistic and Gompertz models can be compared to the other distribution functions (which are nested under the generalized gamma). This comparison can assist the analyst in choosing among non-nested models.

Martingales, Deviance, and Score Residuals for Parametric Models

As with the Cox-Snell residuals, other kinds of residuals are estimable from parametric models. It is worth noting, however, that martingale residuals are sometimes referred to as "martingale-like" residuals. The reason is that martingale theory does not directly extend to the parametric setting and so, strictly speaking, martingale residuals are not directly estimated (Collett 1994). Nevertheless, because of the result shown in equation (8.6), martingale-like residuals can be estimated from Cox-Snell residuals. The application of diagnostic methods based on martingale, deviance, or score residuals discussed in the context of the Cox model can be extended to the parametric setting. Hence, diagnostic methods discussed in terms of the Cox model may also be used in the parametric setting.

Conclusion

Diagnostic methods in much of the applied research we have seen are underutilized. In this chapter, we have illustrated how the use of event history residuals can help the researcher in assessing model fit, functional form, influence, and the proportional hazards property. In general, most statistical software packages now routinely have options for generating the kinds of residuals discussed in this chapter. As such, diagnostic methods based on residual analysis should be routinely used in the analysis of duration data.

CHAPTER 9

Some Modeling Strategies
for Unobserved Heterogeneity

A variety of problems can emerge in typical event history data sets and concomitant models. One of the most prevalent problems in duration analysis involves the issue of unobserved heterogeneity. In this chapter, we consider the issue of unobserved heterogeneity and modeling strategies that can help gain leverage on the problem. Following this, we return to the issue of censoring and truncation in duration data. This discussion will lead naturally to the consideration of yet another modeling strategy that is appropriate when events, for some subpopulation in a sample, never actually occur (such observations are usually regarded as right-censored). This discussion will lead us to consider the so-called "split-population" model.

Heterogeneity

Heterogeneity can be induced in a model any time relevant covariates are not included in the model's specification. Relevant covariates may be left out because they are unmeasurable, unobservable, or because the analyst may not know that a particular covariate is even important. Heterogeneity can lead to problematic inferences insofar as parameter estimates can be inconsistent, standard errors can be wrong, and estimates of duration dependency can be misleading.[1] Given the problems resulting from heterogeneity, it is important for analysts to think seriously about heterogeneity in developing event history models. Indeed, Manton, Singer, and Woodbury (1992) argue "that model

---

[1] There is a vast body of research that has focused on the problems of heterogeneity in duration models, e.g., Holt and Prentice 1974; Heckman and Singer 1984; Gourieroux, Montfort, and Trognon 1984; Struthers and Kalbfleisch 1986; Hougaard, Myglegaard, and Borch-Johnsen 1994; Greene 1997; Scheike and Jensen 1997; Hougaard 2000.

specification must involve considering the likelihood and testing for the presence of unobservable variables to be considered complete" (quoted in Trussel 1992, 2).

Often more complicated models than the ones considered heretofore will be necessary either because of heterogeneity problems or because the substantive research question demands a more complicated approach. In the next section, we consider a modeling approach that attempts to account for sub-group unobserved heterogeneity through the use of "frailty" models. In Chapter 10, we will consider models for multiple outcomes. Such models can mitigate heterogeneity problems by directly accounting for the fact that multiple events (or repeated events) can occur.

Frailty Models

One of the most fertile areas of research in duration modeling techniques involves the estimation and use of so-called "frailty" models (Hougaard 2000 provides an excellent and detailed presentation of these kinds of models). The models get their name because they are used, ostensibly, to account for unobserved heterogeneity that occurs because some observations are more failure-prone—and hence, more "frail"—than other observations in a data set. Moreover, frailty models have been proposed as a method to account for temporal dependence among observations within subgroups (Klein and Moeschberger 1997). The basic idea is to introduce into the hazard rate an additional random parameter that accounts for the random frailties. These frailties may be individual-specific or group-specific. Models constructed in terms of group-level frailties are sometimes referred to as *shared frailty* models because observations within a subgroup share unmeasured "risk factors" that prompt them to exit earlier (or later) than other sub-groups in the population (Hill, Axinn, and Thornton [1993]). Models based on individual-level frailties (i.e. each observation in the sample has potentially its own unique frailty) are conventionally referred to as frailty models or individual-level frailty models. The differences, at least conceptually, between the two classes of models are not drastic and the approach to deriving an estimable model is fundamentally the same and is outlined below.

Individual Frailty

Suppose we have a sample of j observations where some observations are more failure prone due to reasons unknown (or unmeasured) and then estimate a standard (i.e. nonfrailty) event history model. The hazard rate (using the proportional hazards framework) with covariates, is given by

$$h(t)_j = h_0(t) \exp(\beta' \mathbf{x_j}).$$

In this setup, the covariates act multiplicatively on the baseline hazard and as such, reveal information on how the relative hazard is increasing or decreasing as a function of $\mathbf{x}$. However, if there are unmeasured or unobserved "frailties" among individuals in the sample, then the hazard rate shown above will not only be a function of the covariates, but *also* a function of the frailties associated with the j individuals. In this case, the hazard could be expressed as

$$h(t_j) = h_0(t) \exp(\beta' \mathbf{x_j} + \psi' w_j), \tag{9.1}$$

where w_j are the frailties and are assumed to be an independent sample from a distribution with mean 0 and variance 1 (Klein and Moeschberger 1997). If $\psi = 0$, then the standard proportional hazards model is obtained. We can see from the hazard rate in equation (9.1) that the source of model heterogeneity is, in some sense, akin to a model misspecification problem. If the relevant factors comprising w_j could be measured, then ψ would go to 0. Unfortunately, the causes of the individual-level frailty may be unknown to the researcher.

A tractable model to account for heterogeneity can be derived, however, if one is willing to make some assumptions regarding the distribution of the frailty. To see this, equation (9.1) can be rewritten as

$$h_j(t) \mid (\beta' \mathbf{x}_j, \nu_j) = h_0(t) \nu_j \exp(\beta' \mathbf{x}_j), \tag{9.2}$$

where $\nu_j = \exp(\psi' w_j)$ and denotes the individual-level frailties. From equation (9.2), it is easy to see that the hazard, or risk, is conditional on both the observed covariates and on the unobserved frailty term ν. For identification purposes, it is conventionally assumed that the mean of ν is 1 and the variance is unknown and equal to some parameter θ (Klein and Moeschberger 1997). In typical applications (i.e. non-frailty applications) of the proportional hazards model, the frailty term in equation (9.2) is assumed to be 1 with probability 1 (i.e. the variance is assumed 0) and so the standard proportional hazards model is obtained.

Given individual-level frailty, the survivor function is conditional on both the covariates and on the frailty term. Using the connection between the survivor function and the hazard function discussed in Chapter 2, the conditional survivor function (omitting subscripts) is given by

$$
\begin{aligned}
S(t \mid \beta' \mathbf{x}, \nu) &= \exp\left(-\int_0^t h(u \mid \nu) du \right) \\
&= \exp\left(-\nu \int_0^t h(u) du \right)
\end{aligned} \tag{9.3}
$$

and the *marginal* survivor function is given by

$$S(t) = E[S(t \mid \beta' \mathbf{x}, \nu)]$$

$$= E\left[\exp\left(-\nu\int_0^t h(u)du\right)\right]$$

$$= L\left[\exp\left(\int_0^t h(u)du\right)\right] \tag{9.4}$$

where L is the Laplace transformation.[2] The Laplace transformation is used to integrate out the unobserved frailties, given by ν. Consequently, to derive the expected value of the survivor function, it is necessary to specify a probability distribution for ν, call this $g(\nu)$. Any continuous distribution with positive support on the positive numbers, a unit mean, and finite variance θ can be used for $g(\nu)$. Several suitable distributions have been proposed by statisticians, among them include the gamma, t, inverse Gaussian, log-normal, and power variance model (cf. Clayton 1978; Hougaard 1986, 2000; Klein and Moeschberger 1997). Of these distributions, the gamma has most readily been adopted in applied research. The choice of the distribution is important as the conclusions about the variance of the random effect may depend on the distribution chosen. Consequently, if we assume that ν has some appropriate probability distribution (with mean 1) and finite variance θ, then a tractable model can be derived. By taking the expected value of the survivor function through integrating out the frailty, the problem reduces to one of estimating the frailty variance term, θ. Again, note that if the frailty variance is 0, the problem simply reduces to estimating the standard proportional hazards model. Ultimately, then, incorporating heterogeneity into the duration model entails estimation of the additional random coefficient, θ. For this reason, frailty models are often referred to as random coefficients models.

To illustrate for the case of the Weibull, the conditional survivor function is given by

$$S(t \mid \nu) = \exp^{-(\nu\lambda t)^p}.$$

With the exception of the frailty term, ν, this expression is identical to equation (3.13). Now suppose that the gamma distribution is specified for $g(\nu)$. We can define the gamma distribution as $g(\nu, \alpha, \beta)$ where $\alpha = 1/\theta$ and $\beta = \theta$. The density function for the gamma is then given by

$$g(\nu, \alpha, \beta) = \frac{1}{\beta^\alpha \Gamma(\alpha)} \nu^{\alpha-1} e^{-\nu/\beta},$$

where $\Gamma(\alpha)$ is the gamma integral $(\int_0^\infty \nu^{\alpha-1} e^{-\nu})$. With gamma frailty, the marginal Weibull survivor function is equal to

$$S(t) = [1 + \theta(\lambda t)^p]^{-1/\theta}$$

---

[2]Hougaard 2000 refers to this distribution as the "marginal survivor function" because it is the observed survivor function after ν has been integrated out.

and the Weibull hazard with gamma frailty is

$$h(t) = \lambda p(\lambda t)^{p-1} [S(t)]^{\theta}.$$

When the variance of the frailty, θ, is 0, the model reduces to the standard Weibull. What makes this approach attractive is that it is possible to evaluate the hypothesis that $\theta = 0$. Evidence against this hypothesis suggests that there is unobserved heterogeneity exerting influence on the hazard function. It is useful to point out that the approach outlined above is a *mixture model* in that the conditional distribution is described by the Weibull, while the mixture distribution is described by the gamma. We now turn to a brief illustration.

Example 9.1: Use of Frailty Model with Conflict Data

To illustrate some of the points just discussed, we use the well-known data of Oneal and Russett (1997) on the relationship among economic interdependence, democracy, and peace that was introduced in Chapter 8. The data consist of 20,448 observations on 827 dyads, i.e., pairs of states such as the United States and Canada, between 1950 and 1985. We model the hazard of a militarized international conflict as a function of six primary covariates (some of which vary over time): a score for *democracy* (a dyadic score for the two countries which ranges from −1 to 1), the level of *economic growth* (the lesser rate of economic growth, as a percent, of the two countries), the presence of an alliance in the dyad (a dummy variable indicating whether the two countries were allied), the two nations' *contiguity* (a dummy variable for geographic contiguity), their military *capability ratio* (a ratio measuring the dyadic balance of power), and the extent of bilateral *trade* in the dyad (a measure of the importance of dyadic trade to the less trade-oriented country; it is the ratio of dyadic trade to the gross domestic product of each country). Liberal theory suggests that all variables except contiguity ought to decrease the hazard of a dispute, while contiguity should increase it. Table 9.1 presents the results of the Cox model and the Cox Gamma Frailty Model.[3]

The important aspect to notice when comparing the results of the two models is that the variance of the random effect is not zero and it is statistically significant. This tells us that there is considerable heterogeneity in the data that is not captured by the six covariates in the model. The "missing" covariates may be simply be unaccounted for in the model or they may be unobserved or unmeasurable.

---

[3] Technically, the Cox model is an Andersen-Gill Cox model, which we present in order to make this model directly comparable to the frailty model; see the repeated events section in the next chapter.

TABLE 9.1: Frailty Model of Conflict

	Cox	Cox with Gamma Frailty
Democracy	−0.44 (0.10)	−0.37 (.11)
Growth	−3.23 (1.30)	−3.69 (1.30)
Alliance	−0.41 (0.11)	−.37 (.13)
Contiguous	1.21 (0.13)	1.20 (.13)
Capability Ratio	−0.21 (0.06)	−0.20 (0.05)
Trade	−13.16 (11.41)	−3.04 (10.31)
Variance of the Random Effect	−	708.95 ($p < 0.001$)
N	20,448	20,448

Shared-Frailty Models

The approach discussed in the previous section centered around individual-level frailty models. In this sense, the model did not account (directly) for subgroup heterogeneity. However, subgroup heterogeneity may be an important issue in many of the kinds of duration data sets that social scientists work with. Specifically, because we often work with data that involve time-varying covariates, our data sets are quite likely to have multiple observations (or repeated observations) of the same unit over time. This is most easily seen in the discrete-time approach (discussed in Chapter 5) where each observation will contribute T records of data. In such a setting, the relevant "subgroup" are the repeated observations of the jth unit. A straightforward extension of the ideas discussed previously can be applied to this kind of setting. The resultant model is sometimes called a "shared-frailty" model (Hougaard 2000).

The basic idea of the shared-frailty model is easy to understand. Suppose we have j observations and i subgroups (for repeated measures data, the j observations will simply be the period-specific records of data for the individual). The hazard rate for the jth individual in the ith subgroup (with frailties) is

$$h(t_{ij}) = h_0(t) \exp(\beta' \mathbf{x_{ij}} + \psi' w_i), \qquad (9.5)$$

where w_i are the *subgroup* frailties, which, as before, are assumed to be an independent sample from a distribution with mean 0 and variance 1. Also as before, if $\psi = 0$, then the standard proportional hazards model is obtained, thus implying the absence of group-level heterogeneity. We can reexpress equation (9.5) as

$$h_{ij}(t) \mid (\beta' \mathbf{x}_{ij}, \nu_i) = h_0(t) \nu_i \exp(\beta' \mathbf{x_{ij}}), \qquad (9.6)$$

where $\nu_i = \exp(\psi' w_i)$ and denotes the *shared* frailties. Note the difference between this expression and that given in equation (9.2). Here, the frailty is shared among the j observations in the ith group. This common frailty gives rise to the nomenclature, shared-frailty. As in the case of individual-level frailty models, it is conventionally assumed that the mean of ν is 1 and the variance is unknown and equal to some parameter θ (Klein and Moeschberger 1997). Again, note if ν is assumed to be 1 with probability 1, then the standard proportional hazards model is obtained. In ignoring the possibility of subgroup heterogeneity, this becomes the default modeling strategy.

To derive an estimable model of sub-group heterogeneity, a distribution must be defined on ν. Again, any distribution with positive support on the real numbers with mean 1 and finite variance is appropriate. Once $g(\nu)$ is defined, the expected survivor function is obtained by integrating out of the conditional survivor function the frailty term ν. In this sense, the approach taken in the shared frailty case is identical to that taken in the individual-level frailty case. It is useful to note the close connection between the shared-frailty model and so-called "multilevel" or hierarchical models. In a typical multilevel model, one has data on individuals and groups. Further, because unmeasured factors common to groups exert a shared influence on group members, it is usually assumed that with such data, there will be extra, unexplained variation due to these group-specific factors (the extra variation is sometimes called "overdispersion").

As such, in the multilevel modeling approach, the variance associated with unmeasured group-level factors is directly modeled as a random coefficient. As with the shared-frailty model, assumptions regarding the distribution of the unmeasured group factors must be made in order to find an estimate of the variance. In the usual presentation of the multilevel model, unmeasured group factors are usually treated as an additional disturbance term. The variance of this term is then estimated as a separate random coefficient and is taken to measure the degree of random, between-group variation. In the case of the shared-frailty model, the approach is identical to that of the multilevel model and so in some sense, the frailty term, ν, can be thought of as a stochastic disturbance upon which we are interested in modeling its variance. Making identifying assumptions about ν allows us to do this (see Goldstein 1995 for excellent coverage of the connection between multilevel models and duration analysis; see also Steenbergen and Jones 2002). Hence, with duration data where j observations are nested within i groups, the shared-frailty model *is* a multilevel model.

Uses of Frailty Models

The use of the frailty approach is attractive as a means to account for possible unobserved heterogeneity. In general terms, unobserved heterogeneity tends to attenuate the "proportionate response of the hazard to variation in x" (Lancaster 1990, p. 67). For covariates that have a positive effect on the hazard, non-frailty estimates will understate the "true" effect; for covariates that have a negative effect on the hazard, non-frailty estimates will overstate the "true" effect. It is important to note that when heterogeneity is present (i.e. $\hat{\theta} \neq 0$), the standard interpretation afforded the proportional hazards property is lost. This is the case because the hazard ratios are now conditional on the unobserved frailty. As θ approaches 0, the proportional hazards property returns. Because the shared-frailty approach provides a way to account for unobserved heterogeneity, this kind of modeling strategy is recommended in situations where a researcher has reason to believe heterogeneity may be a problem. This will usually occur when one has data consisting of repeated observations, which is very common in event history analysis.

However, the models do have some important caveats to be aware of. First, of all, the models can be sensitive to the distribution posited for ν. That is to say, estimates of the frailty variance can vary from distribution to distribution. Second, estimation of the marginal survivor function can be highly nontrivial for some distribution functions that are defined on ν (Hougaard 2000). Third, even though alternatives to the gamma frailty model have been proposed, the gamma is usually the default choice; however, as Hougaard (2000) notes, the gamma has some undesirable properties. Chiefly, the gamma frailty model may give "strange results" because the non-proportional hazards may have a larger influence on the estimates than the actual degree of dependence found in the data (Hougaard 2000, p. 256).[4] The frailty model approach would seem most useful when one is explicitly interested in modeling the dependency structure among the observations. If the assumptions regarding ν are justifiable, then estimation of the additional random coefficient can provide the researcher with information about where the possible unobserved heterogeneity is "coming from." Finally, some have advocated the use of the shared-frailty approach in the estimation of competing risks models (cf. Crowder 2001; Gordon 2002; Hougaard 2000). We visit this issue in the next chapter.

In the remainder of this chapter, we consider a variant of the event history model that explicitly deals with a special problem than can arise in some settings: the systematic non-occurrence of an event. The model we consider is known as the split-population model, and has been proposed as model to more directly account for right-censoring and unobserved heterogeneity (where heterogeneity is induced by a subgroup of observations that never fail).

The Split-Population Model

The split-population model is unique in that it does not assume that eventually every observation will experience the event. Instead, the model splits the population into two groups—one that will experience the event and one that will not. Consider studies of militarized disputes, where it is commonly the case that many dyads in a data set may *never* experience the event of a militarized dispute (cf. Oneal and Russett 1997; King and Zeng 2001b) or commonly in

---

[4]Hougaard (2000) suggests the use of the family of positive stable distributions, as they have more desirable properties regarding the marginal distribution of the survivor function; however, he notes that estimation under these distributions is considerably more difficult.

studies of criminal recidivism, some individuals will not return to prison (cf. Schmidt and Witte 1988) and duration of smoking (Forster and Jones 2001). In these examples, heterogeneity can be induced in traditional estimates of duration dependency because a large portion of the cases, the dyads, span the observation period having never experienced the event (and most likely never will experience an event). The problem is that there are essentially two populations in the composition of the data: one having "true" risk and one having (effectively) no risk of experiencing an event. Under such circumstances, traditional duration models can be problematic because unrealistically high failure rates will be chosen.

It is an assumption of all duration models discussed to this point that if t is sufficiently large, then the probability of an event occurrence will approach one. For parametric models where a cumulative distribution function, $F(t)$, is posited, it is assumed that this function will approach 1 as t increases (Schmidt and Witte 1988, 1989). This assumption presumes that *all* candidates *eventually* exit the primary, or *all* dyads *eventually* engage in a dispute if we observe them long enough. This assumption is unlikely to be true in these applications and in other social science applications as well.

To account for the problem of incorrectly assuming all observations will eventually fail, Schmidt and Witte (1984, 1988, 1989) developed the so-called "split-population" model. These models have a long lineage in biostatistics (Boag 1949; Berkson and Gage 1952) and were popularized in the social sciences by Maltz and McCleary (1977) and importantly, by Schmidt and Witte (1984, 1988, 1989).[5] The model gets its name from the fact that the observations in an analysis come from a population that is essentially split: one group has some risk of experiencing an event, another group does not. The substantive problem that motivated Schmidt and Witte was recidivism after incarceration; not all former prisoners would commit a crime subsequent to release from prison. In studying the timing until criminal recidivism, a nontrivial number of former prisoners never experience the event of returning to jail. To present the model, we adapt the notation used in Schmidt and Witte (1988, 1989).

Schmidt and Witte assume there is some unobserved variable indicating whether or not an observation will eventually experience an event. Letting Z denote this variable, then let

$$\Pr(Z = 1) = \delta$$

and

$$\Pr(Z = 0) = 1 - \delta,$$

where δ is a parameter indicating the estimated probability that observations experience an event. In the case of criminal recidivism, δ is the estimated

---

[5]Split population models are also referred to as cure models in the biostatistics literature; part of the population is "cured" and thus has a failure rate of zero.

probability an individual will return to crime. It should be clear that if $\delta = 1$, then all observations are assumed to eventually experience an event.

Next, we define a cumulative distribution function for the duration times of individuals who eventually experience the event and denote this as

$$F(t \mid Z = 1), \tag{9.7}$$

with corresponding density

$$f(t \mid Z = 1).$$

The distribution function in (9.7) is conditional on whether or not an observation eventually fails. As Schmidt and Witte (1989, 148) note, this distribution function is irrelevant for individuals for whom $Z = 0$.

Since we do not directly observe Z, Schmidt and Witte (1989) define an indicator R, which is a dummy variable, to denote whether or not an observation experienced an event. For those who experience the event, the probability density is given by

$$\Pr(Z = 1)f(t \mid Z = 1) = \delta f(t \mid Z = 1), \tag{9.8}$$

and for those who do not experience an event, i.e., for whom $Z = 0$, Schmidt and Witte (1989, 148) define the probability that an event is never observed as

$$
\begin{aligned}
\Pr(R = 0) &= \Pr(Z = 0) + \Pr(Z = 1)\Pr(t > T \, Z = 1) \\
&= 1 - \delta + \delta[1 - F(T \mid Z = 1)]. \tag{9.9}
\end{aligned}
$$

Schmidt and Witte (1988, 67) show the log-likelihood function for the full data is obtained by combining (9.8) and (9.9) to obtain

$$
\begin{aligned}
\log L = \sum_{i=1}^{N} R_i[\log \delta + \log f(t_i \mid Z_i = 1)] \\
+ (1 - R_i)\log[1 - \delta + \delta(1 - F(T_i \mid Z_i = 1))]. \tag{9.10}
\end{aligned}
$$

The appeal of the log-likelihood expressed in this way is that observations that never experience an event by the end of the observation period contribute information only to the second part of the function. As such, the log-likelihood "splits" the two populations, hence the name of the model. Indeed, (9.10) is conceptually similar to the log-likelihoods derived earlier for other models. In those cases, observations that never experience an event are treated as right-censored and thus only contribute information regarding the survival function. The basic difference here is that one is explicitly accounting for the fact that some observations may *never* experience an event, no matter how long t is.

The log-likelihood in (9.10) may be parameterized in terms of any of the log-linear parametric models discussed in Chapter 3, for example, the Weibull, exponential, log-normal, and log-logistic (Schmidt and Witte 1988). It is easy to see how this is done: one simply defines a cumulative distribution function for (9.7). The only additional complication is the presence of the δ parameter in the log-likelihood. Schmidt and Witte (1989, 151) propose augmenting the model by estimating δ as a logit model. Practically, this is accomplished by estimating

$$\Pr(R_i = 1) = \frac{1}{1 + \exp^{\beta' \mathbf{x}}}, \qquad (9.11)$$

which is a logit model where $\beta'\mathbf{x}$ are the covariates and parameters. The model in (9.11) will give an estimate of δ. If δ is not significantly different from 1, then a model not accounting for the "splitting" is obtained. Thus, if one estimates a "splitting Weibull" model and δ is not different from 1, then the model reduces to a standard Weibull duration model. If δ is less than 1, then evidence exists that the population is split.[6] This kind of interpretation afforded the δ parameters is why the parameter is sometimes referred to as the "splitting parameter." It is important to note that the covariates used to model whether the event occurs in (9.11) need not be the same set of covariates used to model the duration until an event. As such, an attractive feature of split-population models is they allow one to test whether the event and the timing of the event depend on different factors. We now present an application to demonstrate the interpretation of the covariates.

Example 9.2: Split Population Model of PAC Contributions

To illustrate the split-population model, we use data on political action committee (PAC) contributions to House incumbents during the 1993-1994 period. The data used in this application are from Box-Steffensmeier and Radcliffe (1996), who analyze data on the timing of all corporate labor PAC contributions. There is a record for every possible combination of a corporate or labor PAC and a candidate pair. We focus on the timing until a large labor PAC contribution is made. Because some PACs will not contribute to certain kinds of candidates (for reasons pertaining to ideology, candidate need, geography, etc.), some PAC-candidate pairs will not experience the event of interest (a contribution). This problem naturally leads to the consideration of a split-population model since the more common event history models make the unrealistic assumption that every PAC will give to every candidate. In our application, $R = 1$ whenever a candidate receives a PAC contribution.

---

[6]Kuk and Chen (1992) introduced a split-population variant of the Cox proportional hazards model, but it has so far received relatively little use in comparison to the parametric models, quite possibly because of the emphasis in split-population applications on prediction. For example, in *Predicting Recidivism Using Survival Models*, Schmidt and Witte (1988) focus on predicting when a person released from jail will return to jail, if ever.

To obtain coefficient estimates, a split-population log-logistic model was estimated. The results are presented in Table 9.2. We first consider the splitting parameter. In a split-population model one wants the estimated splitting parameter, δ, which represents the probability of a PAC eventually giving a contribution, to be as close as possible to the observed failure rate, or equivalently, to the observed "split" in the data. For these data, about 43.5 percent of the PAC-candidate pairs experienced the event. The estimated value of the splitting parameter, 44 percent, is presented in Table 9.2. The models do very well in estimating the actual contribution "failure" rate, providing confidence that the correct parametric model is used and showing that the use of the split-population model is absolutely necessary since the estimate for the splitting parameter is significantly different 1. Estimating a traditional event history model would be a grave error since a 100 percent contribution rate would be imposed in contrast to the estimated 44 percent.

We now briefly consider the parameter estimates, which are estimated simultaneously. The first column of estimates in Table 9.2 presents the parameter estimates for the duration model of PAC contributions. The duration coefficients are simply log-logistic coefficients, and may be interpreted as discussed in Chapter 3. For this model, positive (negative) coefficients are associated with a longer (shorter) time-to-contribution. For the model of whether or not a contribution was given, negative (positive) coefficients are associated with an increase (decrease) in the log-odds of contributing. Together with the significance values, the results give a picture of the determinants of contributions, and if given, the timing.

Because we are primarily interested in illustrating the use of the split-population model and the interpretation of the splitting parameter, we refer the reader to Box-Steffensmeier and Radcliffe (1996) for further details about variable definitions and measurement and for comparisons to small labor PACs and both large and small corporate PACs. We focus on the PAC resources and geography variables to illustrate the interpretation of the model. PAC resources and geography have a central role in the allocation decisions of large labor PACs. Four covariates are of interest. The first is the lagged value of labor PAC receipts (for the 1991-92 campaign cycle). This covariate is denoted as "lagged PAC receipts" in the table. The second covariate is the lagged PAC receipts covariate squared. Thus, prior PAC receipts are entered into the model as a quadratic term. The third covariate, denoted as "percent union" in the table, represents the percentage of the district's population who are labor members. The fourth covariate, denoted as "state share" in the table, represents the proportion of the PAC's incoming contributions that come from the same state as the candidate.

The evidence confirms the hypothesized importance of PAC resources. PACs with a larger budget are able to make more contributions and to give them earlier in the cycle. There is evidence of declining marginal returns

TABLE 9.2: Split Population Model of PAC Contributions

	Timing of Contribution	Log-Odds of Contribution
Variable	Estimate (s.e.)	Estimate (s.e)
Constant	6.12 (.17)	4.01 (.32)
Candidate Power		
Education Comm.	.06 (.04)	−.005 (.14)
Prestige	.04 (.03)	−.25 (.07)
Seniority	.34 (.20)	1.12 (.43)
Dem. Leader	−.20 (.04)	−.63 (.14)
Rep. Leader	−.28 (.15)	.09 (.19)
Candidate Ideology		
Republican	−.09 (.07)	1.65 (.11)
COPE	−.19 (.11)	−3.66 (.21)
Candidate Need		
Vote %	.24 (.13)	1.89 (.28)
Quality Chal.	.00 (.05)	−.37 (.10)
Quality Chal. in Primary	.07 (.07)	.31 (.16)
District Income	−.68 (2.07)	−3.52 (.46)
PAC Share	−.16 (.11)	−2.66 (.23)
Cash-on-Hand	.36 (.08)	.26 (.15)
PAC Resources and Geography		
Lagged PAC Receipts	−.31 (.02)	−.40 (.05)
(Lagged PAC Receipts)^2	.03 (.01)	.03 (.01)
Percent Union	−.58 (.23)	−2.79 (.54)
State Share	.59 (.18)	−.81 (.46)
Splitting Parameter	.44 (.003)	
Shape Parameter (σ)	.504	
−2 Log Likelihood	18,953	
N	10,168	

to scale, as squared receipts are statistically significant and have the opposite sign. There is also substantial evidence that PACs contribute where they have members. The percentage of district residents who are members of labor unions is a strong predictor of the likelihood of contributions and incumbents with more union constituents also received earlier contributions from large labor PACs. Traceable contributions *to the PAC* from inside the state are weak predictors of the likelihood of large labor PAC contributions to the candidate. In terms of the log-logistic model, in-state contributions to the PAC appear to delay the PAC's eventual contribution to the candidate. Labor PACs, particularly larger ones with established payroll deduction systems, rely substantially less on large contributions, making this a less important predictor of labor PAC contributions.

The split-population model is a plausible modeling strategy for many social science problems. In the PAC application, because over half of the PAC-candidate pairs never experienced the event, heterogeneity could be induced in the model because the observed data are effectively "split" into two populations: one likely to exchange a contribution, and one not. The split-population model is desirable because the right-censoring "process" is directly modeled as a function of covariates. With the split-population model, not only can leverage be gotten on the duration until an event occurs, but also on the probability that an event will occur or not occur. As such, the split-population model is appropriate when a researcher's problem has the complication that a nontrivial number of observations may never experience the event of interest. For social science applications, where "rare events" are often endemic to the data, use of the split-population model may naturally follow the research question.

Conclusion

In this chapter we have considered several approaches to handling common problems that emerge in event history analysis. Generally, the modeling strategies outlined in this chapter center around the problem posed by heterogeneity. As such, the frailty model and split-population model would seem to be attractive approaches for some settings. However, in other applied settings, the methods outlined here will not be satisfactory. Specifically, it is common in event history processes that multiple kinds of events (or repeated events) can occur. As such, treating every problem as if it were a single-state, non-repeating process would be limiting. Ignoring the possibility that multiple events can occur when in fact they *do* occur in the observed data can easily lead to the kinds of heterogeneity problems discussed in this chapter. In Chapter 10, we explicitly consider models for the complications posed by competing or repeating events.

Models for Multiple Events

The models discussed to this point have all involved so-called "single-state" processes, or equivalently, one-way transition models. In such models, there is a singular event of interest and once the event is experienced—or once an observation fails—the observation leaves the risk set and is assumed to be no longer at risk of returning to the previously occupied state. Concomitantly, in a single-state process, we assume that an observation is *only* at risk of experiencing a single event; that is, the observation is *not* at risk of making a transition to another state. Is this a reasonable assumption? Often it is not, and, at a minimum, it is an assumption that should be tested. In this chapter, we consider some models that account for repeatable events.

Additionally, in previous applications, we did not attempt to account for the *different kinds* of events that could occur. Some research problems, however, may lead one to consider how observations are at risk of experiencing one of several kinds of events. Problems of this kind are sometimes referred to as multi-state processes or competing risks processes because survival times may terminate in a variety of substantively interesting ways. In this chapter, we consider event history approaches to deal with the issue of competing risks.

The issues of repeatable events and competing risks serve to highlight the greater concern of this chapter: how does one employ event history models in the face of complicated social processes? To be sure, many longitudinal problems of interest to social scientists can readily be handled by the kinds of models discussed to this point; however, it is not at all uncommon for an analyst to study a problem that is considerably more complicated than the single-state models previously discussed. The fundamental problem in an analysis of multiple events data is that the traditional duration model assumes that the event times are independent. In multiple event data this assumption is highly likely to be violated. Ignoring the correlation could yield misleading variance estimates and possibly biased estimates of the coefficients (Aalen 1992; Greene 1997). Cook and Lawless' exhortation to give "careful thought before adopting any model for complex multiple event processes" can hardly be emphasized enough (1997, 842).

The phrase "multiple events" is generic. Therneau and Grambsch (2000) and Cleves (1999, 32) provide a useful categorization of the different kinds of multiple events. We adopt this classification here. Generally, we can think of events as being "ordered" or "unordered." Furthermore, we can think of multiple events as being of the same type, such that the same event happens more than once. In contrast, we can think of these multiple events as being of different types, such that different events can occur within an individual's lifetime.

In this chapter, we consider the various kinds of multiple events that can be observed in event history data. In the next section, we deal with the relatively straightforward problem of accounting for unordered events of the same type. Following this, we consider models for ordered repeatable events, which means events occur in a natural sequence. Finally, we discuss competing risks models for multi-state processes, i.e., unordered events that are not the same type. Much of the presentation in this chapter will be based on developments of the Cox model.

Unordered Events of the Same Type

We first consider event history data that involve the consideration of unordered events of the same type. Events of this type can occur more than once to an observation, but the event occurrences are assumed to be unordered, i.e., sequence is nonexistent or unimportant. In the study of unordered events of the same type, parameter estimates from the duration model are still consistent and asymptotically normal (under certain regularity conditions), but the variance-covariance matrix needs to be adjusted to account for dependence among related observations (Lin and Wei 1989, Lee, Wei, and Amato 1992). The basic problem that can emerge is that the estimated standard errors are often wrong in the face of clustered data. Moreover, standard errors are frequently attenuated, or smaller than they should be, when there is clustering in the data. Hence, statistical inference with clustered data can be misleading if one does not account for the serial dependence among the repeated observations as well as the heteroskedasticity problems that can emerge with clustered data.

What is needed is an estimate of the variance-covariance matrix that is robust to the problems clustering presents. In the context of the fully parametric model, robust methods for maximum likelihood estimation have been developed by Huber (1967) and White (1982), among others, to account for the kinds of problems produced by clustered data. In the context of the Cox model, Lin and Wei (1989) developed a robust estimator of the variance-covariance matrix for the maximum partial likelihood estimator. The general approach taken by these kinds of robust estimators is that the model is estimated as if the observations were independent and then the variance is "fixed" to account for the correlation among the repeated observations. The clustering correction assumes that the observations are independent across groups or clusters but not necessarily within groups conditional on the covariates. Because the issue of "clustering" is relevant with TVCs, we refer the reader back to Chapter 7 for further discussion of the Huber, White, and Lin and Wei robust estimators.

Of course it is up to the analyst to determine the appropriate variable upon which clustering occurs. Determining the appropriate variable is often an easy matter, since cases are often clustered within themselves due to repeated (but unordered) measures on the same observation. However, sometimes clustering may occur based on geography or some other attribute. It is important to note that if the clustering variable is incorrectly defined, or if the clustering itself is on unimportant variables, then one may prefer to use robust standard errors. As Blalock elaborates, "If you are studying delinquency and match according to hair color, you will probably be worse off than if you did not match at all" (1979, 239).

Repeated Events Models

In this section, we consider the complication associated with repeated events. Event history structures that incorporate repeated events assume that the same type of event can occur to an observation multiple times. Throughout this section, we assume that there is a natural sequence of the repeated events and accounting for this sequence is almost always important.[1] For example, in the

---

[1]It is useful at the start for us to distinguish between duration models for repeated events and event *count* models. Moving from the study of how many events occur (through the use of a count model) to considering how often *and when* events occur in the context of a repeated events duration model can have analytical payoffs. Since counts of an event generally do not occur simultaneously, count models are throwing away the longitudinal information (Lawless 1995; Lindsey 1995; 1998). Event history models go further than count models by allowing the analyst to also consider the progress of the subject over time. That is, "global counts may hide evolution of the state of the [subject] over time. This will appear as overdispersion, which may wrongly be interpreted as differential frailty among [subjects] ... if the timing of each event is recorded, then one can distinguish, with the appropriate models, between frailty and contagion" (Lindsey 1998, 1745 and 1748). Unlike the methods presented in this chapter, count models do not distinguish potential differential effects of the covariates on, say the eighth event and third event. Lindsey (1998) argues that "summarizing events on a [subject] in a single count carries the implicit assumption that the intensity of events remains constant over the total observation period! All information on the evolution ... over that period of observation has been discarded ... interval censoring is always present but is only important if the rate of the events per time unit of observation is too high" (Lindsey 1998, 1749).

Alt, King, and Signorino (2001) are more balanced, focusing on the connections among binary, count, and duration data and deriving models for each to highlight the identical underlying data generation process. While we recognize that event history models are not a cure-all, we think that political science as a discipline has been slow to fully recognize and account for the longitudinal nature of our data and questions. Thus we side more with Lindsey in advocating that data should be

study of the duration of unemployment or smoking, individuals often experience repeated events or spells. Failing to account for the repeatability of the event is tantamount to imposing an independence assumption on the occurrence of the events, which is likely to be a poor assumption. If one assumes that the first event is no different from, say, the fifth event, then one may miss important and useful information regarding the timing of the repeated event, conditional on the occurrence of past events.

The study of repeated events is an area of considerable scholarly attention, e.g., Bowman 1996; Therneau and Hamilton 1997; Wei and Glidden 1997 and associated discussions; Kelly and Lim 2000; Box-Steffensmeier and Zorn 2002; Box-Steffensmeier and DeBoef 2002. There are two general approaches. First, variance-corrected approaches estimate a model and then "fix up" the variance to account for the fact that the observations are not independent, i.e., they are repeated and therefore correlated. Second, random effects, or frailty, approaches assume that there is stochastic variation across the regression parameters that is attributable to unmeasured factors pertaining to the observation. In this section, we consider models that have been proposed for repeated events.[2] We first turn attention to variance-corrected models, and then consider random coefficient models.

Variance-Corrected Models for Repeated Events

There are three general modeling frameworks under the variance-corrected approach: Andersen-Gill (Andersen and Gill 1982); marginal (Wei, Lin, and Weissfeld 1989); and conditional (Prentice, Williams, and Peterson 1981). All three adjust the variance of the parameter estimates by clustering on subject to account for the repeated nature of the data. The hazard rate for the jth cluster and kth failure in a Cox model is

$$h_k(t) = h_o(t) \exp^{\beta' x_{kj}} .$$

If the hazard rate is allowed to vary by the kth failure in a repeated events model by the use of stratification, i.e., the data are stratified according to the kth event, then the hazard rate is given by

$$h_k(t) = h_{ok}(t) \exp^{\beta' x_{kj}}$$

---

disaggregated as much as possible and the longitudinal information and associated dependencies accounted for in our models.

[2]Some studies have dropped all repeated events (typically losing a considerable amount of observations and obviously not having a random sample left after discarding all multiple events beyond the first occurrence) and instead use only the first occurrence of an event; the repeated nature of the data set is ignored. This model makes the strong assumption that the time to the first event is representative of the time to all events and in most cases this assumption will not be justified. At a minimum this assumption deserves empirical testing, for example, by asking whether inferences markedly change when one accounts for repeated events. Unless the theoretical question is exclusively about "time to first event," such as age at first marriage, we heartily discourage dropping all repeated observations.

(see Lin 1994). Marginal and conditional models use stratification. Even with clustering, the estimates of the covariate parameters, β, are consistent in a correctly specified model; the estimated covariance matrix is incorrect because the additional correlation found in the data attributable to clustering is not taken into account (Cleves 1999, 31). Instead of using the estimated covariance matrix, which is conventionally written as $\mathbf{I}^{-1}$, a robust covariance matrix is usually substituted in models with repeated events. This matrix, as we mentioned in Chapter 7, is given by

$$V = I^{-1}G'GI^{-1},$$

where G is a matrix of the group efficient score residuals (Cleves 1999, 31; Andersen and Gill 1982; Lin 1994). The three modeling frameworks all use this kind of variance correction and are distinguished by the assumptions they make about the composition of the risk set, which is defined in the data setup.

Cook and Lawless (1997) and Lipschutz and Snapinn (1997) emphasize the importance of the theoretical risk set and careful interpretation of covariate effects based on the estimated model. Lipschutz and Snapinn focus on "two specific features of the models that can have a great impact: the event time definition and the risk set definition" (1997, 846-47). All variance corrected models except the conditional gap time model are modeling total elapsed time while the conditional gap time model uses information about the time in between events. Lipschutz and Snapinn (1997) persuasively argue that the study of elapsed time is appropriate only when the repeated events are thought to be developing simultaneously. So, if one is studying coups and the coups are developing simultaneously, perhaps because different factions are planning the coups and will act based on varying conditions, then the use of elapsed time makes theoretical sense.[3] However, if the risks develop sequentially, that is, the risk of a second coup does not begin until after the first coup has occurred, then the use of gap time is more appropriate. The choice between elapsed time and gap time is handled easily in the data setup. Table 10.1 shows that the interval variable now restarts at zero after an event occurs. For the conditional gap time model, the dependent variable is reset to zero after each event. So for company id. 3 and strata 2, the interval is (0, 3] rather than (3, 6].

The conditional model's preservation of the order of sequential events makes it an intuitively attractive alternative in contrast to the other variance

---

[3]Lipschutz and Snapinn (1997) also make the important point that total times by subject are highly correlated parameter estimates. Analyses based on total times that identify a large covariate effect for the first event will usually identify a similar effect for subsequent events, even when an analysis of gap times suggests that the covariates no longer have an effect (1997, p. 847).

corrected options (Box-Steffensmeier and Zorn 2002).[4] Recent statistical studies back up this choice as well. Kelly and Lim (2000) is an especially important study that used both simulated and actual data to evaluate four key components of event history models (risk intervals, baseline hazards, risk sets, and correlation adjustments). Their systematic study resulted in an endorsement of the use of conditional gap time models for studies of repeated events. Bowman (1996) reached similar conclusions in his study of simulated data when he compared the level of significance, power, bias, and mean squared error. The statistical debate about the best model for repeated events when using the variance corrected approach appears to be converging on a single best solution, the conditional gap time model. Thus, we focus our discussion on the conditional gap time model in the following example.

In Table 10.1, we are interested in the timing of Environmental Protection Agency (EPA) enforcement inspections. The company identification variable identifies the company that was inspected, the interval variable shows the start and stop time (or duration information), status is equal to 1 when an event (a surprise inspection) occurs, and 0 when the observation is censored. There is one covariate measuring the number of employees in the company. Finally "strata" is the event number, i.e., was it the first inspection, the second, or the third? We see from the data that companies number 3, 6, and 8 have had more than one inspection; company 3 has been inspected twice and companies 6 and 8 have been inspected once during the time frame of the study.

To estimate the conditional gap time model, we cluster on company id and stratify by event number, i.e., failure order, which allows each strata to have *its own baseline hazard rate* while the coefficients are restricted to be the same across strata. One may posit that this is important since the baseline hazard for the timing of EPA inspections may be different for the first inspection than for the third inspection, i.e., if a company has already had two inspections during the time frame of the study, perhaps due to complaints, they may be more likely to be inspected again. It is an empirical question that can easily be answered with the conditional model. In contrast, models that do not stratify by event

---

[4]The data setup and estimation of the alternative variance corrected models (the Anderson-Gill, marginal, and conditional time-from-entry) are straightforward (Cleves 1999). Another suggested approach to account for repeated events in political science has been the addition of a counter variable indicating event number (Beck, Katz, and Tucker 1998). The covariate is simply a TVC that counts the number of previous k events. There is little discussion of this model in the broader statistical literature and some claim the lack of attention reflects a healthy skepticism about the usefulness of counters (Therneau and Grambsch 2000). Wei and Glidden (1997) argue that the number of prior event occurrences *may* capture the dependence structure among recurrence times, but there is little guidance in the literature about when it might work and when it may not. An event counter introduces a rudimentary form of event dependence, by allowing the baseline hazard to increase by a set proportion with each subsequent conflict. A monotonic change across events is a strong assumption and in most cases there will be reason to believe that a simple monotonic change in the baseline hazard will not fully capture the effects of repeated events.

TABLE 10.1: "Time-from-Entry" Model Data Setup

Company Id.	Time From Previous Event (Start, Stop]	Gap Time Interval (Start, Stop]	Status/ Censoring Indicator	Number of Employees	Strata
1	(0, 6]	(0, 6]	0	10	1
2	(0, 13]	(0, 13]	0	31	1
3	(0, 3]	(0, 3]	1	25	1
3	(3, 6]	(0, 3]	1	25	2
3	(6, 10]	(0, 4]	0	25	3
4	(0, 8]	(0, 8]	0	58	1
5	(0, 15]	(0, 15]	0	6	1
6	(0, 4]	(0, 4]	1	120	1
6	(4, 9]	(0, 5]	0	120	2
7	(0, 12]	(0, 12]	0	64	1
8	(0, 11]	(0, 11]	1	44	1
8	(11, 15]	(0, 4]	0	44	2

number cannot answer this question because they assume the baseline hazard rates are the same across all events.

In the conditional model, an observation is not at risk for a later event until all prior events have occurred (Prentice et al. 1981). That is, the conditional model is based on the idea that an observation is not at risk for the kth event until the kth-1 event has occurred. Therneau and Hamilton (1997) clarify this point in the following example. Assume that events occurred on days 100 and 185 for a subject and that the subject is observed for 250 days. For the conditional models, we assume the subject cannot be at risk for the second event until the first event occurs. Hence, the observation is at risk of event 2 from day 100 to 185. In contrast, other variance corrected models, such as the marginal model, assume the subject is at risk for the first and second event from time 0 to 185 (1997, 2035).

Conditional models can be estimated separately by strata as well. This allows one to "back out" the *strata specific* coefficients (in contrast, if the models are estimated on the full data set with stratification, the hazard rate varies by strata but *one* set of coefficients for the *overall* effect of the covariates is provided). We now turn to a repeated events example.

Example 10.1: A Repeated Events Model for Militarized Intervention Data

To illustrate and interpret the conditional gap time model, we use the militarized intervention data introduced in Chapter 2 and modeled in Chapter 5 from Pearson and Baumann (1993). Table 10.2 presents the results for the conditional gap time model. Because this is a Cox model, the sign on the coefficient

TABLE 10.2: Conditional Gap Time Model for Repeated Events

Variable	Estimate (standard error)
Relative Capabilities	−.43 (.16)
Allied	.24 (.10)
Territorial Contiguity	−.25 (.11)
Intervenor Democracy	.011 (.01)
Target Democracy	.019 (.01)
Authority Breakdown	−.48 (.18)
LR Test	32.9
df	6
N	520

corresponds to the increase or decrease in the risk of an intervention terminating. Thus, a positively (negatively) signed coefficient implies shorter (longer) durations.

Figure 10.1 gives the estimated baseline hazard rate for the conditional gap time model. The figure looks considerably different from the baseline hazards figures we have seen throughout the book; previous figures for a traditional Cox model show one baseline hazard when the repeated nature of the data is ignored whereas this figure shows separate baseline hazards by event number. This difference emphasizes an advantage of the conditional models—the hazard rate is allowed to vary by event number. So the baseline hazard rate for event ten, for example, is not constrained in the conditional models to be the same as that for event one.

In Table 10.3, we give the frequency of events for each strata. One should be aware of the small number of events in the higher strata. There are three approaches to dealing with the problem of low numbers of events in higher strata (Therneau and Hamilton 1997). First, one can simply acknowledge that estimates for the higher strata have a smaller n and are therefore more unstable; second, truncate the data when the n per strata falls; third, combine the higher level strata into one (1997, 2041). The last approach is the recommended strategy, as it can restore some stability in the estimates for higher strata and does not result in the discarding of data. In the table below, grouping strata 5 and higher would be reasonable.

Frailty Models and Repeated Events Data

The second approach suggested for modeling repeated events is the frailty approach (also known as the random coefficients approach, as noted in Chapter 9).[5] The frailty model takes into account the correlation between repeated

---

[5]Fixed effects models also allow for unit-specific effects and consider repeated events as a special case of more general unit-level heterogeneity. However, the effects are a fixed quantity to be estimated and have consistency problems, e.g., Andersen, Klein, and Zhang 1999.

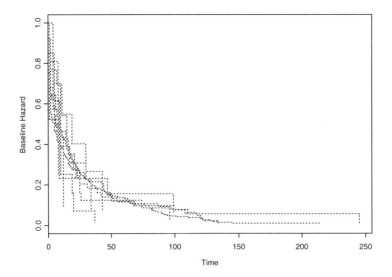

FIGURE 10.1: *This figure gives the estimated baseline hazard rate from the conditional model using the time-from-previous event.*

event times by including a random effects term in the hazard. The underlying logic of frailty models is that some observations (or groups or clusters) are intrinsically more or less prone to experiencing the event of interest than are others, and that the distribution of these individual-specific effects can be known, or at least approximated.[6] Accordingly, a specific parametric distribution is often assumed for the frailties. Because the hazards are necessarily positive, the distribution is usually chosen from the class of positive distributions; in applied work, the most widely used are the gamma and Gaussian distributions, with the gamma being by far the most frequent. In contrast to the Gaussian distribution, the gamma distribution is asymmetric, implying that although most of the observations have a frailty near zero, there is a proportion with large negative values, re: clusters of observations with exceptionally low risk (Therneau and Grambsch 2000, 234). Conditional on the chosen parametric distribution, the event times are assumed to be independent, so inference may be made in standard fashion, though robust standard errors are still used.

---

[6]Whether one expects that some observations are more likely to fail than others starts as a theoretical question. In some cases we have clear expectations that some observations are more apt to experience the event than others. If there is no good measure for this "tendency," however, we can begin to account for the frailty through statistical adjustments.

TABLE 10.3: Event Strata for Intervention Data

Strata	Frequency of Events	Percent
1	281	54.0
2	114	21.9
3	54	10.4
4	28	5.4
5	13	2.5
6	11	2.1
7	7	1.3
8	5	1.0
9	5	1.0
10	2	.4
Total	520	100.0

Oakes (1992) first proposed using an Andersen-Gill frailty model to account for the dependence of repeated events. Repeated events result in within subject variation due to having multiple observations on one subject. When these observations are combined into one analysis there is a lack of independence. The frailty model attempts to adjust for the lack of independence through the frailty parameter. A frailty model allows the underlying intensity function to depend on the number of previous events experienced by the subject (Bowman 1996, 19).

It is well known that the two approaches of variance corrected and frailty modeling sometimes lead to different empirical conclusions (Clayton 1994; Lin 1994; Gao and Zhou 1997; Klein and Moeschberger 1997; Therneau and Hamilton 1997; Wei and Glidden 1997; Hosmer and Lemeshow 1999; Kelly and Lim 2000). It remains for future research to definitively determine under which conditions the alternative modeling strategies of variance corrected versus frailty for repeated events are preferred. For now, we discuss both, emphasizing general recommendations.

Frailty models have been the target of two primary criticisms. First, neither theory nor data typically provides much guidance for imposing a specific distribution on the frailties, and "parameter estimates can be highly sensitive to the assumed parametric form of the error term" (Blossfeld and Rohwer 1995, 255). Second, the random effects are generally required to be independent of the model's covariates; failure to meet this assumption can yield estimates that are badly biased and inconsistent (Hausman 1978).

Research on how to best choose a distribution has been a popular topic since Heckman and Singer's (1984b) work, e.g., Pickles and Crouchley (1995), Sastry (1997). One suggestion is for analysts to try a number of empirical distributions and if the results are generally robust, conclusions can be drawn with more confidence. This is particularly true if the random effects model coefficients are robust when compared to those from the variance corrected

TABLE 10.4: Cox Random Effect Models for Repeated Events

Variable	Cox with Gamma Frailty Est.(s.e)	Cox with Gaussian Frailty Est.(s.e)
Power Balance	−.51 (.18)	−.48 (.17)
Alliance	.22 (.11)	.24 (.11)
Contiguity	−.32 (.12)	−.36 (.12)
Intervenor Democ.	.02 (.01)	.02 (.01)
Target Democ.	.02 (.01)	.02 (.01)
Variance of		
Random Effect	.44	.67
N	520	520

approach. In addition, Guo and Rodriguez (1992), Commenges and Andersen (1995), Xue (1998), and Andersen et al. (1999) all discuss approaches to testing for random effects that do not require specification of the unknown error term, i.e., nonparametric approaches.[7]

Table 10.4 presents the results for a random effects Cox model with gamma and Gaussian frailty using the militarized intervention data. The gamma distribution with mean one and unknown variance is the most commonly used distribution (Clayton 1978). We see that the empirical results are indeed robust across these two distributions and when compared to the conditional gap time model in Table 10.2, which eases concerns about the sensitivity of the results to the chosen frailty distribution.

The variance of the distribution of the random effects is not zero and is statistically significant at the .001 level using a Chi-square distribution for both random effect models. We conclude that the observations from the same cluster are not independent; clustering by dyad is important. The larger the variance, the greater the heterogeneity in frailty across clusters and the greater the correlation among observations in the same cluster (Sastry 1997, 30).

Using a random coefficients model is an important and promising approach for alleviating heterogeneity problems emanating from repeated events or more general sources of unknown heterogeneity. Furthermore, random coefficient models have the important advantage of being able to incorporate multilevel (or hierarchical) data structures in an event history model (Steenbergen and Jones 2002). Sastry (1997) points out that "although (nested) multilevel random effects models are often appropriate in these types of studies [durations] (Goldstein 1995), multilevel random effects models for survival analysis have been proposed only recently (Rodriguez 1994; Sargent 1996)" (1997,

---

[7]The typical risk set considered in frailty models is that of Anderson-Gill model. However, a hybrid frailty model that takes the conditional gap time model and incorporates the frailty parameter seems particularly promising because it allows heterogeneity and event dependence to be incorporated (Box-Steffensmeier and DeBoef 2002). The risk set definition and stratification of the conditional model are part of the hybrid frailty model.

426). Bandeen-Roche and Liang (1996) point out that these multilevel random coefficient models are particularly appropriate for geopolitical type data. In their study they propose clustering by households, villages, and regions. They may also be useful for addressing concerns over the dyadic focus in international relations by being able to assess the influence of national, dyadic, alliance, and regional-level variables. By incorporating regional-level variables, we can empirically assess the effects of dependence across units in space, i.e., spatial correlation. In addition to being useful for data that are naturally clustered at multiple levels, the model is also applicable to survey data collected from a hierarchically clustered sample. We now move to the problem of events that are different.

Competing Risks Models

It is not uncommon for social scientists to be interested in the occurrence (or nonoccurrence) of different kinds of events. For example, in understanding regime stability in developing countries, one may be interested in studying how long the ruling regime survives before it falls. However, the singular interest in the event of "regime falls" or "regime does not fall" may be too simplistic, or may mask other kinds of interesting information. Instead, analysts may be interested in the different *ways* in which a regime may fall. For example, it may fall because of a coup d'etat, due to an election, or from one of many kinds of causes. Diermeier and Stevenson (1999) move the extensive cabinet duration literature in exactly this direction by distinguishing "... whether the cabinet ended with a chamber dissolution or was replaced by a new cabinet without an intermediate election" (1999, 1060). Moreover, different covariates may be hypothesized to influence one kind of event occurrence, but not another. Because regimes may fall in different kinds of ways, it may be natural to consider an event history model that can account for the occurrence of different kinds of events.

Event history processes where multiple kinds of events can occur are sometimes referred to as "multi-state" processes, because it is assumed that an observation can make a transition into one of several states. This kind of process is also sometimes called a "competing risks" problem because the observation is at risk of experiencing one of several kinds of events. The nomenclature for this kind of process is inconsistent in the literature. Lancaster (1990) for example, treats the competing risks problem as a special case of a multistate process. Still others refer to such processes as multiple destination problems or dependent risks problems (although this last term can be misleading as we discuss below). For our purposes, the focus will be on the class of problems typically referred to as competing risks problems—an analysis of different kinds of events.

We discuss modeling strategies that can be used if one's research problem requires the consideration of multiple kinds of events. The competing risks model is the natural choice for this kind of problem. There have been many variants of competing risks models proposed in the literature (cf. Kalbfleisch and Prentice [1980], Allison [1982, 1984], Han and Hausman [1990], Lancaster [1990], Sueyoshi [1992], Hill et al. [1993], Collett [1994], Petersen [1995], Therneau and Grambsch [2000], Crowder [2001], Gordon [2002]), each varying in terms of the assumptions made regarding the dependency of the competing events and how the composition of the risk set is compiled. To motivate the models of this section, consider how the hazard rate can be expressed in terms of competing risks. We will assume that there are $K, k = 1, 2, \ldots r$ possible events that an observation is at risk of experiencing. Sometimes, these K events are referred to as "destinations" or states to which an observation can make a transition. Accounting for the K events in the hazard rate gives

$$h_k(t \mid \mathbf{x}) = \lim_{\Delta t \to 0} \frac{\Pr(t \leq T \leq t + \Delta t \mid T \geq t, \mathbf{x})}{\Delta t}, \tag{10.1}$$

which differs from the hazard rate for a single-state process because the rate is subscripted for each of the k events that could occur. As such, models used for competing risks problems typically model the type-specific hazard rate. Note that the hazard rate expressed in (10.1) does not condition on the state occupied prior to the occurrence of the kth event. As such, this model presumes that all observations occupy the same state and progress through time until one of k possible events are experienced. As an example, in the analysis of legislative careers, we may be interested in understanding the "type-specific" factors (or covariates) that lead to different kinds of career termination, for example electoral defeat, retirement, or pursuing higher office. At the start of a career, all legislators are occupying the same "state space" in that they are currently holding office. Over time, the risk set will decrease as members' careers terminate for one of several reasons, such as death, scandal, or retirement. The duration model for this kind of problem would specify each of the k destinations or outcomes as a function of covariates. Further, the covariates need not be the same across the k outcomes.

As an alternative way to express the hazard rate in (10.1), Petersen (1995) conditions the hazard rate on the state the observation is occupying immediately prior to the occurrence of the k event. This rate is given by

$$h_k(t \mid \mathbf{x}, k^-) = \lim_{\Delta t \to 0} \frac{\Pr(t \leq T \leq t + \Delta t \mid T \geq t, \mathbf{x})}{\Delta t}, \tag{10.2}$$

where k^- represents the state that is occupied prior to the transition (or occurrence of an event). As an example of a process where accounting for the previously occupied state might be of interest, suppose we were studying the duration of time that an electoral district supports a political party in a multiparty system. If there are 3 political parties in the system, then after an

election, an electoral district is "at risk" of switching support to 1 of the 2
other parties in subsequent elections. Thus, the state of support the district is
in immediately after an election determines the destination states to which a
transition can be made. Models that account for the rates of transition to the
other destinations, conditional on the currently occupied state, are sometimes
referred to as "destination-specific" hazard models (Petersen 1995). Under certain conditions (which are discussed directly), deriving models for these kinds
of processes is reasonably straightforward. In the remainder of this section,
we consider some modeling strategies that can accommodate the complication
posed by competing risks kinds of problems.

Latent Survivor Time Approach to Competing Risks

A commonly applied approach to the competing risks problem assumes that
there are $K, k = 1, 2, \ldots r$ specific outcomes or destination states and that
there is assumed to exist a *potential* or latent failure time associated with each
outcome. Hence, for K outcomes, there are theoretically $T_k = (T_1, T_2, \ldots, T_r)$
duration times but only the shortest duration time is actually observed; that is,
$T_k = \min\{T_1, T_2, \ldots, T_r\} = T_C$, where T_C is the duration time associated
with observed event or "cause" of failure (Crowder 2001). As Crowder (2001)
notes, "once the system has failed, the remaining lifetimes are lost to observation" (p. 38). Hence, the remaining failure times are latent, but are assumed to
exist.

   The appeal of this approach is that it is reasonably straightforward to implement, albeit some important assumptions have to be made. The basic result
that drives the model is that if there are k specific outcome states, then the
overall survivor function can be partitioned into marginal survivor functions,
each corresponding to one of the k destination states. In turn, the overall likelihood function can be partitioned into the product of the k-specific likelihoods.
To see this, suppose that there are n observations at risk of failing in one of
k ways. The individual contribution of the ith individual failing by event k is
given by

$$\mathcal{L}_i = f_k(t_i \mid X_{ik}, \beta_k) \prod_{k \neq r} S_r(t_i \mid X_{ir}, \beta_r),$$

where the subscript k denotes the kth event and r in the product term implies
that the product is taken over the survivor times for all states except k. The
likelihood function for the full sample is then given by

$$\mathcal{L} = \prod_{i=1}^{n} f_k(t_i \mid X_{ik}, \beta_k) \prod_{k=1}^{r} S_k(t_i \mid X_{ik}, \beta_k).$$

However, since only T_C is observed (i.e. only one failure among the K possible
outcomes is observed), the overall likelihood can be partitioned in terms of the

number of observations failing by each of the K outcomes:

$$\mathcal{L} = \prod_{k=1}^{r} \prod_{i=1}^{n_k} f_k(t_i \mid X_{ik}, \beta_k) S_k(t_i \mid X_{ik}, \beta_j).$$

This partitioning is easier to see if we define a censoring indicator such that

$$\delta_{ik} = \begin{cases} 1 & \text{if } i \text{ failed due to } k \\ 0 & \text{otherwise} \end{cases}$$

When $\delta_i = 1$, the observation is observed failing due to risk k (and hence we only observe T_C); when $\delta_i = 0$, the observation is right-censored. Incorporating δ_{ik} into the likelihood function, the likelihood of the sampled duration times may be expressed as

$$\mathcal{L} = \prod_{k=1}^{r} \prod_{i=1}^{n} f_k(t_i \mid X_{ik}, \beta_k)^{\delta_{ik}} S_k(t_i \mid X_{ik}, \beta_j)^{1-\delta_{ik}}. \tag{10.3}$$

The basic idea here is that the overall likelihood function factors into k sub-contributions, where failures due to risks other than k are treated as right-censored. In turn, $k-$specific hazards (or sub-hazards, as they are sometimes called [Crowder 2001]) can be generated from equation (10.3). Implementation of this model is straightforward because it simply requires that K models be estimated where all events other than k are treated as randomly censored. For example, if there are three possible destination states, then three *single* state models are estimated where events due to the other two events are treated as right-censored. The latent variables approach has been extended to both the parametric and semi-parametric (i.e. Cox model) setting (see David and Moeschberger 1978; see also Hougaard 2000 and Crowder 2001).

For this model, the assumption must be made that the K risks are conditionally independent. That is, given the covariates, the survival times for risk k are independent of the survival times for risk r. If this assumption cannot be sustained, then the assumption of random or ignorable censoring on the remaining r events cannot hold. Moreover, the theoretical assumption must be made that any of the K possible events *could have* occurred had the clock just kept "ticking" long enough. Given these assumptions, the modeling approach outlined above seems to be an attractive approach to handling the problem of competing risks. For a nice application using this approach, we recommend Diermeier and Stevenson (1999). We illustrate this approach to the competing risks model with an application on U.S. House careers.

Example 10.2: Competing Risks Model of Congressional Careers

In this application, we revisit the data set on the duration of U.S. House members' legislative careers (Jones 1994). These data were examined in Chapter 5

TABLE 10.5: Cox Competing Risks Model of Congressional Careers

	Pooled	General	Primary	Retire	Ambition
Party	.04 (.08)	−.20 (.13)	−.13 (.27)	.20 (.14)	.31 (.15)
Redistrict	1.42 (.21)	1.11 (.31)	.98 (.55)	1.00 (.32)	1.31 (.32)
Scandal	1.55 (.26)	2.35 (.37)	2.61 (.43)	.62 (.40)	−
Open Gub.	.22 (.10)	.09 (.16)	.18 (.32)	.03 (.17)	.47 (.16)
Open Sen.	.30 (.11)	−.25 (.21)	−.47 (.44)	.04 (.21)	.99 (.16)
Leadership	−.51 (.27)	−.69 (.56)	−	−.13 (.31)	−.71 (1.03)
Age	.03 (.01)	.03 (.01)	.03 (.02)	.08 (.009)	−.06 (.01)
Prior Margin	−.02 (.01)	−.06 (.01)	−.00 (.00)	−.01 (.003)	.001 (.003)
Log-Likelihood	−2131.80	−921.31	−303.88	−839.43	−808.78
N	5399	5399 (284)	5399 (66)	5399 (247)	5399 (216)

Data are from Jones 1994. Coefficients are Cox estimates (based on the conditional logit formulation). The first column provides estimates for the pooled model; the last four columns give the event-specific estimates. The number of events for each k risk is given in parentheses.

and Chapter 7. In previous applications, the event of interest was whether or not a U.S. House member's career ended due to electoral defeat; however, there are conceivably many ways in which a legislative career can end. Specifically, members can leave office on their own terms, through retirement or through the decision to seek alternative office, which we refer to as "ambition" (see Rohde 1979). These kind of events denote "voluntary termination," as the member is opting out of the House, rather than seeking reelection. Moreover, a member can *lose* office in two distinct ways: in the general election and in the primary election. Simply treating career termination as a function of electoral defeat ignores the fact that there are many ways members exit office. Because of this, a competing risks model may be appropriate as there are 4 distinct ways a House career can end.

To illustrate the approach discussed in this section, we first estimated a "standard" single event model where we did not discriminate among the various risks. Hence, the event is career termination of any type. In this sense, each of the 4 risks are pooled. In contrast, we estimated a competing risks model using the approach discussed above. A Cox model was applied in both cases. The results are shown in Table 10.5. The first column, labeled "pooled," gives the results from the single-event model; the remaining four columns give the Cox estimates of the type-specific hazards. The labels on the columns correspond to each of the four ways in which a career can terminate.

Eight covariates are included in the model. The covariates denoting party identification, redistricting, scandal, leadership, and prior electoral margin were defined in Chapter 7. The covariates denoted as "Open Gub." and "Open Sen." denote whether or not there was an open gubernatorial or open U.S. Senatorial seat available during the election cycle. These two covariates are used to account for the opportunity structure for higher-office seeking, or "ambition." Rohde (1979) has shown these two factors strongly influence ambition decisions. Also included as a covariate in the model is the incumbent's age. Presumably, the risk of retirement is most strongly related to the age of the incumbent. A variety of functional forms were tested for the age covariate using martingale residuals (Chapter 8) and likelihood ratio tests and the linear term provided the best fit.

In comparing the pooled Cox results to the competing risks estimates, it is clear that the two approaches yield different results regarding the impact a covariate has on career termination. While in most cases, the signs on the coefficients from the pooled model are the same in the sub-models, the pooled results cannot (obviously) distinguish among event types and so represent a sort of "average" effect across the four event types. In the competing risks model, however, we obtain more refined estimates on how a covariate relates to a *particular* risk. For example, the impact of scandal is much higher for the risks of electoral defeat (primary or general) but has less of a relationship to the risk of retirement. That is, scandal moderately increases the risk of retirement but strongly increases the risk of electoral defeat. Scandal-plagued members who pledge to "stay in and fight" face a substantial increase in the risk of losing. The "−" symbol for the risk of ambition indicates that the coefficient tended to infinity and was unreported: there were no cases where a scandal-plagued incumbent sought higher office (this symbol is also used in place of the estimate of the leadership covariate on defeats in primaries, as there were almost no cases where a member in the leadership lost in a primary).

In regard to an incumbent's age, we see that for retirement, each 1 year increase in age is associated with about an 8 percent increase in the risk of retirement; however, for "ambition," a 1 year increase in age is associated with about a 6 percent *decrease* in the risk of exiting the House to seek higher office. In the pooled model, the relationship between age and career termination is moderately positive and suggests an increase in age by 1 year increases the risk of career termination (due to any type) by about 3 percent. The overall relationship between age and career termination is demonstrated much more clearly in the competing risks model.

In general, the competing risks estimates reveal considerably more information about the process of career termination than that given by the pooled model. To illustrate further differences between the pooled and competing risks model, we computed the baseline hazard estimates and graphed them. These graphs are shown in Figure 10.2. In the upper left panel, the baseline hazard from the pooled model is presented. The graph is suggestive that the hazard of career termination is rising over time. However, the sub-baseline hazards tell a different story. For defeat in the general election, the risk seems to decline over time; for primary defeats, the baseline hazard is very noisy (and

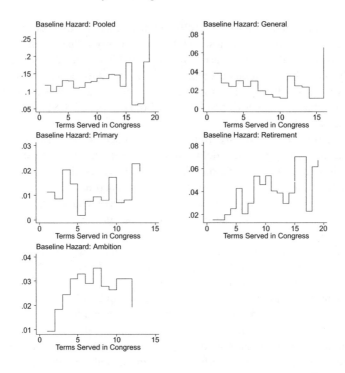

FIGURE 10.2: *This figure graphs the estimated baseline hazard rates from a Cox competing risks model of career termination. The top left panel is based on the pooled model; the top right panel is based on losing in the general election. The middle left panel is based on losing in the primary election. The middle right panel is based on retirement. The bottom left panel is based on exits due to seeking higher office.*

is most likely flat); for the risk of retirement, the baseline hazard generally increases; and for the risk of ambition, the baseline hazard seems to rise and then fall, suggesting the risk is nonmonotonic with respect to time.

As is standard with Cox estimates of the baseline hazards, they are highly adapted to the observed data. If the baseline hazard functions were of critical importance to the analyst, then Cox alternatives might be preferred. The extension of this kind of competing risks model to the parametric setting is straightforward. In the next section, we consider a complementary approach to addressing competing risks problem through the use of a standard logit model.

Multinomial Logit Approach to Competing Risks

In Chapter 5, we discussed how parameters for event history models could be estimated using a logit model. A straightforward extension of the ideas presented in Chapter 5 leads to the consideration of a *multinomial logit* model for competing risks problems (Allison 1982; Yamaguchi 1990). The multinomial logit (hereafter MNL) model is essentially a series of "linked" logit models. So if there are k possible events (destinations, outcomes, states) that an observation is at risk of experiencing, the MNL model estimates $k - 1$ logit models to obtain parameter estimates on the type-specific or destination-specific hazards (in the latter case, one would first condition on the state occupied at the start time of the analysis). The $k - 1$ logits produced by the MNL model are interpretable as logit models. To see this more clearly, note that the hazard probability for the MNL model is

$$\lambda_{(ik)} = \frac{\exp \beta_k' \mathbf{x}}{\sum_k^K \exp(\beta_k' \mathbf{x_i})}. \tag{10.4}$$

To identify the model, the parameter estimates for an arbitrarily chosen baseline category are taken as 0. Thus, if there are $k = 3$ possible outcomes, then the type specific hazard probabilities from the multinomial logit model are given by

$$\lambda(y_i = 1 \mid \mathbf{x}_i) = \lambda_{i1} = \frac{1}{1 + \exp(\beta_2' \mathbf{x_i}) + \exp(\beta_3' \mathbf{x_i})},$$

for the baseline category ($k = 1$),

$$\lambda(y_i = 2 \mid \mathbf{x}_i) = \lambda_{i2} = \frac{\exp(\beta_2' \mathbf{x_i})}{1 + \exp \beta_2' \mathbf{x_i} + \exp \beta_3' \mathbf{x_i}},$$

for $k = 2$, and

$$\lambda(y_i = 3 \mid \mathbf{x}_i) = \lambda_{i3} = \frac{\exp(\beta_3' \mathbf{x_i})}{1 + \exp \beta_2' \mathbf{x_i} + \exp \beta_3' \mathbf{x_i}},$$

for $k = 3$ (where y_i denotes the outcome variable). The form of (10.4) is clearly similar to the logit model for single-state processes presented in Chapter 5. Sometimes the MNL model is referred to as a "baseline category logit" model. This is the case because there are $k - 1$ nonredundant logit equations that are referenced to the baseline category (Agresti 1990). As a method to account for complications posed by competing risks, the MNL model is an attractive choice for much the same reasons the binary logit model is chosen in the context of single-way transition models. It may be estimated by maximum likelihood and the parameters are interpretable as logit coefficients. To illustrate the use of the MNL model for a competing risks problem, we present an application.

TABLE 10.6: Competing Risks Model of Congressional Career Paths

	General	Primary	Retire	Ambition
Party	−.18 (.13)	−.11 (.26)	.18 (.14)	.31 (.15)
Redistrict	1.37 (.35)	1.42 (.59)	1.36 (.28)	1.55 (.31)
Scandal	2.61 (.37)	3.10 (.44)	1.09 (.41)	−
Open Gub.	.12 (.16)	.20 (.31)	.04 (.17)	.49 (.16)
Open Sen.	−.21 (.21)	−.42 (.44)	.07 (.21)	1.01 (.16)
Leadership	−.60 (.54)	−	−.39 (.30)	−1.53 (1.03)
Age	.04 (.01)	.04 (.02)	.08 (.01)	−.06 (.01)
Prior Margin	−.06 (.01)	−.005 (.01)	−.01 (.003)	.00 (.00)
$\log(T)$	−.26 (.09)	−.06 (.20)	.53 (.12)	.51 (.12)
Constant	−3.13 (.38)	−6.15 (.75)	−7.89 (.50)	−1.14 (.41)
Log-Likelihood	−2972.58			
N	5399			

Example 10.3: MNL Competing Risks Model of Congressional Careers

We apply the discrete-time formulation of the competing risks model using the MNL estimator discussed above. The data in this application is identical to that used in Example 10.2. Of interest is modeling the type-specific hazards of career termination. The model estimated in this application is identical to the model discussed in Example 10.2. The only additional covariate is a measure of time dependency. For this illustration, we included the natural log of the number of terms to account for any duration dependency in the data.[8] The type-specific hazard estimates are given in Table 10.6. As the coefficients are interpretable as logit coefficients, the estimates give the log-odds of event k occurring for a unit change in the covariate.

To interpret estimates, it is often useful to convert the log-odds coefficients to odds ratios by exponentiating them. For example, we see that the odds of seeking higher office when there is an open Senatorial seat is about 2.75 times higher than when there is no open seat. For termination due to retirement, we see that for a one year increase in the incumbent's age, the odds of retirement increase by about 1.08, or 8 percent. It is worth pointing out that the estimates in Table 10.6, while similar to the estimates in Table 10.5, do differ by a fair amount on some of the covariates. This is the case because the reference category in the multinomial logit model is the "0" category, which denotes the "non-event" of the incumbent winning election. The reference category, so to speak, in the competing risks model of the previous section is comprised of all other outcomes except the event of interest. Given the assumption of random censoring, any outcome other than outcome k is treated as randomly censored. The logit analog to this type of model would be to estimate 4 stand-alone logits where the reference category was comprised of every event except the one

[8]Other functional forms were tested and based on likelihood ratio tests, the log transformation provided the best fit.

being directly modeled. In the MNL approach, we are essentially estimating the equivalent of 4 stand-alone logits *but* where the baseline category is getting reelected.

This application illustrates how the MNL model can be used to account for the occurrence of multiple kinds of events. The choice of the MNL would seem attractive for many problems of interest. Moreover, since the relevant statistical theory underlying this model is a direct extension of the binary logit model—a model which social scientists routinely work with—the use and interpretation of the MNL model in the context of the competing risks problem is reasonably straightforward. However, the MNL model makes certain assumptions regarding independence of the competing risks (which are similar to the assumptions made in the previous section). We will return to the problem of dependent risks shortly.

The two approaches to addressing the competing risks problem are attractive insofar as event-specific estimates of the covariates can be obtained with relative ease (under a host of assumptions). However, there may be some applications where one has competing risks data but has no particular reason or theory to expect that the covariates act differently on the k possible outcomes. In the next section, we discuss the use of a stratified Cox model to account for competing risks in this kind of situation. Additionally, this model assumes that multiple k events can be experienced by an observation.

Stratified Cox Approach to Competing Risks

In the models discussed in the previous sections, the assumption was made that once one of the k events was experienced, the observation exited the risk set and was no longer at risk of experiencing the remaining $k - 1$ events. Indeed, this assumption gave rise to the latent variable approach: since only 1 outcome is observed, only the shortest failure time is observed, even though it is assumed that the observation was at risk of experiencing any of the k events. In the congressional careers example, this implies that once a career ends in any given way, the member is no longer at risk of experiencing the other events because the process of interest—the career—has terminated. In other social science problems, however, this kind of process may not hold. Fortunately, accommodating this kind of competing risk problem is straightforward. To elaborate, suppose there are $k = 5$ possible (unordered) events that could occur to an observation. Because there are no restrictions on when and how many of these 5 events an observation can experience, we must assume that *for each* of the 5 events, the observation is at risk for all of them. Hence, the data structure will consist of multiple records per observation with each observation having at minimum 5 records of data—one for each possible event. The point is, since we assume each of the k events can be experienced (which is in contrast to the congressional careers application), the data setup requires a unique record of data for each of the competing risks. In Table 10.7, we give an example

TABLE 10.7: Example of Data for a Competing Risks Model

Case Id.	Event Time	Event Status	Event Type
1	6	1	1
1	8	1	3
1	11	1	5
1	14	0	2
1	14	0	4
2	2	1	5
2	14	0	1
2	14	0	2
2	14	0	3
2	14	0	4

of competing risks data set up in this way. The first five records correspond to case 1. We see at time 6, this case experienced an event (event status = 1) and that event was of type 1. At time 8, this observation then experienced event type 3. By the last observation period, time 14, the observation still had not experienced events 2 and 4. Case 2 in the table only experienced 1 of the 5 events and that was at time 2. This case went the remainder of the study without experiencing any kind of event.

If one assumes that the covariate effects are common to each event type, but the baseline hazard for each risk is allowed to vary across risks, then a stratified Cox model can be used to estimate the parameters of interest. The stratified Cox model, in this context, would estimate a single set of parameters for each of the event types. However, if one stratifies on the different kinds of events ($k = 5$), then one can back out of the stratified Cox model a unique baseline hazard function for each of the k risks. This approach to the competing risks problem may be appropriate for many kinds of competing risks problems that emerge in social science, especially where the occurrence of an event does not imply the observation exits the sample. Below, we present an illustration.

Example 10.4: State Adoption of Restrictive Abortion Legislation Using a Stratified Cox Model

To illustrate the stratified Cox approach, we reconsider the data discussed earlier in the book on states' adoption of restrictive abortion legislation in the wake of *Roe v. Wade*. In previous illustrations using these data, the event of interest was singularly defined: adoption of legislation limiting abortion rights. However, as Brace and Langer (2001) note, there are several kinds of restrictive abortion laws that a state could adopt. Specifically, states can adopt laws that: 1) require informed consent; 2) require parental consent; 3) require spousal consent; and 4) limit funding for abortions.

TABLE 10.8: Cox Competing Risks Model for Policy Adoption

Variable	Competing Risks Cox Model Estimate (s.e.)	Standard Cox Model Estimate (s.e.)
Mooney Index	−.20 (.07)	−.19 (.07)
South	.61 (.28)	.49 (.28)
State Ideology	−.02 (.01)	−.02 (.01)
Log-Likelihood	−520.14	−673.17
N	2554	2554

For this application, we assume that each state is at risk of adopting any of these four kinds of policies and further, no assumption is made that once a state adopts one of the five policies, it exits the risk set. As such, a state can adopt all of the policy types (or none, if it is fully right-censored). In our model of policy adoption, three covariates are considered. The first is a dummy variable denoting whether or not the state was in the South; the second is the Mooney index of pre-*Roe* abortion attitudes (described in Chapter 6); and the third is a measure of "average" state ideology. This score is based on the average of the ideology score of the state, the state Supreme Court, and the public (see Brace and Langer 2001 for more details). The measure is scored such that higher values denote more liberal states and lower values denote more conservative states. The results from the stratified Cox model are presented in Table 10.8, column 1. The model was estimated using the event type as the stratification variable.

Note that for this model, we have a single set of coefficient estimates. The idea here is that the covariates are the same across event types *but* that the baseline hazard is allowed to vary by event type. Hence, through stratification we can account for any heterogeneity that may arise due to differences in the baseline hazards of the various risks. From the model, we see that state ideology is negatively related to the hazard of adopting restrictive abortion legislation. The more liberal a state is, the longer it takes for a state to adopt restrictive abortion legislation. The hazard of adopting restrictive abortion legislation is almost twice that of non-Southern states. Finally, regarding the Mooney index, we find that states which were more permissive regarding abortion rights prior to the 1973 Supreme Court decision have a lower risk (about 18 percent lower) of subsequently adopting restrictive abortion legislation after the broadly written *Roe vs. Wade* decision.

To see how the baseline hazards vary by policy type, we computed them from the Cox estimates and graphed them. They are shown in Figure 10.3. The first four panels in the figure correspond to the baseline hazards for each of the four policy types. The top left panel gives the estimates for informed consent. The baseline hazard suggests that the risk is rising slightly over time. The top right panel gives the estimates for parental consent policies. The risk of this event type, too, is also rising slightly over time. The policy types corresponding to limiting funding and spousal consent (the middle two graphs) yield a relatively flat baseline hazard. For both of these policy types, few states have adopted laws this restrictive. The sharp rise at the end of the baseline hazard for spousal consent is due to a single state adopting such a law some 20 years after the *Roe v. Wade* decision.

Finally, the second column of Table 10.3 gives the estimates from an unstratified Cox model. We see that by ignoring the heterogeneity in the baseline hazards associated with the distinct policy outcomes, the unstratified Cox model understates the impact of the south variable. Moreover, the stratified model provides a better fit to the data based on the AIC criteria. Hence, between the stratified and unstratified estimates, we would choose to report the results from the competing risks model. To further compare the stratified estimates of the baseline hazards to the unstratified estimates, the bottom right panel graphs the baseline hazard from the unstratified Cox model of policy adoption. We can see that the unstratified model's baseline hazard suggests a relatively flat hazard over time. However, because we have some evidence that the hazard for parental consent and informed consent are rising, the model allowing the baseline hazards to vary by event type is preferable to the unstratified Cox model.

This variant of the Cox competing risks model would seem most naturally applied when a researcher had little reason to expect covariate effects to appreciably vary across event types. This expectation, of course, will not always hold. If one believes the relationship between a covariate and the hazard varies across event types (for example, it is negatively related to one kind of risk, positively related to another), then the modeling approaches discussed in the previous two sections would seem appropriate. However, as noted above, these models are conditional independence models. If the risks are dependent, then an alternative modeling strategy may be necessary. In the next section, we consider the issue of dependent risks.

Dependent Risks

Consider the multinomial logit approach where it is assumed that, conditional on the covariates, the ratio of the probabilities of any two alternatives is independent of each of the other alternatives. This assumption is known as the independence of irrelevant alternatives, or IIA, assumption. In the context of the competing risks problem, it implies that the hazards for each of the k events are independent (Hill, Axinn, and Thornton 1993). There are a wide variety of statistical procedures to test for the validity of the IIA assumption, see for example Hausman and McFadden (1984),Small and Hsiao (1985), or Zhang and Hoffman (1993). If the assumption of independent risks does not hold, then an

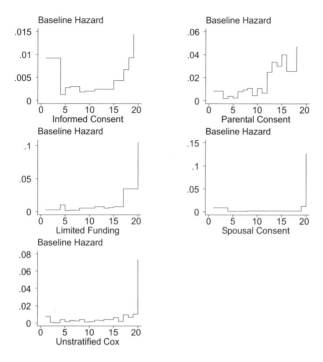

FIGURE 10.3: *This figure gives the estimated baseline hazard rate from the stratified Cox competing risk model. The first 4 panels correspond to the four event types. The last panel gives the baseline hazard from the unstratified Cox model.*

alternative modeling strategy may be necessary. Such modeling strategies may require the consideration of "dependent risks."

Extending the discussion beyond the MNL model, if one's research problem leads to the consideration of dependent risks, then a natural question to explore is why the risks might be dependent. In some sense, dependent risks is a specification problem. The factors producing the correlated hazards are often not observed or are difficult to explicitly take into account (or measure). Hill, Axinn, and Thornton (1993) refer to such factors as "shared unmeasured risk factors." They argue such conditions as unobserved frailty (or the propensity to experience certain events at higher rates) or unmeasured covariates can lead to correlated competing risks, or dependent risks. If a researcher can determine and then measure these underlying risk factors that produce dependent risks, then accounting for them explicitly in a model can mitigate or even eliminate the problem of dependent risks, since the dependence is conditional on the covariates.

Nevertheless, in some applications, dependent risks may be an issue that needs to be addressed, especially if the relevant covariates that would "explain" the dependency are unobserved or unknown. A variety of models for dependent risks have been proposed, though interestingly, there are few applications in the social sciences where dependent risks problems have been explicitly considered. We discuss some of the approaches that have been proposed.

Han and Hausman (1990) propose the estimation of a dependent competing risks model through the use of a bivariate cumulative (ordered) probit model with an additional parameter indicating the degree of correlation between *two* competing outcomes. The baseline hazard in the Han and Hausman (1990) model is unrestricted and so it can take any form for the k events. This approach is useful because no parametric assumptions are made regarding the shape of the underlying hazard, although the covariates are parameterized in terms of the bivariate normal. The model proceeds by assuming there are $K = 2$ competing risks, but that the competing outcomes may be dependent (i.e. correlated). For each risk, a stochastic disturbance term, ϵ_1 and ϵ_2, is defined and the correlation between these two terms is estimated. The data setup for the Han and Hausman model requires that T be decomposed into $t = 1, 2, \ldots, T$ discrete periods. To get estimates of the risk dependence, a bivariate ordinal probit model is then estimated where the dependent variable in the model is the ordered time periods.

The Han and Hausman model has not been widely applied. This is primarily due to two reasons. First, the model as presented in their 1990 article is restricted to two competing outcomes. Extensions beyond $K = 2$ would require the use of numerical methods of Gibbs sampling techniques. Second, most commercial software packages do not have canned routines to estimate the Han and Hausman competing risks model.[9] The basic idea behind the Han and Hausman model is very similar to recently proposed models that adopt the frailty modeling approach to the competing risks problem.

Under the frailty model, it is assumed that observations (or subgroups) in a data set have unobserved "frailties" making them more prone to failure. Because the factors producing these frailties are often unknown or unmeasured, an additional variance term (or heterogeneity term) is added to the duration model to account for the observation-level or group-level heterogeneity that may exist in the data. In the context of the competing risks problem, we noted previously that it is often assumed individuals in a study are at risk of experiencing *any* of K distinct events; however, because only the minimum of the K latent duration times are observed, we only observe the "first" event, even though the individual is presumably at risk of experiencing any of the K outcomes.

---

[9]It is worth pointing out that Han and Hausman also propose use of the ordered probit (logit) approach for single state duration models. Implementation of their model in standard software packages is very easy: estimate an ordered probit or ordered logit model. The resulting model is equivalent to their flexible parametric model proposed in their 1990 article.

Because of the shared risk an observation has of experiencing the K events, there may be dependency among the risks. This is equivalent to saying that the observed duration time for event k is related to the unobserved, or latent survival times, of the remaining $K - 1$ risks. The implication is that each of the K risks may be correlated. Because of this problem, some researchers have proposed the use of frailty modeling techniques to directly estimate the extra variance (i.e. the frailty variance) and the correlation among the frailties. Notably, Gordon (2002) proposes a parametric bivariate competing risks model where the risk-specific frailties are jointly estimated along with the frailty correlation. This correlation can then be used to assess the degree of dependency between the competing risks. The principal issue in implementing Gordon's model is estimation. Unlike the frailty models discussed in Chapter 9, there is no analytical solution for the marginal survivor function (i.e. the "expected" survival function that is obtained after integrating out the frailty) in the Gordon model. Instead, numerical methods or MCMC procedures are necessary to derive the expected survival function. Approaches similar to Gordon's (2002) work have been proposed by Gelfand et al. (2000).

As is suggested by our discussion to this point, estimation of dependent risks model is, in many settings, difficult. As noted, the principal difficulty stems from the fact that often, analytical solutions are unavailable. For researchers interested in applying such models to their problem, this can pose a high hurdle as it requires use of techniques (and understanding of such techniques) that are not (yet) widely used in social science. Moreover, most of the work applying frailty models to the competing risks problem has tended to be developed in the context of $K = 2$ risks. While both the Han and Hausman model and the approach suggested by Gordon are extendable to the $K > 2$ case, the estimation problem gets more difficult as more random coefficients (i.e. the variances and covariances of the frailties) must be estimated. Work in this area is rapidly developing, however.[10]

Conclusion

The models presented in this chapter substantially extend the scope of event history analysis beyond the single-spell models that are typically used by social scientists. Moreover, the occurrence of multiple kinds of events (whether in the form of competing risks or repeatable events) is common to many of the kinds of processes social scientists study. The types of models discussed

---

[10]It should be noted that questions about the identifiability of dependent risks models have been perennial in the literature (see Bagai and Rao [1992] and Kuk and Chen [1992]). Han and Hausman (1990) argue that under mild regularity conditions, the dependent risks problem is identified, and Sueyoshi (1992), extending the work of Han and Hausman (1992), demonstrates identifiability of the dependent competing risks problems with the inclusion of TVCs.

here also represent the frontiers of research on extensions of the event history model. In particular, refinements to the application of the frailty (or random coefficients) approach to competing risks and repeated events problems is on-going. However, apart from the frailty approaches discussed here (which constitute only a portion of the possible modeling strategies available to the analyst), there are a wide variety of well known and well understood models that can sensibly be applied to problems dealing with multiple kinds of events. As these models become more developed, we encourage and strongly recommend that social scientists begin to think more directly about what constitutes an event. As event history processes are more explicitly defined, use of the models discussed in this chapter will become more widespread. In the concluding chapter, we make specific recommendations regarding the use of event history methods.

CHAPTER 11

The Social Sciences and
Event History

It has been our intent to demonstrate how the multitude of methods discussed in this book are naturally relevant for social science analysis. We have stressed throughout that many of the problems, hypotheses, and theories underlying social science research have at their core an implicit or explicit interest in the notions of timing and social change. Event history models are ideally suited for such problems. Given the kinds of questions social scientists ask and the applicability of event history analysis, the models we have considered would seem to have great import for analysis.

We have presented a number of examples of event history analysis with social science data that highlight the interest in both the occurrence of an event and the history leading up to the event. Moving from a focus solely on whether an event occurred to additionally considering *when* an event occurred can result in much greater analytical leverage on the problem at hand. Similarly, moving from the study of how *often* an event occurs, for example through the use of event count models, to how often *and when* an event occurred, for example through the use of a repeated events model, can have analytical payoffs.

Based on the interest in social science theory regarding longitudinal processes, and given the inherent problems of traditional models in handling event history data, we hope readers recognize that event history models are a valuable method for addressing substantive social science problems. As such, application of event history models should be a matter of course when one has a substantive problem that requires the comparative analysis of longitudinal data. Since these problems abound in social science, the event history model is a natural model.

In the remainder of this chapter, we review some of the major topics considered in this book and make some suggestions for the direction event history analysis should take within the broader field of social science methodology. To provide some context for these recommendations, we first highlight some issues that emerge in the application of event history analysis to social science data.

Common Problems in the Analysis of Social Science Event History Data

Clearly much of the important work that we have drawn upon in this book emanates directly from biostatistics and medical statistics (cf. Collett [1994], Therneau and Grambsch [2000], Hougaard [2000], and many others). Yet it is important to point out that social scientists must deal quite often with problems that are not so prevalent in these sciences. In this section, we discuss some of these problems and then make some suggestions as to how to deal with them.

The "Patient Never Dies"

One immediate observation comes to mind when thinking about the application of duration modeling methods to social data. For many longitudinal processes of interest to social scientists, what it means to "exit the risk set" is not always so obvious. To explain, in the application of survival analysis to medical data, it is frequently the case that patients or recruits to a study are examined over time and the effectiveness of a treatment, for example a drug, on the onset of an illness is of primary interest. In such settings, patients are studied to examine how long they survive until an event occurs (where the event may be death, the diagnosis of a particular condition, response to some treatment, and so forth). Typically, in such studies, when an event (or events) of interest occurs, the subject exits the risk set and "leaves" the study. However, for many problems social scientists are interested in, observations are continually at risk; that is to say, observations *never* "exit the risk set."

For example, in the analysis of international conflict, dyads, or country pairs, are presumably *always* at risk of engaging in a conflict. Consequently, data on conflict processes are routinely characterized with repeated (and sometimes numerous) events occurring between countries (recall Table 2.2 from Chapter 2). Similar issues emerge in cross-national or cross-regional data used in comparative politics research. In analyses of regime change, for example, it is quite likely that some subset of countries are perennially at risk of fostering a regime change: regimes may fall many times. The basic point here is that event history analysis of social science data frequently will have to address the fundamental problem that the "patient" never dies, so to speak.

Unfortunately, analysts frequently proceed by implicitly assuming that once some event of interest is experienced, the observation does exit the risk set, even though it may remain at risk indefinitely. Indeed, as we noted in Chapter 10, it is very common for analysts to treat events that occur repeatedly *as if* they were stand-alone processes: once a conflict between country X

and country Y terminates, subsequent conflicts between X and Y are treated anew. Assuming a single-spell process makes estimation of duration models very easy as it avoids the complications posed by the occurrence of multiple events. Yet this approach is problematic. Since the "patient"—the dyad, for example—remains perpetually at risk, these complications not only arise but are, presumably, of substantive interest to researchers.

Ignoring the repeatability of events induces a strong and probably wrong assumption that past and future events are independent of each other. This independence assumption is precisely the assumption that is made when we treat processes leading to repeated events as if they are stand-alone or isolated processes. This is probably not the best place to start modeling efforts. Explicit consideration of the repeated events problem through the use of the models discussed in Chapter 10 seems an obvious recommendation to address this sort of problem. Put another way, the recommended default modeling strategy should be the use of repeated event type methods and *not* single-spell duration models when issues discussed in this section emerge.

Failure to Discriminate among Event Types

A second problem common to much of the applied work in social science has to do with the definition of what constitutes "an event." Indeed, as we discuss below, this problem is closely related to the problem posed by repeatability of events. The basic issue here is that many processes of interest to social scientists can presumably terminate, or end, in a variety of ways. Again using the conflict processes research as an example, it is very clear that disputes can end in a variety of ways. Compromise, stalemate, military victory, and so forth, are just a few of the "terminal states" of a militarized dispute. Yet despite the fact that processes may culminate with the occurrence of one of a variety of outcomes, the usual practice has been to treat distinct outcomes as being equivalent to a singular outcome. This, in turn, is equivalent to saying that it makes no difference *how* a process (or spell) ends; interest simply centers on *if* the process ended. In the conflict example, this would imply that the factors leading to a dispute ending in, say, a stalemate are equivalent to the factors leading to a military victory.

Collapsing or combining multiple events into an indicator of a singular event certainly makes the modeling problem easier: a single-spell duration model can easily be applied. But as with the problem of repeated events, collapsing events in this way masks (or may mask) important substantive information about the process of interest. Moreover, as we saw in Chapter 10, failure to discriminate among the various kinds of events that can occur may induces heterogeneity problems into the estimates, particularly if the type-specific hazard rates vary by event type (recall the pooled estimates in the examples given in Chapter 10). Fortunately, there are attractive alternatives to the simple approach of combining event types. Specifically, the wider consideration of models for competing risks would seem to be a direction social science methodology should head and a preferred strategy over the oft-used practice of ignoring variation in event types.

Poor Measurement of Survival Times and TVCs

The failure of analysts to account for competing outcomes serves to highlight a third problem common to the application of duration modeling methods in social science: events data are often poorly constructed *or* are not nicely amenable to event history analysis. To explain, consider applications of survival analysis to problems of interest in medical sciences. Unlike applications in medical sciences where it is obvious *at the start* of data collection efforts that survival analysis is the appropriate statistical approach to modeling the data, social scientists frequently rely on archived data or data collected for purposes *other* than duration analysis. This fact can make it incredibly difficult to construct (or reconstruct) the event history process, particularly when it is unclear precisely when a process of interest began and ended (as this information may not be readily available to the researcher). The inability to precisely reconstruct an event history, no doubt, invites bad measurement, inaccurate measurement, or the absence of measurement of important covariates and in some instance, of the survival time.

In order to ameliorate these problems, we frequently "aggregate" the time scale to account for the fact that event times and survival times are imprecisely measured. For example, otherwise continuous time processes frequently have survival times measured in terms of years, which is a very broad measure of time. This aggregation problem is not isolated to social science applications, obviously; however, aggregation *can* have potential implications for one's analysis. In the parlance of the literature, the basic problem that arises is sometimes called "time aggregation bias." This can occur when there is measurement error that is associated with how we measure or aggregate time. The "bias" refers to the potential problem that parameter estimates may be biased because although we have access to yearly data (for example), the theoretical research question requires monthly observations (for example). There is only a small body of empirical literature on time aggregation bias in event history models, e.g., Bergström and Edin (1992), and Petersen (1995), and the results are mixed regarding the degree of bias found in the parameters.[1]

Indeed, in many applications, aggregation "bias" will not be problematic, as most social science theories and hypotheses (as far as we are aware) are not usually specified in terms of days, weeks, months, or years. Put another way,

---

[1] ter Hofstede and Wedel (1999) conclude that the effects of time aggregation bias on the baseline parameters are small, particularly for the continuous time model, but their simulation evidence is limited.

theory, in most applications, will be robust to aggregation problems! However, analysts should be careful in constructing the time scale. Specifically, as the time scale becomes more highly aggregated, continuous-time approaches will become less appropriate and discrete-time approaches will become more natural. Thus, in contrast to other disciplines where "continuous-time" models are usually the default modeling strategy, for many applications in social science, discrete-time models like the variant of the Cox model discussed in Chapter 4 and 5 or the logit approach discussed in Chapter 5 may be better suited to social science duration data than are the parametric models considered in Chapter 3.

The imprecision with which time is measured raises the specter of other problems social scientists should be wary of. As we discussed in Chapter 7, time aggregation can make it difficult to discern if a change in the value of TVC occurred before or *after* an event. With yearly data, for example, one may not know if the event occurred on January 1 or December 31. If yearly TVCs are incorporated into the analysis, it is essential that one ensures the TVCs are not changing simultaneously with the event occurrence, or are changing after the occurrence of an event. Lagging the covariates usually helps to solve this problem, but analysts should be particularly careful in applying TVCs to duration models with highly aggregated time scales. These issues were discussed at length in Chapter 7.

Of course all of these problems are exacerbated by the fact that social scientists, as noted above, frequently rely on second-hand data to construct event history processes. Apart from aggregation issues and simultaneity issues regarding TVCs, another implication of relying on archived data or on data not collected for the purpose of longitudinal analysis is that we may not have much information on important covariates of interest, especially on TVCs. King and Zeng (2001b, 2001c) succinctly note this problem in the use of dyadic dispute data. Because such data (for example the Oneal and Russett data) were not originally collected with event history analysis in mind (Beck, Katz, and Tucker [1998] demonstrated how such data could be treated as duration data) and further, because there are thousands of possible dyads in a data set, information on theoretically relevant TVCs is usually not present. Instead, the extent to which covariates are available in such archived data sets usually entails simpler-to-measure covariates such as territorial contiguity or other time *independent* covariates.

The basic solution to the kinds of problems discussed in this section is simple: collect more and better data! Unfortunately, this is easier said than done, particularly with archived data or with data that were not constructed to facilitate longitudinal analysis.[2] Fortunately, the problem of having poor

---

[2]Indeed, this problem, in part, motivates the work of King and Zeng (2001b, 2001c). They note that because of the sheer size of dyadic data sets in international relations, it is infeasible to collect information on important covariates for every observation. They propose the use of a matched case-control design which essentially leads to data reduction, making it easier (or more feasible) to collected data on important covariates for a subset of observations.

event-type data is receding as social scientists are doing a better job of explicitly constructing cross-sectional and time-serial data. Below, we will discuss further the issue of data collection efforts.

The Meaning of Time Dependency

The issue of time dependency has emerged frequently throughout this book, and most directly in Chapter 6. Yet the issue is so relevant to the choice of modeling strategies that it bears revisiting. In our view, most applications calling for the use of event history analysis proceed with an interest in how some covariate or set of covariates influences the risk that some important event will occur. Less interest seems to center on duration dependency or on the time-path that some process takes. Indeed, there are few applied settings in social science where interest in duration dependency is of real substantive concern (though see Bennett 1997 and 1999 for a counter viewpoint). The reasons for this are simple. As discussed in the previous section, we often deal with survival data that are collected with a fair degree of imprecision in them. Moreover, we frequently rely on highly aggregated time scales upon which to estimate our models. It seems to us that as the level of imprecision in our measurement of survival times increases, the extent to which we should substantively "care" about the nature (shape, direction, etc.) of the underlying time dependency should decrease. That is, it is hard to envision what such dependency actually means, substantively, given the imprecision in our data.

Yet even if survival times are accurately measured, as *is* the case much of the time, focusing on duration dependency will still be of little utility in most social science applications. Given the demonstrable fact that duration dependency is highly sensitive to the posited model coupled with the fact that most theories and hypotheses explicitly deal with the connection between an outcome variable and some important independent variable(s), duration dependency usually should be regarded as a nuisance. The implication of this is that modeling strategies that are agnostic to the shape of the baseline hazard rate *should be preferred* to modeling strategies that impose restrictions on the form of the baseline hazard. Of course our recommended modeling strategy throughout this book has been the use of the Cox model, or one of its variants.

Having laid out some common problems and issues facing social scientists, we now turn attention to some specific recommendations regarding the use of event history methods in social science.

What Should Social Scientists Do?

A wide variety of modeling strategies have been discussed in this book. Moreover, a host of analytical and substantive problems that emerge in social science duration data have been addressed both in this chapter and in previous chapters of the book. As we bring the book to a close, it is useful to make some specific recommendations regarding the implementation of event history methods in social science. Specifically we discuss the role theory should play in the analysis of event history data; the implications such theorizing has on data collection efforts; the choice of the appropriate modeling strategy given the type of event history data the analyst has to work with; and the interpretation of event history model estimates.

Connecting Theory to Events

As we noted in the first chapter of this book, numerous theories and hypotheses with which social scientists regularly work have implications that *directly* lead to the consideration of longitudinal processes. As the kinds of models discussed in this book all deal in some respect with "risk" and "survival," many of the problems social scientists deal with make event history analysis natural, given the problem under study. Indeed, it is our view that the methods discussed in this book can be used to gain some leverage on novel aspects of a problem. That is to say, if a theory has observable implications relating to the timing of change, then the models presented here may yield previously unconsidered insights into the problem.

Moreover, if timing and change are theoretically relevant issues to a problem, then a recommended "strategy" for theorizing would be to consider more fully the process under study. As noted previously, for reasons of model tractability or reasons of convenience, analysts frequently ignore or waste valuable information regarding complicated event structures in the data. Nevertheless, if one is theoretically interested in event history processes, then it seems incumbent on the analyst to theorize more precisely about *why* events happen repeatedly or *why* events of a certain kind occur, but other kinds of events do not occur for some observations. Quite often, the specificity of theory is at the level of "what influences the occurrence of an event?" Yet if there are multiple events, repeated events, or events that *never* occur for some observations, then the richness of the theory may be improved by thinking about, or discriminating among event types. This in turn may lead to more precise statements regarding the relationship between important covariates and events that are of theoretical interest.

More generally, if one's research problem has clear implications that naturally lead to the consideration of the event history modeling approach, this in turn should influence (and hopefully improve) our data collection efforts. We discuss these issues next.

Data Collection Efforts

Most of the problems discussed in the previous section can be avoided with the careful collection and recording of events data. In general, when it comes to constructing event history data, "more is better," which is to say, precision in coding the occurrence of events *as well as* precision in recording when TVCs change values can eliminate substantial analytical and logical problems later. To facilitate data collection efforts, we have found that the following set of questions can help guide the researcher.

When does the "clock start ticking?"

Proper application of the models discussed in this book requires a defensible and sensible definition of when the risk period for a process begins. In other words, the researcher needs to know when the clock starts ticking. For some processes, this may be obvious, for others, it is not. For example, in modeling regime transition in comparative politics, the researcher must explicitly define the period at which regimes become at risk of failing. On the surface, this seems easy to define: a regime only becomes at risk of failing once it attains power. Yet the ease in defining the risk period is illusory. Because regimes may rise and fall *repeatedly* in some subset of countries, the question is naturally raised as to *which* regimes are going to be studied. Usually, this question is answered empirically, in the sense that data availability influences the observation plan. That is, a particular year may be chosen as the start of the observation period and regimes from that point onward are studied. The year that is selected may be chosen because prior to that year, data on important covariates were unavailable. In this sense, the researcher is stuck because no matter how far back in time the analyst wishes "to go," data limitations are prohibitive. Justifying the start time of the observation period in terms of the availability of data is a perfectly reasonable (and usually unavoidable) thing to do, but it raises additional questions, which we discuss below.

Which events are of interest?

If the observation plan is largely determined by issues pertaining to data availability, then the researcher needs to determine which events, among the many possible events that could occur, are of most interest. This question will frequently arise in social science settings. As we noted earlier in this chapter, the kinds of "units" social scientists study, for example, individuals, states, countries, dyads, and so forth, may be perpetually at risk of experiencing an event. To illustrate, suppose we are interested in studying the transition of regimes from authoritarian to more democratic regimes. Further, suppose that due to data availability problems, we must start our analysis in 1950. In this case, we might study all countries that, as of 1950, were under an authoritarian regime and study the duration of time until the transition is made to a more democratic regime. As a specific example, consider the country of Peru. Using the data and coding scheme of Gasiorowski (1995), as of 1950, Peru was in the midst of an authoritarian regime; however, sometime in 1956, Peru transitioned from an authoritarian regime to a less authoritarian regime. On the face of it, Peru went 6 years (from 1950) before making the transition (i.e. experienced the event). In collecting event history data, the analyst would now have to address a fundamental issue. If interest only centered on the "first" event, then data on Peru over the period 1950-1956 would need to be recorded.

Unfortunately, a focus on the first event would make little substantive sense for two reasons. First, the event is arbitrarily defined insofar as it is the first event *since the start of the observation period*. In reality, the event history process leading to regime transition in Peru could have occurred numerous times *prior* to 1950. That is to say, there may have been several authoritarian regimes that rose and fell before the start of the observation period. Second, there may be repeated occurrences of authoritarian regime transition *after* the "first" event occurs. Indeed, looking at Peru's history, we see that an authoritarian regime assumed power in 1962 and then transitioned to a less-authoritarian regime in 1963. Then, in 1968, an authoritarian regime regained control until 1977, when another transition occurred. Here, we observe three spells of authoritarian regimes; which of these spells should we study? The simple answer is "all of them." There is probably no justifiable reason to arbitrarily choose one among the three observed spells, and so each of the spells is important to consider.

The issue as far as data collection efforts are concerned is ensuring that the researcher can identify the fact that this country had multiple spells and occurrences of the same event. This is easily done by making sure there is an identifying variable in the data set that can be used to cluster the observations together. Additionally, it is probably wise to identify the sequencing of the multiple spells as well as have recorded in the data set the time that elapses *since* the previous spell ended. The reason for this recommendation is simple. If one knows the sequencing of events and the interval in between spells, one can use this information to help in the estimation of models more appropriate for repeatable events. Not having this information available, or worse, not using this information even if it is available, could result in the estimation of models that make a fairly herculean assumption about the independence of events. It is our observation that this issue will emerge very frequently with social science duration data.

What is the *process* of interest?

Duration data where an event can occur repeatedly or where different kinds of events can occur multiple times leads to an important question: which of the possible event history processes is of theoretical interest? The answer to this question will have direct bearing on the construction of one's event history data and on subsequent analysis. Continuing with the regime transition example, it is important to recognize that there are *two* kinds of processes that are taking place. The first process is transition from an authoritarian regime to a less authoritarian regime. However, since we know that countries may have multiple incidences of authoritarian regimes, it *must* be the case that these same countries will have multiple instances of the intervening spell corresponding to non-authoritarian regimes. Said differently, once a country makes the transition to a less-authoritarian regime, it then becomes at risk of making a transition back to an authoritarian regime. As such, there is an implied second event history process that is observed.

Typically, analysts will focus on one-way transitions; however, since many of the problems social scientists are interested in lead to data with multiple events, ignoring the intervening spells may be unwise. Suppose that the duration of time spent in the intervening state influenced the likelihood that a country would make the transition back to the original state? If so, then at minimum, it would behoove the analyst to ensure that data were collected on the duration time of the intervening spell, *as well as* on the spell of interest. Moreover, it may be of substantive interest to record data on covariates thought to influence the duration of the intervening spell and then model this process directly.

Are there different kinds of events that can occur?

Closely related to the discussion above lies the issue of competing outcomes. For example, unemployment may end due to full-time work, part-time work, or disability. Distinguishing among the three may be vitally important and the covariate effects may differ in magnitude or even direction across the options. As noted earlier in this chapter, many processes of interest to social scientists can conceivably terminate or fail in a variety of ways. If discriminating among event types will be of importance to the analyst, then data should obviously be collected with this issue in mind. In general, we recommend that the researcher maintain as much information as possible regarding event types when constructing event history data. It is far easier to treat distinct events as indicative of a singular outcome than it is to go back to a data set and reconstruct multiple events from a single event indicator. Moreover, as we discussed in Chapter 10, models for competing risks may be theoretically preferable to one-way transition models for many kinds of problems. Hence, recording this information directly will clearly facilitate the use of such models subsequently.

Are TVCs going to be used in subsequent analyses?

It is quite common that social scientists will be interested in incorporating TVCs into their event history models. As we saw in Chapter 7, inclusion of TVCs into any of the kinds of models presented in this book pose few problems; however, there are issues pertaining to data collection efforts the analyst should be aware of. Most importantly, the researcher should record as precisely as possible the time at which a TVC changes value. Given the problems associated with imprecisely recording when TVCs change relative to event occurrences (discussed above and in Chapter 7), these problems can largely be avoided if the researcher is careful in how a TVC is recorded into a duration data set. Constructing data using the stop-start format discussed in terms of the counting process framework (see Chapter 7) can help clarify this issue as it requires the analyst to explicitly split the spell into a series of "stops" and "starts" that correspond to changes in a TVC.

Recommendations for Modeling Strategies

The last set of recommendations we make are in regard to modeling strategies available to social scientists. These recommendations presume one has satisfactorily addressed important issues pertaining to data collection and further (and more importantly), one has a compelling theoretical and substantive reason to consider duration modeling methods. We begin with recommendations on model selection and proceed, as in the last section, with a series of questions.

Is duration dependency a "nuisance"?

The question of duration dependency, again, rears its head. Our view has been that time dependency in social science applications is chiefly a nuisance—that is, a function of the posited model and not a particularly interesting feature of social processes *given that the researcher has specified the survival time as a function of theoretically relevant covariates*. Given our view of duration dependency, the recommended modeling strategy is clear: apply the Cox model (or derivations of the Cox model discussed in this book). The Cox model makes no assumptions about the distributional characteristics of the baseline hazard rate, yet can provide estimates of the covariates of interest that have desirable properties allowing the usual kinds of hypothesis tests. Moreover, baseline estimates, though highly adapted to the observed data, can be retrieved from Cox estimates. Further, as we showed in Chapter 10, the Cox model has been readily extended to the case of competing risks and repeatable events data structures. In short, the Cox model is widely applicable to most of the kinds of problems social scientists address.

What issues emerge in the application of the Cox model?

One issue that used to be raised against the application of the Cox model (and parametric models) was the prevalence of tied events in duration data. This is no longer an issue. As we noted in Chapter 5, the default strategy among most software programs for handling ties under the Cox model is the use of the

Breslow approximation. Principally, this is the case because of the relative ease with which the Breslow estimator can be applied. The computational issues with more precise approximation methods for handling tied data no longer hold. There is no reason *not to use* Efron or exact approximation methods nowadays. Moreover, the exact discrete approximation of the Cox model that we discussed in Chapters 4 and 5 (which gives rise to a conditional logit model) can be applied to discrete duration data—data that by definition have many tied outcomes. Hence, even in the face of discrete-time data, the Cox model can be applied. Further, it is our view that the Cox approach in such a setting will be preferable to the logit-based approach. We return to this issue shortly.

A second issue that *is* of concern in applications of the Cox model is the proportional hazards assumption. Fortunately, this assumption is a testable assumption, as we illustrated in Chapter 8. We strongly recommend that in applications of the Cox model, the analyst should take the time to test this assumption using the approaches outlined previously. Analysts should also be aware that other models maintain the proportional hazards assumption, most notably the Weibull model. As with the Cox model, this assumption should be evaluated as a matter of course.

In what settings might one use parametric methods?

As we discussed in Chapter 6, there may be some settings where parametric approaches might be preferable to Cox alternatives. First, if one is interested in making out-of-sample predictions or forecasts based on model estimates, then in general, parametric-type models will be preferred to Cox models (Hougaard 1999). Second, if an analyst has substantive interest in the underlying duration dependency, then parametric approaches will produce better estimates of this quantity. Examples of settings where substantive interest in duration dependency might be high include reliability testing and epidemiology. As noted above, for several reasons, it is difficult to think of social science applications where the underlying time dependency will have substantive import.

What issues emerge in the application of parametric models?

If an analyst proceeds with the parametric modeling approach, there are several recommendations to be made. To start, we strongly recommend *against* selecting a parametric model for reasons of computational convenience or ease-in-interpretability. The prevalence of the Weibull, no doubt, stems from the fact that for many years, it was the "default" distribution function of many software programs. Yet, if one has an ostensible reason to be interested in the underlying time dependency, then it makes no sense to arbitrarily choose a parametric form. In Chapters 3, 6 and 8, we discussed techniques that could be used to help adjudicate among competing parametric models. We strongly recommend the analyst use some (or all) of these approaches to evaluate the parametric model selected. Specifically, use of the generalized gamma model, Cox-Snell residual plots, and the AIC (for non-nested parametric models) can give the researcher some justification for the model that is selected. Moreover, use of estimated baseline hazards from a Cox model can help the analyst in choosing a parametric model. One attractive alternative to the parametric models discussed in Chapter 3 is the use of "flexible" parametric models like those discussed in Chapter 6 (based on the work of Royston and Parmar 2002). These kinds of models provide a more general fit of the baseline hazard rate, but unlike Cox estimates, are less closely adapted to the observed data.

What about discrete-time data?

It will be common in social science applications for analysts to have essentially discretized duration data, even for otherwise continuous time processes. The reason is that we often use TVCs that change at each observation period, which in turn, produces unit-period data (i.e. the number of records per individual is equal to T). Further, since we often have to rely on highly aggregated time-scales (yearly data, for example) on processes that are continuous, the data are more appropriately viewed as discrete data, not continuous data. In settings where data are highly discretized, we recommend the following modeling strategies. The exact discrete approximation of the Cox model is our first recommendation. Recall from Chapters 4 and 5 that this approximation method is equivalent to a conditional logit model where cases are matched in terms of the ordered failure times. The appeal of this approach is that the analyst needs to make no assumptions regarding the form of the baseline hazard rate, which of course is standard for the Cox model.

Alternatives to the exact discrete approximation of the Cox model are the logit, probit, and complementary log-log approaches discussed in Chapter 5. These approaches are attractive insofar as they are easy to implement, familiar to social scientists (at least the logit and probit models), and straightforward to interpret. For these reasons, such models will remain popular in the literature.

What issues emerge in the application of "logit-type" models?

As we discussed in Chapter 5, special issues arise in the consideration of logit models (or its close alternatives) with discrete grouped duration data. Principally, because data of this type consist of repeated observations of some unit, it is highly recommended that the analysts account in some way for the temporal dependence that will presumably exist among the repeated observations. In Chapter 5 and 7 we discussed this issue, but it bears reviewing here in this summary. It should be routine for analysts to account for duration dependency exhibited among the observations by including as a covariate, some measure of the duration time. There are a variety of ways to do this and they were discussed in detail in Chapter 5. The usual approach to addressing this kind of problem in discrete duration data has been to treat the elapsed duration time, or some transformation of it, as a covariate. However, there are subtle issues the analyst should be aware of when accounting for duration dependency in this way. Just as imposing some arbitrarily chosen distribution function on a set of data is inappropriate, so too is simply including time (or a transformation of time such as the natural log) as a covariate *without any specification tests*. Fortunately, simple likelihood ratio tests can help the analyst in selecting the "functional form" of this duration dependency indicator. An attractive alternative to the standard kinds of transformations (discussed in Chapter 5) on the duration time is through the use of smoothing functions, such as splines or lowess techniques (Beck, Katz, and Tucker 1998; Beck and Jackman 1998). These functions generally will provide a better fit to the data than alternative approaches. In Chapter 6, we illustrated some of these approaches.

Of course most of these issues are avoided if one simply ignores the form of the underlying duration dependency. This, again, is achieved through a Cox model. As discussed previously, use of the exact discrete approximation will result in a discrete-time model, but one without having to directly account for duration dependency in the ways discussed in the previous paragraph.

What about complicated event structures?

One recommendation we make is to strongly encourage social scientists to consider the possibility that single-spell duration models may not be the best modeling strategy to start with. If event structures are complicated in that events can occur repeatedly or multiple kinds of events can occur, then a standard application of a duration model for single-spell data will be wrong. Apart from the fact that such a model does not do a good job of describing the underlying process, strong assumptions regarding the independence of events or the homogeneity among observations are induced. Unfortunately, such assumptions are often wrong. Models for competing risks and repeatable events, which help mitigate these problems, are obvious recommended strategies when such complications arise. In Chapter 10, we discussed various approaches to handling these kinds of event history problems. The important point to make is that such complications will arise *very often* in social science duration data. Our view is that wider applicability of these kinds of models can, for some problems, reveal considerably more interesting information than what can be generated from a standard model assuming a single-spell process.

So when faced with events that can be repeated, it is critical to test and possibly account for the correlation among those repeated events. If not all observations will fail, the use of split-population or cure models will be critical to the inferences drawn. Similarly, asking more specific substantive questions and using a competing risks model to assess how the spell ended, i.e., to distinguish among the possible terminating events, can generate additional information and lead to new insights. The exciting variety of event history models that exist opens new research frontiers for modeling processes where questions about timing and change are important.

What about interpretation of event history results?

In reviewing applied work using event history analysis, we have seen a tendency for analysts to simply report coefficient estimates derived from some model and go no further in interpretation. This is unfortunate because as we have seen throughout this book, all event history models reveal information pertaining to both survival and risk. The problem is that sometimes, the analyst has to work to back this information out of a model. It is imperative that analysts extend their presentation beyond tabular displays of results and illustrate how covariates work to increase or decrease the risk (or survival) that "something" of interest will occur. Duration models are particularly amenable to use of graphic displays; however, use of first differences and predicted hazards based on interesting covariate profiles will also significantly improve the ability of the researcher to convey his or her results. All of these approaches have been discussed and illustrated in nearly every chapter of this book.

Tied closely to careful interpretation of event history results is the necessity for researchers to assess the fit and adequacy of their model by implementing some of the diagnostic measures discussed in Chapter 8. Such techniques can help assess the adequacy of a model's fit, the proportional hazards assumption (if it is made), functional form of a covariate, and influence. In Chapter 8, we illustrated how such techniques could be implemented.

Some Concluding Thoughts

Given the prevalence of theories and hypotheses related to timing and change, the methods discussed in this book will no doubt come to be widely applied in the literature; indeed, such models have already been used pervasively in many social science subfields. We conclude this section by discussing some directions we think the application of duration models to social science data needs to take (or will take).

There should be a more explicit consideration of constructing event history data. We outlined the problems social scientists often face with secondhand data. Data explicitly collected for the purposes of longitudinal analysis (like duration analysis) will substantially improve our ability to implement the kinds of models discussed in this book. Moreover, such data will mitigate or obviate the problems we discussed earlier related to poor measurement of events and event times. Second, there should be a greater attempt to account for problems posed by multiple events. As this issue is a common problem social scientists must deal with, models appropriate to such problems should become more widely applied. Third, social scientists should begin to think more directly about unobserved heterogeneity in their data. Because event history analysis entails the comparative analysis of distinct units (i.e. individuals, states, countries, dyads, governments, etc.), it may be the case that some observations are simply more failure-prone, or "frail" than other observations. This frailty, which will usually be unobserved, can have implications for one's analysis (which we discussed in Chapter 9). The further development and use of frailty models (or random coefficients models) in social science is an approach that should become more widely used.

Conclusion

A considerable amount of ground has been covered in this book. Our intent was to provide social scientists a thorough introduction to event history methods and demonstrate their natural applicability to problems of social science. To be sure, given the wide range of topics covered, some of the issues we raised were not dealt with in great detail. For this reason, we strongly encourage readers to access and study many of the original statistical works from which we drew for this book. The reader should also be aware that many new approaches, especially regarding nonparametric estimation, are continually being proposed, developed, and incorporated into the wider body of research we have attempted to cover in this book. In short, these methods are evolving. The larger point we want to stress, however, is that the approaches discussed in this book often naturally follow many of the kinds of research questions social scientists ask. As such, we hope that these methods, which are already being widely used in social science research, can be further used to help generate novel inferences about timing and change.

Appendix
Software for Event History Analysis

There are a wide variety of statistical software packages available for event
history analysis. We briefly discuss some of these packages. In this book, the
software package Stata was primarily used to estimate most of the models. For
some illustrations, the software package S-Plus was utilized. The data sets and
code used to estimate most of the models in this book are available via Brad
Jones's Web site:

   http://www.u.arizona.edu/~ bsjones/eventhistory.html.

Stata (http://www.stata.com/)
   The software package Stata (Stata Corporation, College Station, TX) can
be used to estimate a wide variety of parametric models as well as extensions
for the Cox proportional hazards model. Moreover, the package has a suite of
diagnostics for both parametric and nonparametric models. Stata and its user
community have continued to greatly expand the functionality of the program
for event history users. One notable strength of Stata is its ability to handle
complicated event history data structures. Cleves, Gould, and Gutierrez (2002)
provide in-depth coverage of Stata's functions for event history analysis.

S-Plus (http://www.insightful.com/products/splus/default.asp)
   S-Plus (MathSoft, Inc., Seattle, WA) provides excellent interactive estimation tools for event history modeling. The event history functions were written
primarily by Terry Therneau, Head of Biostatistics at Mayo Clinic. It is easily
extended to incorporate user-written code. Further, S-Plus is known for its emphasis on graphics, which is particularly important in an event history context.
The GUI (Graphical User Interface) is one of the main advantages of S-Plus
over R, the open-source equivalent of S-Plus.

R (http://www.r-project.org)
   R (R Foundation for Statistical Computing, Vienna, Austria) is comparable to S-Plus in that this package is the open-source equivalent to S-Plus

(i.e., both packages are based on the S language). The major difference between the two packages, as noted earlier, is in terms of the GUI. Because R is the open-source equivalent to S-Plus, the software package is available freely for downloading.

LIMDEP (http://www.limdep.com/)

LIMDEP (Econometric Software, Inc., Plainview, NY) can estimate a wide variety of parametric duration models, including encompassing models like the generalized F or generalized gamma models. LIMDEP can also estimate split-population models. Diagnostics for duration models are not readily available in this package.

SAS (http://www.sas.com)

SAS (SAS Institute, Cary, NC) is a widely used statistical package that is known for its ease of data manipulation. The package has a wide variety of modules to estimate event history models as well as produce model diagnostics. SAS (along with S-Plus) is widely used in biostatistics survival analysis research. Therneau and Grambsch (2000) provide extensive examples of SAS and S-Plus code in their book.

SUDAAN (http://www.rti.org/sudaan/home.cfm)

SUDAAN (RTI International, Research Triangle, NC) is a statistical package designed for the analysis of cluster-correlated data, such as survey data. The package has a variety of capabilities for estimating event history models for these kinds of data. Diagnostic methods are available in SUDAAN.

MLwiN (http://multilevel.ioe.ac.uk/index.html)

MLwiN (Centre for Multilevel Modeling, London, UK) is a program designed for multilevel modeling. The program has capabilities to estimate event history models with multilevel (or hierarchical) data, including a multilevel nonparametric frailty model.

SPSS (http://www.spss.com/)

SPSS (SPSS Inc., Chicago, IL) provides basic/introductory event history modeling options but does not have the extensions and options of other programs.

This list is not meant to be exhaustive, particularly as new software options are continually becoming available. These programs, however, are the ones most commonly used in social science event history analysis.

References

Aalen, Odd O. 1978. "Nonparametric Inference for a Family of Counting Processes." *Annals of Statistics* 6:701–726.

Aalen, Odd O. 1992. "Modeling Heterogeneity in Survival Analysis by the Compound Poisson Distribution." *The Annals of Applied Probability* 2:951–72.

Agresti, Alan. 1990. *Categorical Data Analysis*. New York: Wiley.

Agresti, Alan. 1996. *An Introduction to Categorical Data Analysis*. New York: Wiley.

Aitken, Murray, Nan Laird, and Brian Francis. 1983. "A Reanalysis of the Stanford Heart Transplant Data: Rejoinder (in Applications)." *Journal of the American Statistical Association* 78:291–292.

Allison, Paul D. 1982. "Discrete–time Methods for the Analysis of Event–Histories." In *Sociological Methodology 1982*, ed. S. Leinhardt. Beverly Hills: Sage.

Allison, Paul D. 1984. *Event History Analysis: Regression for Longitudinal Data*. Sage University Paper Series on Quantitative Application in the Social Sciences, series no. 07–041. Newbury Park: Sage.

Allison, Paul D. 1995. *Survival Analysis Using the SAS System*. Cary: SAS Institute.

Allison, Paul D. 1996. "Fixed Effects Partial Likelihood for Repeated Events." *Sociological Methods and Research* 24:207–22.

Alt, James E., and Gary King. 1994. "Transfers of Governmental Power: The Meaning of Time Dependence." *Comparative Political Studies* 27:190–210.

Alt, James E., Gary King, and Curtis Signorino. 2001. "Aggregation Among Binary, Count, and Duration Models: Estimating the Same Quantities from Different Levels of Data." *Political Analysis* 1:21–44.

Andersen, Per Kragh, O. Borgan, R.D. Gill, and N. Keiding. 1993. *Statistical Models Based on Counting Processes*. Springer–Verlag, NY.

Andersen, Per Kragh, and R.D. Gill. 1982. "Cox's Regression Model for Counting Processes: A Large Sample Study." *The Annals of Statistics* 10:1100–20.

Andersen, Per Kragh, John P. Klein, and Mei–Jie Zhang. 1999. "Testing for Centre Effects in Multi–Centre Survival Studies: A Monte Carlo Comparison of Fixed and Random Effects Tests." *Statistics in Medicine* 18:1489–1500.

Ansolabehere, Steven, and Gary King. 1990. "Measuring the Consequences of Delegate Selection–Rules in Presidential Nominations." *Journal of Politics* 52:609–621.

Aranda–Ordaz, F.J. 1981. "On Two Families of Transformations to Additivity for Binary Response Data." *Biometrika* 68:357–363.

Bagai, Isha, and B.L.S. Prakasa Rao. 1992. "Analysis of Survival Data with Two Dependent Risks." *Biomedical Journal* 7:801–14.

Bandeen–Roche, Karen J., and Kung–Yee Liang. 1996. "Modelling Failure–Time Associations in Data with Multiple Levels of Clustering." *Biometrika* 83:29–39.

Beck, Nathaniel. 1998. "Modelling Space and Time: The Event History Approach." In E. Scarbrough and E. Tanenbaum, eds., *Research Strategies in the Social Sciences.* New York: Oxford University Press, 191–213.

Beck, Nathaniel, and Simon Jackman. 1998. "Beyond Linearity by Default: Generalized Additive Models." *American Journal of Political Science* 42:596–627.

Beck, Nathaniel, and Jonathan N. Katz. 1995. "What to Do (and Not to Do) with Time–Series–Cross–Section Data in Comparative Politics." *American Political Science Review* 89:634–647.

Beck, Nathaniel, and Jonathan N. Katz. 2001. "Throwing the Baby out with the Bathwater: A Comment on Green, Kim, and Yoon." *International Organization* 55:487–95

Beck, Nathaniel, Jonathan N. Katz, and Richard Tucker. 1998. "Taking Time Seriously: Time–Series–Cross–Section Analysis with a Binary Dependent Variable." *American Journal of Political Science* 42:1260–1288.

Bennett, D. Scott. 1996. "Security, Bargaining, and the End of Interstate Rivalry." *International Studies Quarterly* 40:157–183.

Bennett, D. Scott. 1997. "Testing Alternative Models of Alliance Duration, 1816–1984." *American Journal of Political Science* 41:846–878.

Bennett, D. Scott. 1999. "Parametric Models, Duration Dependence, and Time–Varying Data Revisited." *American Journal of Political Science* 43:256–270.

Bergström, R., and P.A. Edin. 1992. "Time Aggregation and the Distributional Shape of Unemployment Duration." *Journal of Applied Economics* 7:5–30.

Berkson, J., and R.P. Gage. 1952. "Survival Curve for Cancer Patients Following Treatment." *Journal of the American Statistical Association* 47:501–15.

Berry, Frances Stokes, and William D. Berry. 1990. "State Lottery Adoptions as Policy Innovations: An Event History Analysis." *American Political Science Review* 84:395–416.

Berry, Frances Stokes, and William D. Berry. 1992. "Tax Innovation in the States: Capitalizing on Political Opportunity." *American Journal of Political Science* 36:715–42.

Berry, Frances Stokes, and William D. Berry. 1994. "The Politics of Tax Increases in the States." *American Journal of Political Science* 38:855–59.

Blalock, Hubert M., Jr. 1979. *Social Statistics.* 2nd edition. New York: McGraw–Hill.

Blossfeld, Hans–Peter, and Gotz Rohwer. 1997. "Causal Inference, Time and Observation Plans in the Social Sciences." *Quality & Quantity* 31:361–384.

Blossfeld, Hans–Peter, and Gotz Rohwer. 1995. *Techniques of Event History Modeling: New Approaches to Causal Analysis.* Mahwah, NJ: Lawrence Erlbaum.

Boag, J. W. 1949. "Maximum Likelihood Estimates of the Proportion of Patients Cured by Cancer Therapy." *Journal of the Royal Statistical Society, Series B* 11:15–44.

Bowman, Michael Emerson. 1996. "An Evaluation of Statistical Models for the Analysis of Recurrent Events Data." Ph.D. diss., Ohio State University.

Box–Steffensmeier, Janet M. 1996. "A Dynamic Analysis of the Role of War Chests in Campaign Strategy." *American Journal of Political Science* 40:352–371.

Box–Steffensmeier, Janet M., and Suzanna DeBoef. 2002. "A Monte Carlo Analysis of Repeated Events Survival Models." Presented at the Political Methodology Annual Meeting. Seattle, WA.

Box–Steffensmeier, Janet M., and Bradford S. Jones. 1997. "Time Is of the Essence: Event History Models in Political Science." *American Journal of Political Science* 41:1414–1461.

Box–Steffensmeier, Janet M., and Peter Radcliffe. 1996. "The Timing of PAC Contributions: A Split–Population Model." Presented at the 1996 Meeting of the American Political Science Association, San Francisco.

Box–Steffensmeier, Janet M., and Christopher J.W. Zorn. 2001. "Duration Models and Proportional Hazards in Political Science." *American Journal of Political Science* 45: 951–967.

Box–Steffensmeier, Janet M., and Christopher J.W. Zorn. 2002. "Duration Models for Repeated Events." *The Journal of Politics* 64:1069–1094.

Brace, Paul, Melinda Gann Hall, and Laura Langer. 1999. "Judicial Choice and the Politics of Abortion: Institutions, Context, and the Autonomy of Courts." *Albany Law Review* 62:1265–1302.

Brace, Paul, and Laura Langer. 2001. "State Supreme Courts and the Preemptive Power of the Judiciary." Paper presented at the Midwest Political Science Association Annual Meeting, Chicago, Il.

Breslow, N.E. 1974. "Covariance Analysis of Censored Survival Data." *Biometrics* 30:89–99.

Chastang, C. 1983. "A Simulation Study in a Two Covariate Survival Model: Importance of the Proportional Hazards Assumption." *Controlled Clinical Trials* 4:148.

Chen, C.H., and P.C. Wang. 1991. "Diagnostic Plots in Cox's Regression Model." *Biometrics* 47:841–50.

Chung, Ching–Fan, Peter Schmidt, and Ann D. Witte. 1991. "Survival Analysis: A Survey." *Journal of Quantitative Criminology* 7:59–98.

Clayton, David G. 1978. "A Model for Association in Bivariate Life Tables and Its Application in Epidemiological Studies." *Biometrika* 65:141–151.

Clayton, David B. 1999. "Poisson Regression with a Random Effect." *Stata Technical Bulletin* 46:30–33.

Cleveland, W.S. 1979. "Robust Locally Weighted Regression and Smoothing Scatterplots." *Journal of the American Statistical Association* 74:829–836.

Cleveland, W.S. 1981. "LOWESS: A Program for Smoothing Scatterplots by Robust Locally Weighted Regression." *American Statistician* 35:54.

Cleves, Mario. 1999. "Analysis of Multiple Failure–Time Data with Stata." *Stata Technical Bulletin* 49:30–39.

Cleves, Mario A., William W. Gould, and Roberto G. Gutierrez. 2002. *An Introduction to Survival Analysis Using Stata.* College Station: Stata Corporation.

Collett, D. 1994. *Modelling Survival Data in Medical Research.* London: Chapman & Hall.

Collett, Dave, and Jonathan Golub. 2002. "Improving Survival Analysis: Time-Sensitive Covariates and Cox Models." University of Reading. Typescript.

Commenges, D., and P.K. Andersen. 1995. "Score Test of Homogeneity for Survival Data." *Lifetime Data Analysis* 1:145–60.

Cook, Richard J., and J.F. Lawless. 1997. "An Overview of Statistical Methods for Multiple Failure Time Data in Clinical Trials – Discussion." *Statistics in Medicine* 16:841–43.

Cox, D.R. 1972. "Regression Models and Life Tables." *Journal of the Royal Statistical Society, B* 34:187–220.

Cox, D.R. 1975. "Partial Likelihood." *Biometrika* 62:269–76.

Cox, D.R., and D.V. Hinkley. 1974. *Theoretical Statistics*. New York: John Wiley & Sons, Inc.

Cox, D.R., and D. Oakes. 1984. *Analysis of Survival Data*. London: Chapman and Hall.

Cox, D.R., and E.J. Snell. 1968. "A General Definition of Residuals (with discussion)." *Journal of the Royal Statistical Society B*. 30:248–275.

Crouchley, R., and A. Pickles. 1993. "A Specification Test for Univariate and Multivariate Proportional Hazards Models." *Biometrics* 49:1067–1076.

Crowder, Martin. 2001. *Classical Competing Risks*. Boca Raton: Chapman and Hall.

David, H.A., and M.L. Moeschberger. 1978. *The Theory of Competing Risks*. London: Charles Griffin and Company.

Diermeier, Daniel, and Randy T. Stevenson. 1999. "Cabinet Survival and Competing Risks." *American Journal of Political Science* 43:1051–1068.

Efron, B. 1977. "The Efficiency of Cox's Likelihood Function for Censored Data." *Journal of the American Statistical Association* 72:557–65.

Fahrmeir, L., and A. Klinger. 1998. "A Nonparametric Multiplicative Hazard Model for Event History Analysis." *Biometrika* 85:581–592.

Firth, D., C. Payne, and J. Payne. 1999. "Efficacy of Programmes for the Unemployed: Discrete Time Modelling of Duration Data from a Matched Comparison Study." *Journal of the Royal Statistical Society Series A – Statistics in Society* 162:111–120, Part 1.

Fleming, Thomas R., and David P. Harrington. 1991. *Counting Processes and Survival Analysis*. New York: Wiley.

Forster, M., and A.M. Jones. 2001. "The Role of Tobacco Taxes in Starting and Quitting Smoking: Duration Analysis of British Data." *Journal of Royal Statistical Society, Series A* 164:517–547.

Gail, M.H. 1972. "Does Cardiac Transplantation Prolong Life? A Reassessment." *Annals of Internal Medicine* 76:815–817.

Gasiorowski, Mark J. 1995. "Economic Crisis and Political Regime Change: An Event History Analysis." *American Political Science Review* 89:882–897.

Gelfand, A.E., S.K. Ghosh, C. Christiansen, S.B. Soumerai, and T.J. McLaughlin. 2000. "Proportional Hazards Models: A Latent Competing Risk Approach." *Applied Statistics* 49:385–397.

Gochman, Charles, and Zeev Moaz. 1993. "Militarized Interstate Disputes, 1816–1976." *Journal of Conflict Resolution* 28:585–616.

Goertz, Gary, and Paul F. Diehl. 1992. "The Empirical Importance of Enduring Rivalries." *International Studies Quarterly* 37:142–172.

Goldstein, Harvey. 1995. *Multilevel Statistical Models*. New York: Halstead Press.

Golub, Jonathan. 1999. "In the Shadow of the Vote? Decisionmaking in the European Community." *International Organization* 53:733–764.

Golub, Jonathan. 2002. "Institutional Reform and Decisionmaking in the European Union." In M. Hosli and A. Van Deemen (eds.), *Institutional Challenges in the European Union*. London: Routledge.

Gordon, Sanford C. 2002. "Stochastic Dependence in Competing Risks." *American Journal of Political Science* 46:200–217.

Gourieroux, C., A. Monfort, and A. Trognon. 1984. "Pseudo Maximum Likelihood Methods: Applications to Poisson Models." *Econometrica* 52:701–720.

Grambsch, P.M., and T.M. Therneau. 1994. "Proportional Hazards Tests and Diagnostics Based on Weighted Residuals." *Biometrika* 81:515–526.

Grambsch, P.M., T.M. Therneau, and T.R. Fleming. 1995. "Diagnostic Plots to Reveal Functional Form for Covariates in Multiplicative Intensity Models." *Biometrics* 51:1469–1482.

Gray, Robert J. 1992. "Flexible Methods for Analyzing Survival Data Using Splines, With Applications to Breast Cancer Prognosis (in Applications and Case Studies)." *Journal of the American Statistical Association* 87:942–951.

Green, David Michael, Chad Kahl, and Paul F. Diehl. 1998. "The Price of Peace: A Predictive Model of UN Peacekeeping Fiscal Costs." *Policy Studies Journal* 26:620–635.

Green, Donald P., Soo Yeon Kim, and David H. Yoon. 2001. "Dirty Pool." *International Organization* 55:441–468.

Greene, William. 1997. *Econometric Analysis*, 3d ed. New York: Macmillan Publishing Company.

Guide to Statistics. 1999. Seattle: MathSoft, Inc.

Guo, Guang, and German Rodriguez. 1992. "Estimating a Multivariate Proportional Hazards Model for Clustered Data Using the EM Algorithm, with an Application to Child Survival in Guatemala (in Applications and Case Studies)." *Journal of the American Statistical Association* 87:969–976.

Gutierrez, Roberto G. 2001. "On Frailty Models in Stata." Unpublished manuscript.

Gutierrez, Roberto G., Shana Carter, and David M. Drukker. 2001. "On Boundary–Value Likelihood–Ratio Tests." *Stata Technical Bulletin* 60:15–18.

Hamerle, Alfred. 1989. "Multiple–Spell Regression Models for Duration Data." *Applied Statistics* 38:127–38.

Hamerle, Alfred. 1991. "On the Treatment of Interrupted Spells and Initial Conditions in Event History Analysis." *Sociological Methods and Research* 19:388–414.

Hamerle, Alfred, and Gerd Ronning. 1995. "Panel Analysis for Qualitative Variables." *Handbook of Statistical Modeling for the Social and Behavioral Sciences.* Ed. Gerhard Arminger, Clifford C. Clogg, and Michael E. Sobel. New York: Plenum Press.

Han, Aaron, and Jerry A. Hausman. 1990. "Flexible Parametric Estimation of Duration and Competing Risks Models." *Journal of Applied Econometrics* 5:1–28.

Harrell, F.E. 1986. "The PHGLM Procedure." *SUGI Supplemental Library User's Guide.* Cary, NC: SAS Institute.

Hastie, T.J., and R.J. Tibshirani. 1990. *Generalized Additive Models.* New York: Chapman & Hall.

Hausman, Jerry J., and B. Singer. 1984. "Specification Tests for the Multinomial Logit Model." *Econometrica* 52:1219–1240.

Heckman, James, and B. Singer. 1984a. "The Identifiability of the Proportional Hazards Model." *Review of Economic Studies* 51:234–241.

Heckman, James, and B. Singer. 1984b. "A Method for Minimizing the Impact of Distributional Assumptions in Econometric Models for Duration Data." *Econometrica* 52:271–320.

Heckman, James, and B. Singer. 1985. "Social Science Duration Analysis." In *Longitu-dinal Data Analysis of Labor Market Data*, ed. James J. Heckman and B.S. Singer. New York: Cambridge University Press.

Hill, Daniel H., William G. Axinn, and Arland Thorton. 1993. "Competing Hazards with Shared Unmeasured Risk Factors." *Sociological Methodology* 23:245–277.

Hjort, N.L. 1992. "On Inference in Parametric Survival Data Models." *International Statistical Review* 60:355–387.

Holt, J.D., and R.L. Prentice. 1974. "Survival Analyses in Twin Studies and Matched Pair Experiments." *Biometrica* 61:17–30.

Hosmer, David W., and Stanley Lemeshow. 1989. *Applied Logistic Regression.* New York: Wiley.

Hosmer, David W., and Stanley Lemeshow. 1999. *Applied Survival Analysis.* New York: John Wiley & Sons.

Hougaard, Philip. 1991. "Modeling Heterogeneity in Survival–Data." *Journal of Applied Probability* 28:695–701.

Hougaard, Philip. 1999. "Fundamentals of Survival Data." *Biometrics* 55:13–22.

Hougaard, Philip. 2000. *Analysis of Multivariate Survival Data.* New York: Springer–Verlag.

Hougaard, Philip, P. Myglegaard, and K. Borchjohnsen. 1994. "Heterogeneity Models of Disease Susceptibility, with Application to Diabetic Nephropathy." *Biometrics* 50:1178–1188.

Hsiao, C. 1986. *Analysis of Panel Data.* Cambridge: Cambridge University Press.

Huber, P.J. 1967. "The Behavior of Maximum Likelihood Estimates under Non–Standard Conditions." In *Proceedings of the Fifth Berkeley Symposium on Mathematical Statistics and Probability.* Berkeley: University of California Press.

Ibrahim, J.G., M.H. Chen, and D. Sinha. 2001. *Bayesian Survival Analysis.* New York: Springer-Verlag.

Jacobson, Gary C. 2001. *The Politics of Congressional Elections*, 5th ed. New York: Harper Collins.

Jaggers, K., and T.R. Gurr. 1995. "Tracking Democracy 3rd–Wave with the Polity–III Data." *Journal of Peace Research* 32:469–482.

Jones, Bradford S. 1994. *A Longitudinal Perspective on Congressional Elections.* Ph.D. diss., State University of New York Stony Brook.

Jones, Daniel M., Stuart A. Bremer, and J. David Singer. 1996. "Militarized Interstate Disputes, 1816–1992: Rationale, Coding Rules, and Empirical Patterns." *Conflict Management and Peace Science* 15:163–213.

Kalbfleisch, J.D., and J.F. Lawless. 1989. "Inference Based on Retrospective Ascertainment: An Analysis of the Data on Transfusion–Related AIDS." *Journal of the American Statistical Association* 84:360–372.

Kalbfleisch, J.D., and R.L. Prentice. 1973. "Marginal Likelihoods Based on Cox's Regression and Life Model." *Biometrika* 60:267–78.

Kalbfleisch, J.D., and R.L. Prentice. 1980. *The Statistical Analysis of Failure Time Data.* New York: John Wiley.

Kelly, Patrick J., and Lynette L.–Y. Lim. 2000. "Survival Analysis for Recurrent Event Data." *Statistics in Medicine* 19:12–33.

King, Gary, James E. Alt, Nancy E. Burns, and Michael Laver. 1990. "A Unified Model of Cabinet Dissolution in Parliamentary Democracies." *American Journal of Political Science* 34:846–871.

King, Gary, and Langche Zeng. 2001a. "Estimating Risk and Rate Levels, Ratios, and Differences in Case–Control Studies." *Statistics in Medicine* 21:1409–27.

King, Gary, and Langche Zeng. 2001b. "Explaining Rare Events in International Relations." *International Organization* 55:693–715.

King, Gary, and Langche Zeng. 2001c. "Logistic Regression in Rare Events Data." *Political Analysis* 9:137–63.

Klein, John P., and Melvin L. Moeschberger. 1997. *Survival Analysis: Techniques for Censored and Truncated Data.* New York: Springer–Verlag.

Kuk, A.Y.C., and C.H. Chen. 1992. "A Mixture Model Combining Logistic Regression with Proportional Hazards Regression." *Biometrika* 79:531–541.

Lancaster, Tony. 1979. "Econometric Methods for the Duration of Unemployment." *Econometrica* 47:939–956.

Lancaster, Tony. 1990. *The Econometric Analysis of Transition Data.* Cambridge: Cambridge University Press.

Lancaster, Tony, and A.D. Chesher. 1984. "Simultaneous Equations with Endogenous Hazards." In *Studies in Labour Market Dynamics*, G.R. Nuemann and N. Westergaard–Nielsen (eds.). Berlin: Springer–Verlag.

Larsen, Ulla, and James W. Vaupel. 1993. "Hutterite Fecundability by Age and Parity: Strates for Frailty Modeling of Event Histories." *Demography* 30:81–102.

Lawless, J.F. 1995. "The Analysis of Recurrent Events for Multiple Subjects." *Applied Statistics – Journal of the Royal Statistical Series C* 44: 487–498.

Le, Chap T. 1997. *Applied Survival Analysis.* New York: Wiley Press.

Lee, E.W., L.J. Wei, and D.A. Amato. 1992. "Cox–Type Regression Analysis for Large Numbers of Small Group Correlated Failure Time Observations." In *Survival Analysis: State of the Art.* John P. Klein and Prem K. Goel, eds. Boston: Kluwer Academic Publishers.

Lin, D.Y. 1994. "Cox Regression Analysis of Multivariate Failure Time Data." *Statistics in Medicine* 15:2233–2247.

Lin, D.Y., and L.J. Wei. 1989. "The Robust Inference for the Cox Proportional Hazards Model." *Journal of the American Statistical Association* 84:1074–1078.

Lin, D.Y., L.J. Wei, and Z. Ying. (1998). "Accelerated Failure Time Models for Counting Processes." *Biometrika* 85:605–618.

Lindsey, J.K. 1995. *Modelling Frequency and Count Data.* Oxford: Oxford University Press.

Lindsey, J.K. 1998. "Counts and Times to Events." *Statistics in Medicine* 17:1745–1651.

Lipschutz, K.H., and S.M. Snapinn. 1997. "An Overview of Statistical Methods for Multiple Failure Time Data in Clinical Trials – Discussion." *Statistics in Medicine* 16:846–848.

Lloyd, Kim M., and Scott J. South. 1996. "Contextual Influences on Young Men's Transition to First Marriage." *Social Forces* 74(3):1097–1119.

Maltz, M.D., and R. McCleary. 1977. "The Mathematics of Behavioral Change: Recidivism and Construct Validity." *Evaluation Quarterly* 1:421–38.

Mansfield, Edward D., and Jack Snyder. 1995. "Democratization and the Danger of War." *International Security* 20:5–39.

Manton, Kenneth G., Burton Singer, and Max A. Woodbury. 1992. "Some Issues in the Quantitative Characterization of Heterogeneous Populations." In *Demographic Applications of Event History Analysis,* ed. James Trussel, Richard Hankinson, Judith Tilton. Oxford: Clarendon Press.

Maoz, Zeev. 1999. *Dyadic Militarized Interstate Disputes (DYMID1.1) Dataset–Version 1.1.* ftp://spirit.tau.ac.il/zeevmaos/dyadmid60.xls. August.

McCullagh, P., and J.A. Nelder. 1989. *Generalized Linear Models.* 2nd ed. London: Chapman and Hall.

McFadden, D. 1974. "The Measurement of Urban Travel Demand." *Journal of Public Economics* 3:303–328.

McLaughlin, S., S. Gates, H. Hegre, R. Gissinger, and N.P. Gleditsch. 1998. "Timing the Changes in Political Structures – A New Polity Database." *Journal of Conflict Resolution* 42:231–242.

Mintrom, Michael. 1997. "Policy Entrepreneurs and the Diffusion of Innovation." *American Journal of Political Science* 41:738–770.

Mintrom, Michael, and Sandra Vergari. 1998. "Policy Networks and Innovation Diffusion: The Case of State Education Reforms." *Journal of Politics* 60:126–148.

Mitchell, Sara McLaughlin, and Brandon C. Prins. 1999. "Beyond Territorial Contiguity: Issues at Stake in Democratic Militarized Interstate Disputes." *International Studies Quarterly* 43:169–183.

Mooney, Christopher Z., and Mei–Hsien Lee. 1995. "Legislative Morality in the American States: The Case of Pre–Roe Abortion Regulation Reform," *American Journal of Political Science* 39:599–627.

Norrander, Barbara. 2000a. "Candidate Attrition During the Presidential Nomination Season." Paper presented at the Annual Meetings of the American Political Science Association, Washington, D.C., Aug.–Sept.

Norrander, Barbara. 2000b. "The End Game in Post–Reform Presidential Nominations." *Journal of Politics* 62:999–1013.

Oakes, D. 1977. "The Asymptotic Information in Censored Survival Data." *Biometrika* 64:441–448.

Oakes, D.A. 1992. "Frailty Models for Multiple Event Times." In J.P. Klein and P.K. Goel (editors). *Survival Analysis, State of the Art.* Netherlands: Kluwer Academic Publishers.

Oakes, D. 1997. "Model–Based and/or Marginal Analysis for Multiple Event–Time data?" In Lin, D.Y. and Fleming, T.R. *Proceedings of the First Seattle Symposium in Biostatistics.* New York: Springer.

Oneal, J.R., and B.M. Russett. 1997. "The Classical Liberals Were Right: Democracy, Interdependence, and Conflict, 1950–1985." *International Studies Quarterly* 41: 267–293.

Parmar, M.K.B., and D. Machin. 1995. *Survival Analysis: A Practical Approach.* New York: John Wiley and Sons.

Peace, D.E., and R.E. Flora. 1978. "Size and Power Assessments of Tests of Hypotheses on Survival Parameters." *Journal of the American Statistical Association* 73:129–132.

Pearson, Frederic S., and Robert A. Baumann. 1989. "International Military Intervention in Sub–Saharan African Subsystems." *Journal of Political and Military Sociology* 17:115–150.

Pearson, Frederic S., and Robert A. Baumann. 1993. *International Military Interventions, 1946–1988.* Principal Investigators, ICPSR 6035. Ann Arbor, MI: Inter–university Consortium for Political and Social Research.

Pearson, Frederic S., Robert A. Baumann, and Gordon N. Bardos. 1989. "Arms Transfers: Effects on African Interstate Wars and Interventions." *Conflict Quarterly* 1:36–62.

Petersen, Trond. 1995. "Analysis of Event Histories." *Handbook of Statistical Modeling for the Social and Behavioral Sciences.* Ed. Gerhard Arminger, Clifford C. Clogg, and Michael E. Sobel. New York: Plenum Press.

Peto, R. 1972. "Contribution to the Discussion of Paper by D.R. Cox." *Journal of the Royal Statistical Society, Series B* 34:472–475.

Pickles, Andrew, and Robert Crouchley. 1995. "A Comparison of Frailty Models for Multivariate Survival Data." *Statistics in Medicine* 14:1447–1461.

Prentice, R.L., B.J. Williams, and A.V. Peterson. 1981. "On the Regression Analysis of Multivariate Failure Time Data." *Biometrika* 68:373–379.

Rodriguez, G. 1994. "Statistical Issues in the Analysis of Reproductive Histories Using Hazard Models." *Annals of the New York Academy of Sciences* 709:266–279.

Rohde, David W. 1979. "Risk–Bearing and Progressive Ambition: The Case of Members of the United States House of Representatives." *American Journal of Political Science* 23:1–26.

Rosenberg, Gerald N. 1991. *The Hollow Hope: Can Courts Bring about Social Change?* Chicago: University of Chicago Press.

Royston, Patrick. 2001. "Flexible Parametric Alternatives to the Cox Model, and More." *Stata Journal* 1:1–28.

Royston, Patrick, and M.K.B. Parmar. 2002. "Flexible Parametric Models for Censored Survival Data, with Applications to Prognostic Modelling and Estimation of Treatment Effects." *Statistics in Medicine* July:1275–1297.

Russett, B. 1993. "Can a Democratic Peace be Built?" *International Interactions* 18:277–282.

Sargent, Daniel J. 1998. "A General Framework for Random Effects Survival Analysis in the Cox Proportional Hazards Setting." *Biometrics* 54:1486–1497.

Sastry, N. 1997. "A Nested Frailty Model for Survival Data, with an Application to the Study of Child Survival in Northeast Brazil." *Journal of the American Statistical Association* 92:426–435.

Scheike, T.H., and T.K. Jensen. 1997. "A Discrete Survival Model with Random Effects: An Application to Time to Pregnancy." *Biometrics* 53:318–329.

Schemper, M. 1992. "Cox Analysis of Survival–Data with Nonproportional Hazard Functions." *Statistician* 41:455–465.

Schmidt, Peter, and Ann D. Witte. 1988. *Predicting Recidivism Using Survival Models.* New York: Springer–Verlag.

Schmidt, Peter, and Anne D. Witte. 1989. "Predicting Recidivism Using Split–Population Survival Time Models." *Journal of Econometrics* 40:141–159.

Schoenfeld, D. 1982. "Partial Residuals for the Proportional Hazards Regression Model." *Biometrika* 69:239–241.

Self, S.G., and K.Y. Liang. 1987. "Asymptotic Properties of Maximum Likelihood Estimators and Likelihood–Ratio Tests under Nonstandard Conditions." *Journal of the American Statistical Association* 82:605–610.

Singer, Judith D., and John B. Willett. 1993. "It's About Time: Using Time Survival Analysis to Study Duration and the Timing of Events." *Journal of Educational Statistics* 18:155–195.

Small, Kenneth A., and Cheng Hsiao. 1985. "Multinomial Logit Specification Tests." *International Economic Review* 26:619–627.

Sobel, Michael E. 1995. "Causal Inference in the Social and Behavioral Sciences." *Handbook of Statistical Modeling for the Social and Behavioral Sciences.* Ed. Gerhard Arminger, Clifford C. Clogg, and Michael E. Sobel. New York: Plenum Press.

Steenbergen, Marco R., and Bradford S. Jones. 2002. "Modeling Multilevel Data Structures." *American Journal of Political Science* 46:218–237.

Strang, David. 1991. "Global Patterns of Decolonization 1500–1987." *International Studies Quarterly* 35:429–454.

Struthers, C.A., and J.D. Kalbfleisch. 1986. "Misspecified Proportional Hazard Models." *Biometrika* 73:363–369.

Sueyoshi, Glenn T. 1992. "Semiparametric Proportional Hazards Estimation of Competing Risks Models with Time–Varying Covariates." *Journal of Econometrics* 51:25–58.

Sueyoshi, Glenn T. 1995. "A Class of Binary Response Models for Grouped Duration Data." *Journal of Applied Econometrics* 10:411–431.

ter Hofstede, Frenkel, and Michel Wedel. 1999. "Time–Aggregation Effects on the Baseline of Continuous–Time and Discrete–Time Hazard Models." *Economic Letters* 63:145–150.

Therneau, Terry M. 1997. "Extending the Cox Model." *Proceedings of the First Seattle Symposium in Biostatistics.* New York: Springer–Verlag.

Therneau, Terry M., and Patricia M. Grambsch. 2000. *Modeling Survival Data: Extending the Cox Model.* New York: Springer–Verlag.

Therneau, Terry M., Patricia M. Grambsch, and Thomas R. Fleming. 1990. "Martingale–Based Residuals for Survival Models." *Biometrika* 77:147–160.

Therneau, Terry M., and Scott A. Hamilton. 1997. "rhDNase as an Example of Recurrent Event Analysis." *Statistics in Medicine* 16:2029–2047.

Trussel, James. 1992. "Introduction." In *Demographic Applications of Event History Analysis*, ed. James Trussell, Richard Hankinson, Judith Tilton. Oxford: Clarendon Press.

Vaupel, J.W., and A.I. Yashin. 1985. "The Deviant Dynamics of Death in Heterogeneous Populations." In *Sociological Methodology* (E.F. Borgotta, ed.), 179–211. San Francisco: Jossey–Bass.

Vermunt, Jeroen K. 1996. *Log–Linear Event History Analysis: A General Approach with Missing Data, Latent Variables, and Unobserved Heterogeneity.* Tilburg: Tilburg University Press.

Warwick, Paul. 1979. "The Durability of Coalition Governments in Parliamentary Democracies." *Comparative Political Studies* 11:465–498.

Warwick, Paul. 1992. "Economic Trends and Government Survival in West European Parliamentary Democracies." *American Political Science Review* 86:875–886.

Warwick, Paul, and Stephen T. Easton. 1992. "The Cabinet Stability Controversy: New Perspectives on a Classic Problem." *American Journal of Political Science* 36:122–146.

Wei, L.J., and David V. Glidden. 1997. "An Overview of Statistical Methods for Multiple Failure Time Data in Clinical Trials." *Statistics in Medicine* 16:833–839.

Wei, L.J., D.Y. Lin, and L. Weissfeld. 1989. "Regression Analysis of Multivariate Incomplete Failure Time Data by Modeling Marginal Distributions." *Journal of the American Statistical Association* 84:1065–1073.

Weissfeld, Lisa A., and Helmut Schneider. 1990. "Influence Diagnostics for the Weibull Model Fit to Censored Data." *Statistics and Probability Letters* 9:67–73.

White, H. 1980. "A Heteroskedasticity–Consistent Covariance Matrix Estimator and a Direct Test for Heteroskedasticity." *Econometrics* 48:817–830.

Willett, J.B., J.D. Singer, and N.C. Martin. 1998. "The Design and Analysis of Longitudinal Studies of Development and Psychopathology in Context: Statistical Models and Methodological Recommendations." *Developmental Psychopathology* 10:395–426.

Xue, Xiaonan. 1998. "Multivariate Survival Data under Bivariate Frailty: An Estimating Equations Approach." *Biometrics* 54:1631–1637.

Yamaguchi, Kazuo. 1990. "Logit and Multinomial Logit Models for Discrete–Time Event–History Analysis: A Causal Analysis of Interdependent Discrete–State Processes." *Quality & Quantity* 24:323–341.

Yamaguchi, Kazuo. 1991. *Event History Analysis.* Newbury Park: Sage.

Zhang, Junsen, and Saul D. Hoffman. 1993. "Discrete–Choice Logit Models: Testing the IIA Property." *Sociological Methods & Research* 22:193–213.

Zorn, Christopher J.W. 2001. "Generalized Estimating Equation Models for Correlated Data: A Review with Applications." *American Journal of Political Science* 45:470–99.

Index

213